Supporting Multilingual Learners' Academic Language Development

A practical and comprehensive resource, *Supporting Multilingual Learners' Academic Language Development: A Language-Based Approach to Content Instruction* introduces a language-based approach to teaching academic language to multilingual learners across the content areas. Luciana C. de Oliveira provides elementary school teachers with everything they need to know to successfully teach grade-level content to multilingual learners. Chapters are organized by subject, addressing the specific language demands of teaching English language arts, social studies, mathematics, and science. Each chapter features examples of implementation in grades K-5, practical strategies, and a wealth of unit plans, tables, figures, and other resources.

The Language-Based Approach to Content Instruction (LACI) in this book provides teachers with a ready-to-use framework of six scaffolding elements that serves as a guide to enable multilingual learners to meet the grade-level standard without simplification. Aligned with WIDA and CCSS standards, this resource provides the tools and methods teachers need to support multilingual learners' academic language development in the content area classroom.

Luciana C. de Oliveira is Associate Dean for Academic Affairs and Graduate Studies in the School of Education and a Professor in the Department of Teaching and Learning at Virginia Commonwealth University, USA.

Supporting Multilingual Learners' Academic Language Development

A Language-Based Approach to Content Instruction

Luciana C. de Oliveira

Routledge
Taylor & Francis Group

NEW YORK AND LONDON

Designed cover image: © Getty Images

First published 2023
by Routledge
605 Third Avenue, New York, NY 10158

and by Routledge
4 Park Square, Milton Park, Abingdon, Oxon, OX14 4RN

Routledge is an imprint of the Taylor & Francis Group, an informa business

Library of Congress Cataloging-in-Publication Data
Names: De Oliveira, Luciana C., author.
Title: Supporting multilingual learners' academic language development : a language-based approach to content instruction / Luciana C. de Oliveira.
Description: First Edition. | New York : Routledge, 2023. | Series: Eye on education books | Includes bibliographical references. |
Identifiers: LCCN 2022046283 (print) | LCCN 2022046284 (ebook) | ISBN 9781032207230 (Hardback) | ISBN 9781032207216 (Paperback) | ISBN 9781003264927 (eBook)
Subjects: LCSH: Language experience approach in education--United States. | Language arts--Correlation with content subjects--United States. | English language--Study and teaching--Foreign speakers. | Academic language--Study and teaching--United States. | Multilingual education--United States.
Classification: LCC LB1576 .D435 2023 (print) | LCC LB1576 (ebook) | DDC 370.117/50973--dc23/eng/20221230
LC record available at https://lccn.loc.gov/2022046283
LC ebook record available at https://lccn.loc.gov/2022046284

ISBN: 978-1-032-20723-0 (hbk)
ISBN: 978-1-032-20721-6 (pbk)
ISBN: 978-1-003-26492-7 (ebk)

DOI: 10.4324/9781003264927

Typeset in Palatino
by SPi Technologies India Pvt Ltd (Straive)

Contents

Figures

Tables

Meet the Author

Dr. Luciana C. de Oliveira is Associate Dean for Academic Affairs and Graduate Studies in the School of Education and a Professor in the Department of Teaching and Learning at Virginia Commonwealth University, Richmond, VA, USA. She has worked for many years as a TESOL teacher, teacher educator, and educational linguist. Her research focuses on issues related to teaching multilingual learners at the K-12 level, including the role of language in learning the content areas and teacher education. She has collaborated with many teachers over the past 20 years in elementary and secondary classrooms, implementing a language-based approach to content instruction (LACI) with multilingual learners. She has authored or edited 30 books and has over 200 publications in various outlets. Dr. de Oliveira has over 30 years of teaching experience in the field of TESOL. She served in the presidential line (2017–2020), as President (2018–2019), and as a member of the Board of Directors (2013–2016) of TESOL International Association, the largest international organization for English language teachers worldwide. She was the first Latina to ever serve as President of TESOL.

Acknowledgments

This book has been in the works for many years. I have some important people to acknowledge. I started to work on the ideas presented here back when I was a PhD student at the University of California, Davis. My two mentors, Dr. Mary Schleppegrell and Dr. Steven Z. Athanases, were instrumental in helping me conceptualize the concepts and ideas presented here. Mary, my dissertation supervisor, taught me about systemic-functional linguistics. We worked together for many years conceptualizing how to implement a functional approach in content classrooms. This initial work with her through my PhD studies and continuing over the next few years were instrumental for the development of the ideas presented in this book. With Steve, I learned about teacher education. His first seminar focused on research in teacher education was an incredible experience that sparked my interest to work with practicing teachers. I also learned how to plan for presentations and publications with him. Steve is someone who is always supporting his doctoral advisees and students to become scholars. I would not have reached this milestone if it wasn't for the two of them!

This book would not have been possible without the collaboration of the teachers featured here for whom I provide the following pseudonyms, Mrs. Karla Dixon, Mrs. Ruby Li, and Mrs. Jana Cabana, who opened up their classrooms to me as a researcher and teacher educator. The classroom environments that they have created for multilingual learners are the kind of general education classrooms we would like to see everywhere, with high challenge and high support for MLs' development of academic language and content learning. I also want to acknowledge my collaboration with Mrs. Lilian Martin (pseudonym) on an integrated social studies and language project in her second-grade classroom.

I also owe enormous debt to my doctoral advisees who have worked with me over the past 16 years in various capacities. Dr. Sharon Smith, who started to work with me as an undergraduate research trainee at Purdue University when she was an undergraduate student, has been a wonderful collaborator over time. When she went to the University of Miami for her PhD, she continued to work with me as a research assistant, joining my research team then. We worked with another PhD student at the time, Dr. Loren Jones, on several publications putting some of the ideas presented in this book in practice with in-service teachers in Florida. Both of them have been great collaborators and writers to develop some of the ideas in this book. I'm also thankful for the detailed notes and care by Dr. Cristiane Vicentini, a PhD student who joined our research group a little later; she collected most of the data presented from the fifth-grade classroom. At the University of Miami, I also worked with Drs. Mary Avalos and Alissa Blair with whom I'm continuing the LACI work in current projects to be developed over the next few years.

At Virginia Commonwealth University, my current institution, I have had the privilege of working with amazing PhD students on my research team, including Jia Gui, Tara Willging, and Destini Braxton. Destini has helped our team consider the needs of practicing mathematics teachers with diverse populations in their classrooms. Both Jia and Tara read all the chapters of this book and provided feedback. Jia also worked on the references and list of tables and figures for the book – amazing tasks that require a lot of attention and careful detail! Joy Beatty joined our team in 2022 and worked on the page proofs and index.

I am also immensely grateful to Dr. Ruslana Westerlund and Dr. Karen Terrell, my critical friends with expertise in SFL for teachers, for their careful reading of Chapter 2 and the tables that appear in Chapter 7. Their feedback helped me add information that they found necessary for better understanding.

I also want to gracefully acknowledge the work of the Routledge production team on bringing this project to fruition. Karen Adler, Senior Editor, was always there to answer my questions and provide support throughout the publishing process.

Finally, I would like to thank my husband Alexander Noguera for pushing me to finalize this book every day for several months in the summer, providing support and encouragement. He was instrumental in making this project come to fruition. He also made sure I took breaks and ate well and on time so I could push through to the end! I would also like to thank my family in Brazil for always supporting me through the years.

1

A Language-Based Approach to Content Instruction (LACI) for Multilingual Learners

Multilingual learners, students who speak languages other than English, have been an increasing population in many parts of the world for several years (de Oliveira & Westerlund, 2021; Gibbons, 2009; Gunderson, 2007, 2009). In Australia, 15% of the primary and secondary school student population is students classified as English Learners (ELs) (Michell, 2021). In Canada, over 2 million students were enrolled in second language programs in 2020 out of a total population of five million students at primary and secondary levels. An increase in the population of students classified as ELs has also been consistent in the United Kingdom, with 19.3% of the primary and secondary school population representing ELs in 2021, an increase of 2% from 2015 (Clark, 2022). In the United States, more than 9% of the U.S. primary and secondary (K-12) student population consists of students identified as ELs, representing over 3.8 million students in the country's schools, as of fall 2020 (National Center for Education Statistics, NCES, 2020). The largest number of these students is found in California, Florida, Illinois, New Mexico, New York, Puerto Rico, and Texas. However, states such as Arkansas, Alabama, Colorado, Delaware, Georgia, Indiana, Kentucky, Nebraska, North Carolina, South Carolina, Tennessee, Vermont, and Virginia have all experienced more than 200% growth in the numbers of ELs in schools over the past 10 years.

The need to prepare teachers to work with these students in many English-speaking countries around the world as well as in all U.S. states, then, is pressing. Given this increase, it is vital for teacher education programs to address the needs of MLs in their courses (Athanases & de Oliveira, 2011).

DOI: 10.4324/9781003264927-1

Many teachers view mainstream U.S. culture and monolingualism as the norm, thereby ignoring linguistic diversity (Osborn, 2007) and perpetuating misconceptions about teaching MLs (de Jong & Harper, 2005). These considerations are relevant in the context of teacher preparation, as teachers' attitudes are likely to affect what MLs learn.

Typically, MLs take English as a second language (ESL) classes or participate in programs where both their native language and English are used to develop their language proficiency before they enter the general education classroom. Yet, the number of ESL specialists in K-12 schools is limited and many school districts do not serve the full number of MLs. Most MLs spend only a portion of their day with bilingual or ESL teachers. These students, then, attend general education classes most of their time in school.

General education teachers who did not have this student population before in their classes are now seeing high numbers of MLs among their students. Because of the growing number of MLs in mainstream classes, *all* teachers – not just bilingual or ESL specialists – need to be prepared for meeting MLs' content and language needs (Lucas & Grinberg, 2008; Viesca et al., 2019). General education, content area teachers need knowledge and practical ideas about addressing the academic language needs of MLs because they have the dual responsibility of facilitating MLs' content learning while also supporting their ongoing English language development (Li & Peters, 2020; López & Santibañez, 2018).

Understanding the Challenges of a Discipline in Linguistic Terms

Subject matter in schools is constructed in language that differs in key ways from the language we use to interact with each other in daily life (Schleppegrell, 2004). This language of schooling, often called *academic language*, is the language children encounter in schooling from the earliest years (Schleppegrell, 2004). Academic language refers to the new set of registers that many children encounter for the first time at school and is a "second" language for all students. Students are expected to learn this new set of registers and participate in classrooms using these registers as they move through the grades. Academic language is generally learned in school from teachers and textbooks, and only with proper instructional support. It includes content-specific vocabulary, formal and precise language, and sentences with a higher lexical density (Schleppegrell, 2004). Academic language draws on the discourses of the subject areas, recontextualized for schooling purposes and becoming more challenging as we move through grade levels. For students with limited opportunities to develop this language outside of school, the classroom needs to offer opportunities to learn language and content simultaneously. Much of the challenge of the content areas is linguistic.

Starting in elementary school, to learn content, MLs need to be able to see how language works in texts, read with comprehension, engage in discussion of complex issues, and critically evaluate the texts they encounter. Research focusing on the linguistic construction of secondary content areas (e.g. Fang, 2006, 2017; Fang & Schleppegrell, 2008, 2010; Fang et al., 2020; Schleppegrell, 2004; Schleppegrell & Colombi, 2002) has shown that authors present disciplinary knowledge very differently from the ways in which meanings are constructed in students' everyday language (de Oliveira, 2011; Fang, 2006; Fang & Schleppegrell, 2008). My work in K-12 classrooms has demonstrated that, as MLs progress at school, they need to understand how authors construct the discipline-specific discourse of the content areas. This research has shown that the key language features found in the content areas at the secondary level are already present at the elementary school level. Therefore, identifying the language demands of the content areas for MLs at the elementary school level is important for teachers so they can develop a better understanding of how authors construct disciplinary knowledge and address these demands in their teaching. This work recognizes that MLs need opportunities for interaction in meaningful contexts supported by explicit attention to language itself.

General strategies, such as creating collaborative groups, using visuals, and building on students' background knowledge, often are cited as strategies that work well for MLs in the content areas (Hansen, 2006; Keenan, 2004). To make content accessible to MLs, many content area teachers draw on a variety of strategies and techniques to simplify the language of texts. While these strategies and techniques may be helpful for MLs at the beginning levels of language proficiency, they are not appropriate for MLs at intermediate to advanced levels, especially as they progress through the elementary grades. Under a watered-down curriculum, MLs may not be taught academic language and they may never learn to read content area texts without modifications or adaptations (Gibbons, 2006).

More Than Just Vocabulary

Academic language in the content areas involves more than just vocabulary. General academic vocabulary words occur across a range of content areas, but each content area has demands in terms of the academic vocabulary it often uses. Vocabulary is a significant component of academic language, but the challenges of academic language go beyond vocabulary challenges. Academic language consists of grammatical patterns through which meanings are made. Vocabulary knowledge is often described as an important element for MLs to comprehend information from texts (Scarcella, 2002), but knowing a word means knowing how to use it effectively in appropriate contexts. As will be shown in this book, knowledge of the academic vocabulary word is not enough to fully grasp the meaning of a text. Much more is needed than lexical understanding. Abstract terms typical of history, for example, occur within grammatical structures that will be difficult for MLs to understand even if they understand the academic vocabulary word. This is often the case with technical terms present in many science texts as well.

All teachers need to develop knowledge about how to make content *accessible* to MLs. In this book, the word *accessible* takes a different connotation than in recent literature on modifying the language of texts to help MLs learn better from them. The notion of making content *accessible* is taken here to mean providing *access* to the academic language that constructs disciplinary knowledge in the content areas by enabling MLs to manipulate language as it is written, without simplification, and by developing teachers' understanding about how disciplinary discourse is constructed.

A Language-Based Approach to Content Instruction

A **language-based approach to content instruction (LACI)** is a teacher preparation model developed over the past 20 years through research in content area classrooms with MLs. This approach has grown from a functional theory of language, *systemic functional linguistics* (SFL; Halliday & Matthiessen, 2014), that describes how speakers use language in social life developed by MAK Halliday and colleagues over the past six decades. LACI also draws on recent scholarship highlighting the linguistic demands of schooling (e.g., Athanases & de Oliveira, 2011; Brisk, 2015; de Oliveira, 2007, 2011, 2017; de Oliveira, Braxton & Gui, 2021; de Oliveira & Dodds, 2010; de Oliveira & Iddings, 2014; de Oliveira & Lan, 2014; de Oliveira & Schleppegrell, 2015; de Oliveira & Yough, 2015; de Oliveira, Jones & Smith, 2021; Fang, 2006; Fang & Schleppegrell, 2008; Gebhard, 2019; Honigsfeld et al., 2018; Schleppegrell, 2004). LACI implements a *functional approach to language development*, providing a simultaneous focus on the meanings that are made (the "content") and the language through which the meanings are expressed. Language is seen as a meaning-making system used to achieve social goals (de Oliveira & Schleppegrell, 2015; Halliday & Matthiessen, 2014).

In a U.S. general-education classroom where MLs learn alongside monolingual English-speaking peers, LACI provides an emphasis on language learning. LACI helps teachers understand how knowledge is created across content areas (de Oliveira, 2016, 2020; Honigsfeld et al. 2018).

By placing emphasis on language learning in the content classroom, LACI assists teachers in using language to teach content. Instead of finding relevant content to further language development goals, this approach focuses on enabling teachers to foreground specific language as a way into the content. Talking about language *is* talking about content. LACI, with a focus on content *through* language, can be a means through which instruction for MLs can be accomplished in meaningful ways in a general education classroom. LACI is a powerful framework for raising teachers' awareness about the challenges of learning content, and enables them to more effectively contribute to the language development of MLs in their general education classes.

LACI differs from content-based instruction (CBI). Content-based instruction (CBI) is an approach that has been implemented in many ESL classes. CBI uses meaningful language to motivate students and enable content learning along with language learning (Davison & Williams, 2001; Karim & Rahman, 2016). In CBI classrooms, a focus on form and meaning should be balanced, indicating that form and meaning are seen as aspects of language that can be addressed separately. The content is considered a means of selecting appropriate, authentic, or motivating language instruction; therefore, teachers must find relevant content to further language development goals.

Background

In this book I report on work that has led to new understandings of the relationship between language and content. Using language analysis to focus on content, and working with teachers who are knowledgeable about content, the approach developed promotes a focus on language in ways that reveal and uncover the many and varied meanings that any text presents. Instead of using content as a vehicle for teaching language, LACI uses language as a means of teaching content.

This approach speaks to concerns about addressing the needs of MLs in the era of standards-based education. The development of the Common Core State Standards (CCSS) (National Governors Association Center for Best Practices & Council of Chief State School Officers, 2010) initiative, starting in 2009, marked a new chapter in this era. The CCSS in English Language Arts, Mathematics, and Science, History/Social Studies and Technical Subjects were designed for a general student population and provide little guidance for teachers who have MLs in their classrooms. The only direction given was a two-page document entitled "Application of Common Core State Standards for English Language Learners" (National Governors Association Center for Best Practices & Council of Chief State School Officers, 2010) that provides very general information about MLs and their needs. This document does not provide any guidance for teachers in how to adapt and use the CCSS with

MLs, and nothing about how to address the demands and expectations of the standards with this student population. LACI clearly addresses the language and content demands and expectations of the CCSS for MLs.

In December 2020, WIDA, an organization dedicated to the academic achievement of MLs, published a new edition of the WIDA English Language Development Standards Framework (henceforth, WIDA Standards or the Standards Framework; WIDA, 2020). The revised edition offers a renewed commitment to equity for MLs by building on students' linguistic and cultural assets, bridging content and language in collaborative environments, and making language visible through a functional approach to language development. The Standards Framework is anchored in four Big Ideas (Figure 1.1).

The four Big Ideas are not new to the WIDA Standards or to the field of TESOL (Shafer Willner et al., 2020). However, they provide a renewed reminder of what is needed to design culturally and linguistically sustaining learning environments where MLs can thrive and reach their full potential (de Oliveira & Westerlund, 2021). The first Big Idea, *Equity of Opportunity and Access*, renews educators' commitment to equity of educational opportunities for MLs by setting high expectations and providing the necessary skills for their success. The second Big Idea, *Integration of Content and Language*, reminds educators and curriculum leaders that language is best developed alongside disciplinary learning, not separately from the content areas. Language and content need to be integrated so it becomes the conduit for learning concepts. The third Big Idea, *Collaboration Among Stakeholders*, reminds educators that it takes more than individual efforts to create inclusive and equitable educational experiences for MLs. Finally, the fourth Big Idea, a *Functional Approach to Language Development*, highlights the idea that language is a resource not only to communicate, but to enact roles and relationships, and

Figure 1.1 The Big Ideas in the WIDA 2020 Edition of the English Language Development Standards.

act on the world. While new to WIDA and perhaps new to many teachers around the U.S., a functional approach has been implemented in many classrooms around the world with great success and in the U.S. over the past 30 years or so (Achugar et al., 2007; Brisk, 2015; de Oliveira, 2016; Gebhard, 2019; Schleppegrell, 2004). LACI, as a way to implement a functional approach to language development, focuses on several scaffolding elements, including what I call *code-breaking* – direct and explicit instruction on the different cultural, linguistic, and disciplinary codes and registers that make up academic language, content, and school.

The development of LACI initiated through my work as a linguistics researcher at the History Project at the University of California, Davis, where I collaborated with history teachers and historians to develop a "literacy in history" curriculum for in-service professional development in a context where virtually every teacher has a range of levels of MLs in the regular history classroom, but few teachers have backgrounds or preparation in ESL teaching or applied linguistics (see, for example, de Oliveira, 2011; Schleppegrell, Achugar & Oteíza, 2004; Schleppegrell & de Oliveira, 2006). This work sparked my interest in the content area classroom and led me to expand my focus to the content areas of English language arts, mathematics, and science.

The work presented here is also informed by classroom-based research done in schools in Indiana, Florida, and New York. In Indiana, I worked closely in a school district with a high number of Latinx MLs – 30% of the student population. As a consultant with this district from May 2007 until August 2013, my work included summer English language learner institutes and several workshops addressing content instruction for these learners. In Florida, I worked in a school self-identified as an "International School of Excellence" which serves an international community of students who come from over 50 countries and speak many languages. I worked at this school as a Professor in Residence, supervising student teachers and working to provide professional learning opportunities for staff from 2015 until 2020. In New York, I have worked with the Division of Multilingual Learners to bring LACI into content-area classrooms, especially social studies, to develop culturally relevant and sustaining pedagogies for MLs that draw on their linguistic and cultural resources while also building new ones for them to participate in new situations.

To develop this approach, I first observed classroom teaching to expand my understanding about the skills and knowledge teachers needed to help MLs fully in the content area classroom. Teachers had a range of strategies for building background knowledge, for helping students predict from headings, layout, visuals and other features, and for using strategies such as collaborative work, group work, graphic organizers and other techniques that have been shown to be helpful for MLs. But teachers had few strategies to employ when it came to actually reading texts and getting meaning from texts. I also identified patterns in content area texts and developed language-focused strategies to help teachers understand the linguistic challenges presented in content area texts and tasks. Over time we discovered the ways of talking about language that teachers found most accessible, and identified the linguistic constructs that teachers most readily adopted in their own teaching. This book presents those constructs and describes the kind of focus on content that they promote. The book describes a language analysis process that illustrates how clause- and discourse-level analyses of the language that expresses content enables teachers to engage MLs in grade-level discussion of important content, even when the students' language proficiency and reading skills lag behind grade level. By putting the language focus into the content classroom, with a functional focus on the meanings expressed in the language, we transcend the form/meaning dichotomy and enable teachers to simultaneously focus on form and meaning by seeing how language choices construct meaning in a particular text. The book places an emphasis on how elementary teachers can select grade-level texts from textbooks and other materials, identify the potential challenges for MLs they may present, and plan instruction to address those challenges.

LACI as a Functional Approach to Language Development

As an approach grounded in SFL, LACI does not separately address language and content, but instead sees the language as the realization of meaning in context. This perspective puts the focus on content, helping teachers understand how the language works to construct knowledge in the disciplines. It offers a way of getting meaning from the text itself, going beyond general reading strategies to provide a means of tackling a content area text, unpacking meanings clause by clause to examine how any content is presented in language. LACI enables a focus on language from each of these three angles: *presenting ideas, enacting a relationship with the reader or listener*, and *constructing a cohesive message*.

In order for teachers to understand how language works in their discipline, they need practice in seeing how language expresses disciplinary knowledge. Since most teaching today is based on adopted standards, teachers should be able to work with texts that they choose to address the standards they must teach. In order to develop lessons, teachers begin with the selection of a key standard. They then design units of study that incorporate language analysis to highlight the key concepts in their content curriculum. For each standard, teachers choose a related passage and develop a guiding question that will focus their analysis and discussion. Then they engage in text deconstruction, first to learn more about it themselves, and then to design activities that could engage their MLs in seeing the multiple meanings embedded in the text. In the following chapters, we will go through this text deconstruction process, showing different key linguistic notions for each content area.

Choosing a particular text and deconstructing its language features provides more than an abstract focus on language. MLs will have opportunities to explore the different patterns of language that construct different types of texts. By focusing on texts, we can show MLs language patterns that present specific content, which encourages conversation in the classroom about which content is presented, who is represented and how, and how the text is organized.

Focus and Organization of This Book

This book focuses on the academic language of the content areas. I draw on research findings and provide practical information in each chapter – the *what* and *how* of a language-based approach to content instruction. I seek to achieve two primary objectives: (1) to describe the academic language of the content areas for MLs at the elementary level; and (2) to provide examples of a language-based approach to content instruction to explore academic language with MLs.

The book provides the information elementary teachers need to focus on grade-level content with MLs. It reports current research to answer the following key questions:

- ◆ What is academic language?
- ◆ What does a language-based approach to content instruction offer teachers of MLs?
- ◆ What are the academic language challenges of the content areas of English language arts, mathematics, science, and history-social studies, *beyond* vocabulary?
- ◆ In what ways can exploring language be incorporated in a content classroom?
- ◆ How can elementary teachers help MLs develop academic language in the different content areas?
- ◆ How does LACI address language and content demands for MLs?

Chapter 2, **A Language-Based Approach to Content Instruction's Six Cs of Support for Scaffolding and Teaching and Learning Cycle**, introduces the six Cs of support that teachers can use to scaffold instruction for MLs. The six Cs are: 1. Connection; 2. Culture; 3. Code-breaking; 4. Challenge; 5. Community and Collaboration; 6. Classroom Interactions. The chapter discusses each of the Cs in detail. This chapter shows how a language-based approach allows for a simultaneous focus on content and language. The chapter introduces LACI's Teaching and Learning Cycle (TLC) as a pedagogical framework to provide learners with explicit knowledge about language and application of genre-based pedagogy based on SFL.

The chapter introduces a functional approach to language development showing how teachers can explore language throughout LACI's TLC. We focus on language from three angles: *presenting ideas, enacting a relationship with the reader or listener,* and *constructing a cohesive message.* These three meanings are always present when language is used and their realization is dependent upon the situational contexts, such as school. The chapter introduces a *metalanguage* – a language to talk about language – that connects linguistic form with meaning to talk with MLs about the grade-level texts they are reading to help them learn about how English works. This metalanguage includes some linguistic constructs that enable a focus on the meanings that the author has embedded in texts. These constructs include being able to divide sentences into their *constituents* and identify the meaning relationships between the parts of a sentence, to analyze *mood and modality* to identify the perspectives presented in the text, and to recognize how *connectors and reference devices* help structure a text and make cohesive links. The language of a functional approach to language development lets us look at whole chunks and label them in ways that relate to their meaning in context. In this chapter, a comparison between functional and traditional grammar terminology is included to help teachers move back and forth from traditional and functional terms. Using a picture book about a little girl's experiences learning English (*I Hate English!* – Levine, 1989), this chapter concludes with an example of how teachers can explore language and meaning.

The chapters that follow – Chapters 3, 4, 5, and 6 – focus on each one of the content areas: English language arts, social studies, mathematics, and science. They each have a similar format, with sections that identify academic language features important for learning that particular subject, a section that has examples of LACI implementation in the classroom by teachers and unit plans that incorporate LACI and highlight different phases of LACI's TLC. Each of these chapters ends with a section entitled "Putting into Practice" so readers can apply what they learned in each chapter. This section features some case studies of practice and reflection questions, based on observations of elementary teachers.

Chapter 3, **Teaching English Language Arts to Multilingual Learners**, starts with an example from a kindergarten classroom and asks readers to identify some of the Cs of support used by the teacher. It then presents examples of LACI in the classroom, showing how a kindergarten teacher and a first-grade teacher explored the language of English language arts with MLs and used LACI's TLC and six Cs of support in classroom instruction. Two unit plans incorporating LACI are included.

Chapter 4, **Teaching Social Studies to Multilingual Learners**, starts by characterizing the academic language demands of social studies, specifically focusing on dense definitions, descriptions, and explanations, mood choices to connect with the reader, and cohesive devices that create links within the text. It presents a sample unit plan to address these demands and explore the language of social studies. The chapter then shows applications of LACI in the classroom, exploring the language of social studies with MLs. The examples come from a second-grade classroom and a fifth-grade classroom.

Chapter 5, **Teaching Mathematics to Multilingual Learners**, starts with examples from a second-grade classroom to frame the chapter. The chapter then characterizes the multisemiotic nature of mathematics. It then focuses on the academic language demands in mathematics, specifically focusing on word problems. Examples of word problems are used to demonstrate the language demands of these word problems. This framework includes five questions that will enable teachers to connect the language used in a word problem with the mathematical knowledge needed to solve the problem. The chapter then shows applications of LACI in the classroom, exploring the language of mathematics with MLs. The examples come from a kindergarten classroom, already introduced in Chapter 3.

Chapter 6, **Teaching Science to Multilingual Learners**, starts by characterizing the academic language demands in science. The chapter then shows applications of LACI in the classroom, exploring the language of science with MLs. The examples come from a fourth-grade classroom. This chapter shows a unit plan which contains how the teacher used LACI's TLC to plan instruction applying LACI's six Cs of support. Two writing samples from a ML are used to show what he was able to do before the implementation of genre-based writing pedagogy in the classroom, and a writing sample after the implementation.

Chapter 7, **Implementing LACI in the Classroom**, reviews the metalanguage developed throughout the book and describes a framework for language analysis and unit planning that teachers can use to analyze the language demands of different content area texts and plan units that teach content *through* language to help MLs *access* grade-level content. This framework provides guiding questions to help teachers identify the content focus of their lesson, select a text to deconstruct with students that addresses the main content focus, conduct a language analysis of their content texts, and plan a unit of instruction to address the language demands of the text by focusing on its content. A sample third-grade lesson plan with the picture book *I Hate English*, introduced in Chapter 2, illustrates how teachers can plan to integrate LACI into their lessons. The chapter also reiterates some main points developed throughout the book, highlighting that language development and content learning occur simultaneously for MLs.

2

LACI's Six Cs of Support for Scaffolding and the Teaching and Learning Cycle

LACI draws on the notion of scaffolding to prepare teachers to meet the disciplinary needs of MLs. Scaffolding is the process of providing support to learners that enables them to access classroom content. This construct builds on Vygotsky's *zone of proximal development* (ZPD; 1978), a concept that identifies the space between students' independent academic achievement levels and the levels of learning they have the potential to reach with the guidance of adults or more advanced peers (de Oliveira & Westerlund, 2023). Development occurs as a result of learners' engagement in activity that places them *beyond* what they know (Walqui & Schmida, 2023). Early scholars in the field (e.g., Wood et al., 1976) recognized that scaffolding was a means for adults to help children work within their ZPD, bridging the gap between their current and future independent performance. This independence is achieved through a teacher or a more advanced peer gradually releasing responsibility as students become capable of successfully completing the assigned task on their own (Bruner, 1983).

In classroom-based research and practice, incorporating scaffolding has provided teachers with the opportunity to raise students' levels of achievement, especially for MLs (Daniel et al., 2016). Teachers implement scaffolding in various ways. At times, they consciously design supports to incorporate for students, especially MLs, but they often also provide unplanned assistance during classroom interactions. Macro-scaffolding refers to the general planned progression of the curriculum, that is, designing and planning over a longer period of time, or "design at the unit level" (Walqui & Schmida, 2023, p. 39).

DOI: 10.4324/9781003264927-2

Meso-scaffolding corresponds to the goals, objectives, procedures, and sequencing of tasks used in specific lessons, that is, shorter-term planning of the steps and sequencing of activities and tasks (Van Lier, 2004; Walqui, 2006) most recently referred to as the "lesson architecture" (Walqui & Schmida, 2023, p. 40). Micro-scaffolding refers to the in-the-moment interactions between the teachers and students, that is, the crucial interactions between teachers and students as teachers contingently support students' participation and offer additional opportunities for students to engage in classroom activities and tasks (Hammond, 2023; Malik, 2017; Walqui & Schmida, 2023). Macro-, meso-, and micro-scaffolding have been central tenets of scaffolding frameworks (de Oliveira & Athanases, 2017; Hammond & Gibbons, 2005; Johnson, 2019). I use notions of designed-in (or planned) scaffolding as incorporating both macro and meso levels of scaffolding (Hammond, 2023). Planned scaffolding includes the ways teachers consciously organize their classrooms, determine instructional goals, and identify and implement tasks. There are seven elements of planned scaffolding: (1) students' prior knowledge and experiences, (2) selection of tasks, (3) sequencing of tasks, (4) participant structures, (5) semiotic systems, (6) mediational texts, and (7) metalinguistic and metacognitive awareness (de Oliveira, Jones & Smith, 2021; Hammond & Gibbons, 2005). Interactional scaffolding consists of classroom talk between teachers and students during various learning activities. In a dynamic environment, teachers find opportunities to provide "on the spot" support through purposeful conversations that build academic literacy, specifically for MLs (de Oliveira & Athanases, 2017). Teachers facilitate conversations allowing students to find and exercise their voices, thus becoming co-constructors of the conversation. The scaffolding provided through conversations works with students in their ZPD and promotes their full participation in typical classroom settings (McNeil, 2012).

These key ideas of scaffolding are critical for the approach presented here. LACI is a concrete, comprehensive approach that teachers can implement in order to provide MLs with access to content through language. Within our educational context, there is a growing demand for methods teachers can utilize to engage MLs (Peercy et al., 2015). LACI, as a teacher education model and a functional approach to language development, provides a guiding framework of six scaffolding elements teachers can use to support MLs during classroom instruction.

LACI raises teachers' awareness about the challenges of learning content and enables them to more effectively contribute to the language development of MLs in their general education classes. The goal is to provide teachers with ways of talking about the language that enable them to focus on the content at the same time that they offer MLs opportunities to develop academic language. In order for teachers to understand how language works in their discipline, they need practice in seeing how language expresses disciplinary knowledge. LACI offers a way of getting meaning from the text itself, going beyond general reading strategies to provide a means of tackling a content-area text, unpacking meanings clause by clause to examine how any content is presented in language.

The Six Cs of Support of a Language-Based Approach to Content Instruction

LACI builds on *six Cs of support* that have identified specific elements of instructional activities for MLs, some of which are well established in the literature (Achinstein et al., 2013). The six Cs are drawn from research with culturally and linguistically diverse students, especially MLs, and are summarized in Figure 2.1 (based on de Oliveira, 2016, 2020). Even though each C

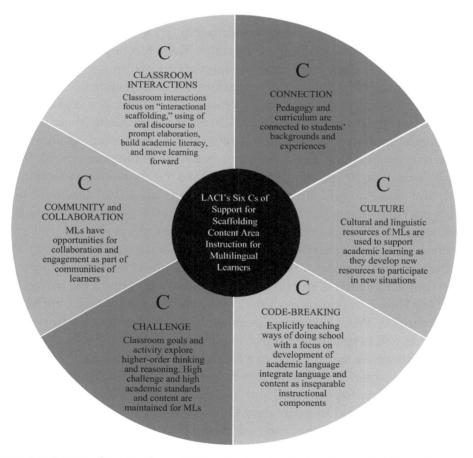

Figure 2.1 LACI's Six Cs of Support for Scaffolding Content Area Instruction for Multilingual Learners.

is presented individually here in order to give specific attention to each, they interconnect and relate to one another.

Connection

The C of **connection** refers to the ways in which teachers can connect various components of the content and curriculum to students' prior knowledge, experiences, and interests (Cochran-Smith, 2004; Villegas & Lucas, 2002). By connecting pedagogy and curriculum to students' backgrounds and experiences, teachers draw on students' knowledge in ways that make content explicit. Connection creates a more inclusive, engaging learning environment and supports MLs in understanding new content while developing their language skills (e.g., Blair et al., 2018; Keefer et al., 2020). One example of connection is leveraging elementary students' experiences and understandings as they are introduced to mathematical modeling (Turner et al., 2019). Turner et al.'s (2019) study shows that students draw on their prior experiences to identify important quantities and relationships, to make assumptions, to analyze and interpret the reasonableness of their solutions, and to revise their models when needed.

Implementing biography-driven instruction (Herrera, 2015) may be particularly useful in considering the C of connection. Teachers can create a supportive learning environment that engages MLs in language practice while infusing cultural relevance into curriculum and instruction by developing a student biography that collects sociocultural, linguistic, cognitive, and academic information. Specifically, teachers can connect to their students' backgrounds and experiences and bring to the classroom students' cultural heritages, bridging the connection between home and school. Within reading instruction, these connections may take the shape of text-to-self, text-to-text, and text-to-world connections (Herrera et al., 2015). Teachers should connect past learning with the new learning by referring to a lesson, a book, an investigation, a chart, a visual that the MLs have experienced previously. Questions to help teachers consider the C of connection include: a) What activities, visuals, pictures, and personal experience do you need to provide MLs to connect to what they bring to the classroom and build the background needed? b) How can you connect the new material to something the MLs are familiar with? c) What concepts, ideas, and information have you taught in the past that will help MLs learn the new material?

Connecting new learning to prior knowledge and experiences is essential; however, all too often, "only a narrow range of these culturally specific home-based [knowledge, experiences, and skills] are rewarded in school, namely those most often found in mainstream homes" (Gee, 1996, p. 24). MLs' home experiences are strengths that can be drawn upon and first-hand experiences with families allow MLs to show what they know.

Culture

The C of **culture** enables students to build on prior knowledge by accessing cultural and linguistic resources (Valenzuela, 1999). By drawing on culture and the diverse "funds of knowledge" (FOK; Moll et al., 1992) MLs bring with them from home, teachers can provide more equitable learning opportunities. FOK, initially defined as "historically accumulated and culturally developed bodies of knowledge and skills essential for household or individual functioning and well-being" (Moll et al., 1992, p. 133), has evolved to now include students' interests more broadly (Hedges et al., 2011) and the ways of knowing that they develop from peer groups, communities, and popular culture (Moje et al., 2004). Students' FOK include the dynamic knowledge, skills, and practices developed in households and communities (de Jong et al., 2013; Moje et al., 2004; Moll et al., 1992). Students' FOK are crucial sources of information that can lead to more effective teaching practices (Hogg, 2011), but it takes purposeful planning that can be challenging, especially when teachers are faced with scripted curricula (Mead, 2021). With the C of *culture*, we position students' cultures and languages as central to their academic success and to classroom activities, rejecting deficit-oriented views and highlighting asset-based approaches (de Oliveira, 2020).

While *culture* is one type of connection, the historical marginalization of cultures other than the dominant U.S. one (White, English-monolingual, middle-to-upper socioeconomic class) necessitates the explicit emphasis of culture by elevating it as a prominent element of this framework. It is important to recognize that culture "involves every aspect of human endeavor" (Paris & Alim, 2017, p. 143), including both more readily identifiable elements such as food, clothing, traditions, and language, and also less visible aspects such as ways of thinking and ethics. An asset-based approach views these different ways of being, speaking, and doing as resources to be used as opportunities for MLs to demonstrate what they know (Gonzalez et al., 2005).

Practices that promote and sustain MLs' multilingualism and promote joy in being multilingual are at the core of the C of *culture*. One example is the concept of *translanguaging*. Translanguaging is the use of a speaker's full linguistic repertoire without regard for strict adherence to the socially and politically defined boundaries of named languages (Otheguy et al., 2015). Translanguaging is a multilingual approach to language development rather than a monolingual approach that has been the "norm" in the TESOL field for many years now (Ortega, 2013). Translanguaging applies an inclusive and holistic process of understanding, as it values the strengths of the languages that students utilize in their daily lives (Lee, 2020).

Pedagogical translanguaging refers to "a theoretical and instructional approach that aims at improving language and content competencies in school contexts by using resources from the learner's whole linguistic repertoire" (Cenoz & Gorter, 2021, p. 1). The use of pedagogical translanguaging allows MLs to employ all of their linguistic resources to increase their participation in classrooms and improve language and content development. With the goal of developing multilingualism, pedagogical translanguaging highlights an integrated approach to languages and MLs' use of their full linguistic knowledge to further their linguistic and academic learning. There is significant evidence in the research literature to support using students' L1 in the classroom and pedagogical translanguaging as integral parts of the teaching and learning process for MLs (Cenoz & Gorter, 2021; García, 2015; García & Kleyn, 2016; Tian & Shepard-Carey, 2020). Even monolingual educators can adopt a pedagogical translanguaging approach, understanding their relationship with language and instruction through language (Fine, 2022; Seltzer, 2019).

For this C, MLs' cultural and linguistic resources are used to support academic learning as MLs develop new resources to be able to participate in new situations, enhancing opportunities for students to learn. Teachers can draw on MLs' bilingual repertoires as supports for culture (Martinez, Hikida & Durán, 2015), as MLs use their bilingualism in classrooms as resources without artificial linguistic boundaries (Gort & Sembiante, 2015).

Code-Breaking

The C of **code-breaking** involves explicitly teaching ways of doing school, academic language, as well as disciplinary, linguistic, and cultural codes of content learning (Fang, 2006; Schleppegrell, 2001, 2004). Code-breaking includes the integration of language and content as inseparable instructional components. Academic literacy then becomes a process of making academic dimensions of subject matter transparent for MLs.

Code-breaking supports the development of *academic language* – or the language used for schooling purposes – as existing on the same continuum and emerging from the same repertoire as *everyday language* used for communicative purposes in everyday life (Schleppegrell, 2013). Academic language includes a range of registers that differ across age levels and the content areas that MLs learn in schools. To use these registers, MLs need to explore how they work by focusing on the language features of the texts they read and write (Moore & Schleppegrell, 2014). This exploration is a major part of code-breaking, as teachers talk with MLs about language. Teachers analyze the texts they teach and develop activities that focus their MLs on language. In this way, MLs learn about the registers that subject-matter authors use. Such activities support reading comprehension and offer the MLs language they can use in their writing.

With the C of code-breaking, we address academic language development in the content areas through **a functional approach to language development**. A functional approach draws on key tenets:

1. Language is a meaning-making resource. Every language has developed *systems* through which different meanings are made. As such, we emphasize how language is involved in the construction of meaning. We are **not** concerned with a set of rules which prescribe correct and incorrect use of language.

2. We consider language at the level of the text, not as isolated, individual words and sentences. Decontextualized exercises at the word or sentence level that are not connected to authentic tasks do not build students' meaning-making resources. Students need to be engaged in deconstruction and construction of texts and to be provided with opportunities for explicit discussion about texts.

3. The ways we use language differ according to the subjects we are discussing, the people with whom we are interacting, and the communication goals we have. Texts vary because our audiences, purposes, and contexts vary. If students have an explicit knowledge of how audiences, purposes, and contexts vary and the role of language in constructing texts, they will be in a better position to make language choices when they build texts of their own. This is an issue of **equity**: We aim to provide access to the disciplines for **all students** through the explicit teaching of the language needed to achieve the learning outcomes of the school curriculum.

4. People *learn language, learn through language*, and *learn about language*. We never stop *learning language* – from an early age to our later years, we are constantly developing new ways of using language in every situation and context in which we are. We learn the language that we experience. In schools, language is the medium of instruction, so we *learn through language*. We also need to *learn about language* – develop knowledge about how language works in various contexts and situations. *Learning about language* helps us make explicit the implicit understandings of how language works – whether content-specific dialogue, sentence structure, or terminology. As such, teachers need shared ways of talking about language with students.

5. Each content area has its own ways of using language to accomplish its purposes. Understanding the different expectations for academic language use in the disciplines is important for students, as they develop language and content simultaneously. The classroom is a prime place to offer opportunities for students to learn how language participates in constructing knowledge in different disciplines. A focus on language in the disciplines has to be oriented toward developing overall subject-matter knowledge.

These key tenets guide a focus on the C of code-breaking. Educators need to be knowledgeable about the language in and through which they are teaching, as they are faced with the dual task of scaffolding students' learning about both content and language. Many scholars have shown how bridging between everyday and academic languages is essential for understanding of content (e.g., de Oliveira, 2016; Gibbons, 2006; Khote, 2018).

Challenge

The C of **challenge** relates to classroom goals and activities that explore disciplinary literacy as well as higher-order thinking and reasoning. High challenge and high academic standards and content should be maintained for MLs (Hammond, 2006; Mariani, 1997). Classrooms with high challenge but inadequate support result in learner frustration while low-challenge but high-support classrooms function in students' comfort zones where little learning occurs. Low-challenge and low-support classrooms result in lack of interest from students and typically do not lead to any significant learning. High-challenge and high-support classrooms offer prime places for MLs to develop their language and content knowledge with the appropriate scaffolding.

A balance of high challenge and high support is ideal and where classroom instruction should be targeted. Teachers need to set high expectations and standards for what is possible for MLs to achieve, focusing on productive, targeted supports to engage them in challenging curriculum (Athanases, 2012; Hammond, 2009). The implementation of high challenge needs to happen with parallel use of strategies that provide necessary and targeted high levels of support and to be interwoven with explicit and systematic teaching of language (Hammond, 2009). Such contexts are accompanied by high intellectual challenges that incorporate explicit explanations about expectations, how to achieve them, and why they are important (Wilson & Devereux, 2014). For MLs in particular, these features, accompanied by welcoming, supportive, and respectful learning environments, affirm students' identities and respect students and what they bring to the classroom.

Figure 2.2 provides a representation of challenge and supportive class-rooms at various levels. In the upper right quadrant in the figure, learning goals are high but achievable, providing the right context for learning and growth. Teachers design effective supports to help students achieve curriculum goals. Remember that ZPD requires MLs be challenged with tasks that are well beyond their present individual capacity – high challenge. High-challenge tasks can be motivating and provide students with opportunities to move towards learning. High challenge, though, is not enough. MLs also need high support because if they consider the task too difficult, they may become frustrated and lose interest, thus hindering optimal learning.

Adapting curriculum is often seen as the way for students who need to develop academic preparation to fully participate in classroom activities. However, such adaptations may result in low-challenge tasks which, in turn, may lead to "busy" and boring work. Low-challenge tasks may be perceived by MLs as irrelevant, leading to them feeling uninterested and overlooked. Students may feel that the task has been "dumbed down," evoking a version of stereotype threat (Steele & Aronson, 1995), wherein the perception may be that the teacher does not consider them to be "smart enough" for more stimulating work. Low-challenge and low-support classrooms provide very low expectations and standards, as shown in the bottom left quadrant of the figure.

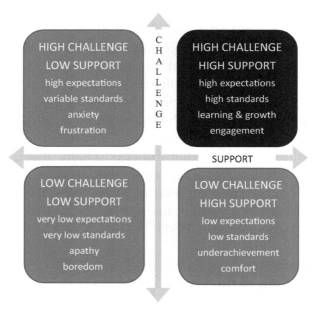

Figure 2.2 Towards High-Challenge, High-Support Classrooms.

Community and Collaboration

The C of **community and collaboration** refers to joint productive activity in which students co-construct knowledge (Brown & Campione, 1994; Lave & Wenger, 1991). Teachers create communities of learners in their classrooms, where all students participate in activities to socially construct knowledge (Nieto, 2000). Building community and collaboration includes using varied participant structures to support the organizational configurations within a unit of instruction: the nature of the task, the degree and nature of scaffolding within it, as well as changes in grouping. The choice of individual, pair, or group work is a decision that is dependent on the learning purposes of the task or activity.

Collaborative work allows students to develop strong relationships with fellow classmates and increase their opportunities to learn from each other, often improving their social relationships (Cooper & Slavin, 2001). For MLs, interactions with peers during collaborative work can affect the development of their language proficiency (Liang, Mohan & Early, 1997; Swain, 2001) and promote second language development (Brooks & Thurston, 2010). When MLs communicate in the second language, they adjust what they say through a process of language feedback and modification when listeners do not understand them (Egi, 2010; Lyster & Izquierdo, 2009). An additional correlation has been found between classroom interaction and engagement with others and improved reading comprehension (Brock, 2007; Ebe, 2011).

Even though studies have shown some challenges in collaborative work for MLs, such as the devaluing of their contributions, power imbalances, and limited opportunities (Kanno & Applebaum, 1995; Toohey & Day, 1999), well-designed pedagogical practices that include open-ended and challenging tasks as well as role distribution, explicit responsibilities, and shared accountability have demonstrated the possibility of balancing inequities, better group integration, and overall positive results (Boaler, 2006; Bunch, 2006; Cohen et al., 1997; Lotan, 2007). MLs are more likely to actively engage in classroom activities when they collaborate with other students in pairs or small groups rather than during whole-class or individual instruction (Brooks & Thurston, 2010), especially when groups are composed of proficient speakers who support and interact with MLs in an environment that supports these relationships and interactions (Wong Fillmore, 1991).

Classroom Interactions

The C of **classroom interactions** considers what teachers can do to more fully engage MLs in teacher–student interactions, especially during teacher-led question-and-answer sequences. Clarity, wait time, question types, higher-order thinking, high expectations, and challenging content influence how teachers interact with MLs. MLs at all English language proficiency levels are able to participate in classroom interactions when teachers create environments in which MLs engage with teachers and other students to share ideas and discuss content and language.

When teachers use classroom interactions, they employ *interactional scaffolding*, an instrumental aspect of classroom discourse for student engagement. Interactional scaffolding is particularly important for MLs due to the opportunities it provides for teachers to gauge MLs' needs and respond appropriately in the moment. Teachers can elicit more from MLs if they know various interactional scaffolding moves that they can make in order to encourage MLs to **say** more and **do** more with language, encouraging their participation

My work on interactional scaffolding (de Oliveira et al., 2020) has identified several interactional scaffolding moves to support MLs. The moves of *linking to prior experience* and *pointing to new experiences* involve referencing students' experiences, both in and out of school. Teachers are able to link students' funds of knowledge (Gonzalez et al., 2005) to broader conceptual frameworks in the curriculum by connecting previous learning to current instruction and preparing students for what will follow. This interactional scaffolding move can be used to address the C of connection, as teachers are making explicit connections to prior experiences and connecting to what will follow as part of their classroom instruction.

Appropriating, recasting, and *recapping* students' contributions take place when actively involving students in the construction of subject-specific discourse. During discussions or exchanges, teachers direct students' contributions by means of summarizing or restating their ideas and employing more academically-appropriate discourse. *Cued elicitation* can further engage students in complex academic conversations, as teachers offer strong verbal or gestural hints about expected responses. Through the move called *moving the discourse forward*, teachers provide students with opportunities to say more by asking *why, how*, and *what* questions, oftentimes asking for a more detailed explanation of a particular point as ways of moving the conversation forward. This allows MLs to **say more** and **do more** with language.

All of these interactional scaffolding moves can be implemented as part of the feedback turn of the Initiation-Response-Feedback sequence, a sequence used in interactions through which teachers offer strong verbal or gestural hints about expected responses, especially targeting specific students for specific purposes. This contrasts with Initiation-Response-Evaluation (IRE; Mercer, 2000) sequence, a three-part exchange initiated by the teacher who first poses a display question (one to which the student clearly knows the answer), the student responds (typically with a single word or short answer), and then the teacher provides some sort of evaluation of the answer (e.g., 'good job'). The IRE pattern can be very limiting for MLs as it leaves little to no space for students to negotiate meaning with others nor the opportunity to produce extended segments of discourse.

Probing is used as a follow-up after a student responds to an initial question, allowing the student to add new information or expand upon their answer. With probing, the teacher typically interacts with individual students. *Elaboration* refers to a teacher supplementing contributions with additional information (typically of a more personal nature), with examples from experience, or with further explanations when discussing a specific topic or concept. The move *clarification* occurs when the teacher clarifies what students say, typically when students provide an answer that the teacher and or students are not sure about. *Purposeful repetition* is used to draw attention; the teacher repeats so all can hear and provides cues to self-correct or extend thoughts. Figure 2.3 shows these interactional scaffolding moves (based on de Oliveira et al., 2020).

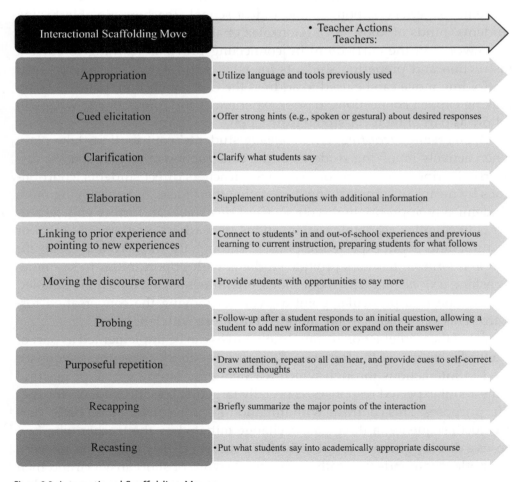

Figure 2.3 Interactional Scaffolding Moves.

Interactional scaffolding moves can be used as a means of creating an environment that supports participation and engagement by all MLs. MLs' participation in the classroom can be enhanced through the use of *purposeful repetition* and *moving the discourse forward*. These enable exploring ideas, cumulative questioning, responding to the ideas of others and building collective understanding more fully (Alexander, 2008) to create a dialogic classroom. Students engaged in dialogue must come to the classroom prepared to reconsider their ideas and thinking, as teacher and students discuss and build knowledge. Moving the discourse forward is especially important for teachers to use with MLs so they are asked to say more and do more with language. Table 2.1 shows a few questions and their purpose to help teachers use them in the classroom.

Table 2.1: Teachers' Questions and Purposes to Move the Discourse Forward

Interactional Scaffolding Move: Moving the Discourse Forward	
Teachers' Questions	**Purpose**
Can you tell me more about…?	To extend thoughts
How do you know that…?	To clarify
Why?	To explain
Would you explain that again?	To rephrase
Is there another example of…?	To provide an example
How is this similar/different to…?	To contrast
What would happen if…?	To consider perspectives
What else?	To say more
Any other ideas?	To further develop ideas

The *six Cs of support* for scaffolding presented here can be used by teachers as they plan instructional activities for MLs. While these Cs are presented individually, they do interconnect and relate to one another. Next, we will focus on LACI's Teaching and Learning Cycle, a framework for scaffolding academic language development through explicit tasks, academic discussions, sustained reading, language development, and writing. It involves immersing students in a content area through the framework's intentional, language-focused support that simultaneously builds deep content knowledge and then scaffolds them toward independence. This approach is quite different from many other approaches to literacy instruction, which teach language and literacy in ways that are isolated from deeper, integrated content and language learning goals.

LACI's Teaching and Learning Cycle: Breaking Down and Building Up Academic Language with MLs

LACI's Teaching and Learning Cycle (TLC) draws on all Cs of support for scaffolding to design instruction for MLs and applies genre-based pedagogy based on SFL (e.g. Brisk, 2015; Derewianka & Jones, 2016; Gebhard, 2019; Hamman-Ortiz et al., 2022; Rose & Martin, 2012). It is based on the notion that high-challenge, high-support classrooms with high expectations and purposeful scaffolding provide the explicit teaching necessary for MLs' language and content development. As a pedagogical framework which provides learners with explicit knowledge about language, LACI's TLC applies the concept "guidance through interaction in the context of shared experience" (Martin & Rose, 2005, p. 253) to break down academic language and build up MLs' knowledge, skills, and abilities for continued access and success. This concept refers to the guidance provided by teachers in talking, reading, and writing about a specific text in the context of a shared experience – a common text, field trip, movie, science experiment, reading, among others.

LACI's TLC enables teachers to:

- ◆ identify the language demands of the texts and tasks assigned;
- ◆ explicitly teach MLs the genres of schooling;
- ◆ focus simultaneously on language and content learning;
- ◆ create high-challenge, high-support classrooms;
- ◆ utilize classroom interactions to build scaffolding throughout the cycle.

Through LACI's TLC, MLs explore disciplinary learning as they dissect and "unpack" – or **break down** – academic language in texts discovering both the language and content they are using and developing. This exploration develops their awareness of how language works as teachers support MLs to notice, explore, analyze, and practice discipline-specific writing.

What Is Genre?

We draw on the notion of *genre*, represented by the culturally expected patterns of types of texts (Martin & Rose, 2008) to explicitly **build up** academic language development. Genre is a recurrent configuration of meanings, described as a staged goal-oriented social process (Martin, 2009, p. 13). It is:

- ◆ staged: because it usually takes us more than one step to reach our goals,

♦ goal-oriented: because unfolding phases are designed to accomplish goals, and

♦ social: because we write for specific audiences.

Genres are socially recognized ways of using language that enable people to present, enact relationships with others, and organize information to achieve various goals. To understand how different written genres accomplish this, it is important to consider the purpose, organization, and specific language features of each genre.

Purpose

Language use is goal-oriented. Written genres are distinguished by what the text is meant to achieve within a particular context and content area – that is, their social purposes. Genres are used to achieve social purposes. Purposes include narrate (e.g., telling about an experience or an event), inform (e.g., telling about a historical event or science facts), explain (e.g., helping others to understand a system or a process), and argue (e.g., persuading others to believe something or act on an issue). Genres produced for different purposes in different contexts have different language features.

Organization

Each genre has evolved and continues to evolve to be organized in expected ways and use specific language features connected to the genre's social purpose. To accomplish their purposes, genres generally move through a number of *stages*. Stages are named according to their function and go beyond a typical three-step structure as an Introduction, a Body, and a Conclusion. In fact, we do not use this terminology when discussing genre stages. Each stage plays a particular role in the developing text. Identification of the organization of a genre through its stages and reflection on what job these stages are performing in the text is important. The stages are not meant to be presented firmly as a prescription – rather, stages are functional for each genre and, therefore, may change as the social purpose changes. For example, a Procedural Recount genre typically has the purpose of recording steps taken to carry out experiments, tasks, and observations. The typical stages are Aim (Materials), Record of Events, and Conclusions. As you will see in Chapter 6, in science, when we write Procedural Recounts about experiments, the Aim stage provides information about the goal of the experiment and usually includes materials required to conduct the experiment. The second stage is Record of Events in which the writer includes the step-by-step process that was followed in the procedure, in this case, the science experiment. The Conclusions stage describes the findings of the experiment.

Language Features

Different genres have typical language patterns to achieve their social purpose. Identifying language features can help teachers and students develop an understanding of how texts achieve their social purposes most effectively. When students recognize patterns of language present in different genres they become familiar with the expectations for that particular genre. While identifying the stages of a text is a useful starting point, we need to dig deeper into the language of the texts to see how an author has made particular choices to make the meaning that they wanted to convey. The role of the teacher is instrumental in extending students' repertoires of language choices, both in their comprehension of meaning in texts and their construction of meaning in texts.

To help teachers identify some common genres for schooling contexts, we developed a table that contains typical genres, their social purposes, typical organization in stages, and language features associated with each genre, following previous work done on genre instruction (Derewianka & Jones, 2016; de Oliveira et al., 2020; Rose & Martin, 2012). Table 2.2 can be used by teachers to develop their awareness of typical genres of schooling. The table is not meant to be 'taught' to students out of context. Rather, it is meant as a resource for teachers to develop their own understanding of genres, stages, and typical language features associated with each genre. A more complete set of genres can be found in Appendix A.

LACI's TLC

LACI's TLC takes students through the phases of building shared knowledge about a topic, sustained reading, deconstruction, joint construction, collaborative construction, and independent construction. Though the cycle allows students different points of entry and enables teachers to start at any one of these phases, it is important to build shared knowledge about any new topic that will be the focus of instruction. This process can be recursive and repeated as students become more familiar with specific genres. While LACI's TLC is portrayed as a cycle, it is important to recognize that each iteration might not include all phases. For instance, when first being introduced to the genre, the cycle may not include an independent construction phase. The teacher also may choose to move back and forth between building shared knowledge and deconstructing texts for a few lessons before even touching the other phases. Therefore, the cycle offers a flexible, nonlinear framework that allows teachers to use their knowledge of their MLs to help them plan how to best address their needs and to integrate other scaffolding strategies into the cycle. LACI's TLC is especially useful for extended units of study, but it can also be adapted, as you will see examples in the next chapters, for use with a shorter

Table 2.2: CCSS Text Types, WIDA Key Language Uses, Example Genres, Purpose, Stages, Language Features, and Examples

CCSS Text Type	WIDA Key Language Use	Example Genre	Purpose	Stages	Language Features	Examples
Narrative	Narrate	Stories	to entertain or engage	Orientation Complication Resolution	◆ simple past tense (*she saw, they looked*) ◆ doing processes [verbs] (*drank, went, did*) ◆ time connectors (*on Saturday, then, next, after church*) ◆ specific participants [nouns] (*Mary, Jose, the cat*) ◆ First person pronouns (*I, we*) ◆ creative or literary elements ◆ personal reactions	Narrative Anecdotes Fables
		Recounts	to tell what happened	Orientation/ background Record/ account of stages	◆ Sequenced in time ◆ simple past tense (*she saw, they looked*) ◆ doing processes [verbs] (*drank, went, did*) ◆ time connectors (*on Saturday, then, next, after church*) ◆ specific participants [nouns] (*Mary, Jose, the cat*) ◆ Typically first person pronouns (*I, we*)	Recounting a historical event Recounting solving math problems

(Continued)

Table 2.2: (Continued)

CCSS Text Type	WIDA Key Language Use	Example Genre	Purpose	Stages	Language Features	Examples
Informational/Explanatory	Inform	Procedures	to instruct how to do something	Purpose Equipment Method/steps Results	◆ doing processes [verbs] mainly commands (*place, give, add*) ◆ generalized participants, referring to whole class of things and specific things ◆ time connectors (*first, when, then*) ◆ *Directions* tend to use declarative clauses in simple present tense with *you/we/one* as a generalized actor. ◆ *Instructions* tend to use imperative clauses.	How to do a craft How to play a game How to go somewhere How to make candy
		Reports	to provide information about a topic	Classification or Positioning Description	◆ relational processes (*is, has, were, have, belong to*) describe characteristics and present generalizations. ◆ doing processes in the present tense (*spread, climb*) describe activity. ◆ generalized participants (*sharks, cultures*) ◆ timeless verbs in simple present tense (*exist, grow*)	Types of sharks A description of Antarctica Greek and Roman cultures
	Explain	Explanations	to explain how things work/why they happen	Phenomenon Explanation	◆ generalized non-human participants (*generators, ecosystems*) ◆ logical organization (*if/then, so, since*) ◆ relational processes (*is, are, has*) ◆ doing processes (*shift, increases*) ◆ timeless present tense (*happens, turns, decrease*)	How a life cycle works What causes hurricanes

Argument	Argue	Arguments	to persuade	Issue/thesis Arguments/sides Reiteration/resolution	◆ generalized participants, both human and abstract ◆ variety of processes – *doing, saying, thinking, feeling, relating* ◆ timeless present tense when presenting position ◆ Nominal expressions name the arguments to be used, drawing on abstractions ◆ connectors of contrast used (*on the other hand, however*)	Essay taking a stance Discussion exploring various sides Formal Debate
		Text Responses	to critique	Context Description Evaluation Reaffirmation/challenge	◆ simple evaluative adjectives (*great, excellent, helpful*) ◆ reasons described in declarative clauses	Product review Interpreting a book message Challenging a book message Opinion of a movie

sequence of lessons (a week or two). The pedagogical practices employed in each of the phases can be used with flexibility. These phases of LACI's TLC start with the whole text as the unit in focus rather than individual sentences or a list of vocabulary words. These phases enable teachers to support their students in developing their knowledge and control of school genres across disciplines.

Setting context occurs at each phase as an important step to build with students as they think of the specific context for reading and writing a specific genre within other possible contexts. Setting context continues throughout the other stages of the TLC so that MLs' understanding of the topic accumulates and becomes progressively advanced. The notion of *building shared knowledge of the topic* as a phase is key, as students develop their knowledge of the content and context of particular texts. Students also build a critical orientation to language by learning about language and about the genre while teachers assess student learning at all phases of activity. The different phases of LACI's TLC aim to provide students with teacher interaction, guidance, and support as students go through these phases. Most recently, after their work in K-5 classrooms, both Brisk (2015) and de Oliveira (2017) included an additional, optional phase entitled *collaborative construction*. Figure 2.4 includes a visual representation of LACI's TLC and the six phases of teaching and learning.

Building Shared Knowledge of the Topic

This phase includes engaging MLs in discussion about the topic that will be the focus of various activities, finding out what they know about the topic, and beginning to develop shared understandings. This phase can include the C of *connection* and the C of *culture*, as teachers connect to MLs' experiences and backgrounds and use their cultures in the classroom. It is important to note that simply drawing on prior experience or personal knowledge is not enough at this phase. Knowledge needs to be developed so it is shared, and all students, including MLs, can contribute equally to discussions about the content. Interactive activities for MLs to use, hear, and see the language associated with the topic emphasize students' engagement through talk, typically around written text, visuals, and images. Activities may include:

◆ Identifying current knowledge of the topic
◆ Guided discussions about the unit's topics and themes
◆ Hands-on activities such as science experiments and community visits
◆ Teacher-guided activities that involve bridging (e.g. shifting between everyday and more academic language to support students; use of

Figure 2.4 LACI's Teaching and Learning Cycle.

classroom interactions with interactional scaffolding moves; dialogic teaching to move the discourse forward)
◆ Multimodal activities that involve examining images and visuals and image–text relationships
◆ Brainstorming and mind mapping
◆ Think–pair–share
◆ Field trips
◆ Videos

◆ Guest speakers
◆ Research activities, such as jigsaw and notetaking
◆ Skimming/scanning material
◆ Anchor charts

Sustained Reading

The **Sustained Reading** phase places emphasis on reading carefully selected texts which can be two to three paragraphs or longer texts, depending on the purposes for reading. This phase continues to build knowledge of the topic, now with an emphasis on further developing MLs' experiences. Teachers should select *mediational texts and artifacts*, any instrumental texts around which significant talk occurs and which serve as ways to link prior or future learning. Teachers can think of the C of *challenge* here as they select texts that are more challenging for MLs. As a first activity, teachers can guide the class to skim the text to get an overall idea of how it will unfold by looking at headings, sub-headings, images, captions, etc. If reading a picture book, teachers can do a picture walk with students, looking first at the images and then making image–text connections as students go through the text with the teacher guiding them. Teachers may go through a series of reading practices with students as part of **Sustained Reading**, including reading aloud, modeled reading, shared reading, guided reading, collaborative reading, and independent reading.

Reading Aloud is an instructional practice in which teachers read texts aloud to children. The reader uses variations in pitch, tone, pace, volume, pauses, eye contact, questions, and comments to create a confident and enjoyable delivery. Reading texts aloud is a very important activity for building the knowledge required for successful reading (Morrison & Wlodarczyk, 2009). *Interactive Reading Aloud* is similar to *Reading Aloud* in that teachers read texts aloud to children, but the difference is that, with the interactive reading aloud, teachers occasionally and selectively pause for conversation and invite students to discuss key ideas, images, illustrations, text features, interesting details, and language. Teachers may ask specific questions about what a phrase means, what characters are doing (if reading a fictional text), what a section means (if reading a non-fictional text), connections to other things they discussed in class, including other texts. Teachers may also confirm and disconfirm predictions and make connections to other materials used in the classroom.

Modeled Reading is a practice in which teachers model, verbally, to the students how they would read the text themselves, including reading the text aloud to students while they listen and observe and demonstrating how they would read a text with challenging sentences, thinking aloud about how they might tackle them and allows students to see a purpose in learning to read.

Shared Reading is an interactive reading experience in which teachers share a text that is visible to the entire class. Students join in or share the reading while guided and supported by the teacher. This is an important practice for MLs as they need to be guided to read key texts strategically. During shared-reading sessions, the teacher reads the text with the class and purposefully engages students by asking questions, answering questions, making connections between images and texts, explaining vocabulary in context, demonstrating comprehension strategies, and drawing attention to relevant language features. This practice presents opportunities for teachers to discuss the language of the text by drawing MLs' attention to specific effective language choices, sentence structure, and text organization.

Guided Reading is a small-group practice in which teachers provide differentiated support for students' developing reading proficiency as they move to new texts at increasingly challenging levels of difficulty. Teachers group students according to different levels of reading proficiency and need, enabling them to work with students with similar needs and proficiency to extend their reading capacity. Teachers work with a particular group on guided reading activities to address specific aspects of reading relevant texts. This practice encourages MLs to apply the reading skills they have learned and become more independent while reaching higher levels of reading competency. Teachers listen to students read the text aloud and respond to cues that indicate they need assistance. *Collaborative Reading* is an instructional practice that involves pairs or groups doing structured reading activities, while the teacher is working with a particular group. This can involve teachers giving students tasks to focus on particular language choices made by authors. *Independent Reading* is similar to collaborative reading but students will be doing activities independently.

Exploring the Language of the Text. Any of the instructional reading practices described above can be part of sustained reading. What is critical for LACI is the selection of a short excerpt or short text to explore with the class that includes content that is important for students to learn, addressing state content standards. Students and teachers explore how the text is written and how it accomplishes its goals through its language choices. This close focus incorporates classroom interactions with students, conducting read-alouds, identifying language features, focusing on grammatical expressions, target vocabulary, and main ideas of texts.

After reading a selection with the class, teachers engage them in exploration of the text to help the class identify an aspect of the text that teachers think is important for student comprehension. This involves learning a language for talking about language, further discussed in this chapter, and connecting language with meaning. It will help students 'unpack' meaning in the texts they read by learning how to deconstruct dense sentences into their meanings, and it will help teachers explore questions such as these:

◆ What is this section of the text about?
◆ How does the author introduce and develop a concept in an informational text? An explanation? An argument?
◆ How does this character change as the story moves along?
◆ How does the author interact with the reader?
◆ How has the author structured this text?

Deconstruction

Teachers introduce mentor texts in a specific genre that students are expected to read and write (e.g., procedural recount, descriptive report, discussion); guide students to deconstruct these texts through demonstration, modeling, and discussions about their purpose, stages, and language features typical of a specific genre; and build up students' knowledge of the content information (i.e., setting context). Teachers project the mentor text for the whole class to see and also give students copies. During this phase, the class is developing a shared metalanguage to refer to various aspects of texts, including the purpose and name of the genre, the labeling of stages, and the terminology used for the various language features.

Mentor texts may include: texts created by MLs in previous classes; texts that the teacher and students co-created in past years; or even published texts that teachers find (i.e., online, in textbooks, magazines, or other sources) that could serve as exemplars for students. Mentor texts model the genre expectations and are different texts from the ones used during the Sustained Reading phase. Preferably, teachers should use two examples of the genre during the Deconstruction phase. One is to demonstrate their purpose, stages, and language features typical of the specific genre while the other is used for students' exploration of purpose, organization, and language features in pairs or groups. It is important to work initially with prototypical examples produced in a similar context to that which the students will be writing, especially important for students with little experience writing the genre (Humphrey & Macnaught, 2011). While mentor texts are commonly used in ELA, with LACI, mentor texts are used in any content area such as math or science to show students models of mathematical or science explanations.

Many activities can be used to familiarize students with the characteristics of the genre. Teachers can perform a variety of tasks through whole class interactions:

- ◆ Exploring the **social purpose** for writing (e.g. narrating, informing, explaining, arguing)
- ◆ Identifying the **typical key stages** that the text goes through in achieving its purpose
- ◆ Identifying **optional phases** within stages
- ◆ Carrying out discussions related to **how the text is organized** and other linguistic styling and organizational choices
- ◆ Identifying **language features** (only between 2 and 3 depending on length and text complexity)

During this phase, the C of *code-breaking* is at the core. However, the C of *classroom interactions* is also very relevant as the teacher engages students in discussion about the mentor text so the use of various interactional scaffolding moves is expected – elaboration, cued elicitation, moving the discourse forward are typical. The C of *connection* can also be used as teachers can connect the information in the mentor text to what students already know.

Joint Construction

Teachers and students work together to write a text in the same genre. In this phase, the teacher and students co-construct texts that are similar to the mentor texts that they already explored in the deconstruction phase. Students start using the language features of the specific genre about which they are learning. In co-constructing texts, teachers are expected to provide a bridge for students between their everyday language and the academic language of school so attention will be directed to text organizational issues such as purpose, stages, and language features. The teacher is typically in front of the room scribing while everyone is writing together. This phase is an engaging task that presents many opportunities for language development for MLs at various levels of English language proficiency while demonstrating how to construct a good example of the genre they are learning.

It is important to note that the preparation for joint construction is critical for MLs (Caplan & Farling, 2017). Teachers should have MLs come to this phase with some preparation so that they have had time to prepare and are ready to contribute. For this preparation, teachers can have students brainstorm ideas in pairs or groups – incorporating the C of *community and collaboration* – and write those ideas using a graphic organizer or other organization tools. This will enable MLs, especially those at lower English language proficiency levels, to be better prepared to share their ideas.

The teacher takes a leading role by guiding the joint construction of the text, shaping the text as it unfolds. The teacher solicits contributions from all students and ensures MLs contribute as well. Students propose words, phrases, and sentences as the teacher demonstrates how to shape the text. The teacher has many opportunities to guide students. For example, teachers may:

◆ develop an overview of the text with students' help
◆ focus on a particular stage of the text
◆ develop a paragraph
◆ demonstrate language choices by recasting what students offer in oral language into more written-like language
◆ ask questions to request student responses
◆ make suggestions
◆ discuss how a specific language choice might be better than another
◆ move the discourse forward by asking students to say more or extend their ideas
◆ focus on choices about the whole text, paragraph or sentence structure
◆ remind students of the stages of the genre and typical genre features
◆ refer back to the deconstructed text as the class composes a new text together

During this phase, there are many opportunities for the teacher to use interactional scaffolding moves, as part of the C of *classroom interactions*, as the teacher and students are highly engaged in the co-construction of text. This teacher-led, whole-class joint construction is considered "the most powerful classroom practice currently available as far as learning written genres is concerned" (Rose & Martin, 2012, p. 73). Students' experience with joint construction shows them what is involved in composing a text, the kinds of decisions writers need to make as they compose, and the language choices that will help them develop their own texts independently.

Collaborative Construction

Collaborative Construction can be added as a bridge between the joint construction and independent construction phases, especially for students in grades K-2 who are novice writers as they often require additional support when writing a difficult genre for the first time (Brisk, 2015). For this phase, the teacher designs pair or group activities for students to work together to develop a new, single text – a clear example of the C of *community and collaboration*. The teacher may elect to just focus on one stage for the collaborative construction. Students work with other students in pairs or small groups to construct a text together, brainstorming and negotiating ideas, writing, revising, etc. The teacher circulates the room and provides further scaffolding as needed, drawing on understandings developed in previous lessons. Teachers continue to support collaborative pairs or groups as needed.

This particular phase of the TLC is promising for MLs, as working in pairs and small groups has shown to be effective in supporting academic language development (Brisk & Tian, 2019), especially when they have the opportunity to interact with their fluent English-speaking peers (Walqui, 2019). Because previous studies have described challenges associated with uncooperative pairs/groups (e.g. Roberts & Eady, 2012; Yarrow & Topping, 2001), it is very important to do purposeful pairings and groupings for this phase of the TLC (Jones & de Oliveira, 2022).

Jones & de Oliveira (2022) propose the following steps to organize a collaborative construction in the classroom:

1) **Introduce the Collaborative Construction Activity**: Explain what collaborative writing is and the purpose it serves so students understand what they will be doing with their partner(s) and why. (This is a step that may need to be revisited as students grow accustomed to writing in this way.)

2) **Select Partners/Groups for the Writing Task**: Select the partners/groups purposefully. Be sure to take into consideration students' literacy levels, language abilities, personalities, prior knowledge, etc.

3) **Model the Collaborative Writing Phase**: After identifying partners/groups, scaffold the collaborative writing phase for students, especially when doing collaborative writing for the first time. Consider dividing the collaborative writing into simple steps that students will be able to follow and model the implementation of these different steps (potentially through a think aloud), focusing on the collaborative aspects in order to prevent students from maintaining their individual working habits.

4) **Engage Students in Writing Conferences**: After the writing is completed, implement 'group conferencing' as an additional form of collaboration between different pairs/groups of students and the teacher. In the first round of group conferencing, pairs/groups of students can present their writing to their peers and receive feedback related to content, format, etc. In the second round, students can work with the teacher to receive support in the revision process prior to creating the final product.

5) **Encourage Student Presentations**: Provide time and space for students to present their final product to the class and other relevant community members (administrators, other teachers, parents, etc.).

Though collaborative construction was not originally part of other genre-based models of the TLC, it was incorporated in this LACI model due to my extensive work in elementary classrooms and identification of additional needs by MLs, especially in the lower grades, as they were learning to read and write.

Independent Construction

Independent Construction is a phase in which students are ready to work independently to construct their own texts in the specific genre. Teachers are expected to minimize their support, scaffolding, and guidance so students have more opportunities for independent writing of the specific genre. If the student is developing a text that is on a different topic from the topics of the other phases but involves the same genre, they may need to conduct additional research into that topic.

Students refer to the deconstructed mentor text, the jointly constructed text, and the collaboratively constructed text to now write a text by themselves independently. They can further consider the audience, edit the text, and expand their language choices. Consultation with the teacher and conferences with peers about writing can also happen within this phase. As students are writing independently, the teacher can go around the room providing feedback and answering questions. Students can also work with other students to share their writing and receive feedback on their drafts from peers. Peer feedback can help students as they work to polish their drafts and publish them. Students proofread their texts to attend to spelling, punctuation, and other mechanics. It is important for teachers to provide guidelines for students to revise, edit, and proofread their texts. Students may share their published texts with others, feeling proud of everything they have accomplished throughout the cycle.

Exploring Language Throughout LACI's TLC

As described above, we want to engage MLs in exploring how language is used in texts and how meanings are presented in various content areas. This exploration affords teachers an explicit pedagogy that keeps language at the core of learning content. Learning language from this perspective means learning the options that are available in the new language to make meanings of different kinds, for particular purposes, in various situations. Teachers involve MLs in talking about the language choices of speakers and writers and develop with them a metalanguage – **a language for talking about language** – that is functional for such discussion. A metalanguage provides a means for focusing on and engaging in talk about wording in the texts MLs read and write.

While most teachers are familiar with traditional metalanguage such as *noun, verb, adjective, conjunction*, and *present tense*, these terms do not always help students understand how language patterns function in texts. Drawing on traditional metalanguage offers ways of bridging between traditional and functional terminology to support teachers who are already familiar with traditional terms. A functional metalanguage helps teachers and students look closely at language to see patterns that are connected to categories of meaning (Moore & Schleppegrell, 2014). This kind of metalanguage is important for MLs to recognize the choices they can make in the new language. Because functional metalanguage connects to meaning, it supports curriculum goals as it offers explicit ways to connect to the knowledge to be learned (Schleppegrell, 2013).

Any time that we use language, we are simultaneously presenting some kind of content, enacting a relationship with a listener or reader, and organizing this content in some way by building a cohesive message (de Oliveira & Schleppegrell, 2015). These three areas of meaning – *presenting content, enacting relationships*, and *constructing a cohesive message* – help us examine language closely. Teachers and students explore texts as they are written, without any simplification.

In terms of presenting ideas, as teachers and language analysts, we focus on the content of the message, looking at verbal and visual resources that construct the content presented in the nouns, verbs, adjectives, prepositional phrases, and adverbs. When we read, write, listen, and speak, we draw on language resources that indicate the kind of relationship we are enacting, whether it is formal or informal, close or distant, and whether it includes attitudes of various kinds. We can explore the verbal and visual resources that construct the nature of relationships among speakers/listeners, writers/readers, and viewers, and what is viewed. Some of the language choices we make are not about presenting content or enacting a relationship but instead are in the service of constructing a message that holds together. For this we explore the resources that are concerned with the organization of the information and elements of texts and images used to present content in a cohesive way.

In working with both pre-service and in-service teachers, we have introduced a functional metalanguage to guide teachers to see how a focus on different language features highlights different aspects of meaning in a text. We develop teachers' awareness about the forms language takes in presenting content, enacting a relationship, and constructing a cohesive message. Next, particular functional constructs that can be used to help teachers develop activities focusing MLs on meanings in texts are highlighted. Teachers then use these constructs to explore the language of the texts in their programs and engage their MLs in talk about text to support better understanding of how English works. Table 2.3 presents an overview of each area of meaning,

Table 2.3: Areas of Meaning, Questions to Guide Language Focus, and Language Focus

Area of Meaning	Questions to Guide Language Focus	Language Focus
Presenting content	1. What is the text/ image about? 2. What are the key concepts developed in the text/image?	Sentence constituents: ◆ Participants (human and non-human e.g., *the enormous tree, magnetism, Maria and her friends*) ◆ Processes (doing, relating, thinking, feeling, and saying verbs) ◆ Circumstances (adverbs and prepositional phrases e.g., *this summer, before school started, loudly*)
Enacting a relationship with the reader	3. What is the author's perspective? 4. How does the author of this text/ image interact with the reader/viewer?	Mood choices: ◆ Declarative ◆ Interrogative ◆ Imperative Modality Evaluative Meanings
Constructing a cohesive message	5. How is the text/ image organized? 6. How does the text/ image construct a cohesive message?	Given/New Patterns Cohesion

includes questions to guide the language focus for each area, and identifies the language focus associated with each area of meaning. Each of these areas of meaning is explored next.

Presenting Content

Presenting content explores the Participants (typically expressed through nouns) engaged in some kinds of Processes (typically expressed through verbs) under certain Circumstances (typically expressed through prepositional and adverbial phrases) (Eggins, 2004; Halliday & Matthiessen, 2014).

While we are focusing on whole texts, we can examine individual units within a full text. The basic unit of language analysis within a text is the *clause*. Sentences can have just one clause, but sometimes a sentence has more than one clause. The basic unit of a clause is a *process*, constructed in a verb or verb group. A clause can consist of just a process (for example, *Come!*), but typically clauses have both processes and *participants*. Participants are constructed in nouns or noun groups that present who is participating in the process. They can be human and non-human. In addition, a clause may have *circumstances* that present meaning related to time, place, manner, cause, etc. Circumstances are constructed in adverbs or prepositional phrases. Clauses also may incorporate *connectors* such as *conjunctions* or other words and phrases that help move the text along. These four elements, *process, participant, circumstance, connector*, give us a metalanguage for talking about the main elements of each sentence in English. This approach to sentence analysis focuses on meaningful chunks, and not on isolated words. We want to see the major meaning components of the sentence and how they work together in the text.

Participants

Participants are the entities involved in the process, typically realized in noun groups (e.g., *the magnet, many metal objects, a scientific phenomenon*). Nouns are used to represent participants in a process. They refer to people, places, things, ideas or concepts. Participants can be one word (*Phillip*) or a group of words (*more settlements than any other place in California*). Each type of process involves different kinds of relationships with participants and these participants take on different roles in different process types.

- ◆ Nouns name people, places, things or ideas. They are what takes part in the actions or happenings. Noun groups can be:
  - ▪ a single word (***Books*** are wonderful resources)
  - ▪ a noun modified with **pre-** and/or **post-modifiers** by adjectives, prepositional phrases, and even whole clauses. These are all single participants: (***Roasted*** *beef; The bedroom **in my house**; a different place **to play**; the most intriguing feature **ever known to people**; something **that we need to consider***).
- ◆ Typical noun suffixes: verb+ *-ment* (enjoyment), verb+ *-er/-or* (writer), verb+ *-ion* (anticipation), adjective+ *-ness* (cheerfulness).
- ◆ Nouns have special endings (inflections) **-s**: for possessives and regular plurals.
- ◆ Nouns can be preceded by articles (*The* or *a, an*) and can be modified by adjectives (***The interesting*** *talk, **a useful** theory*).
- ◆ Participle and infinitive clauses can function as participants (noun groups): *Steve loved **having a friend**. **To have a great trip around the world** was his biggest dream.*
- ◆ Nouns can function as the subject of a clause. They can also be direct and indirect objects, complements of linking verbs, and objects of prepositions.

Processes

Verbs are used to represent experience by telling us what is 'going on' in the text. In functional language, we call verbs *processes* because we are focused on the representation of experience that the verb provides, and because often a group of verbs, rather than a single verb, constitutes the process. Different types of processes have different language patterns associated with them. There are five major process types, expressed through verbs, shown in Table 2.4, with some examples:

Processes can be:

◆ a single word (*Phillip **participates** in meetings; We **calculated** the perimeter*)
◆ a number of words (*Phillip **gave up** his throne after the rebellion. He **didn't want to fight** against the troops.*)
◆ Sometimes more than one verb is part of a single process (*looked up to watch, began leaving*)
◆ Forms of *have* and *be* often occur together with a main verb (***has started; is watching***)
◆ Modal verbs (***will, should, can, may, might**, etc.*), negatives, and adverbs (*we **will win**; He **won't fight**; **has left***)

Table 2.4: Process Types, Typical Function, and Examples

Process Type	Typical Function	Examples
doing verbs	represent actions	*participate* *run* *move* *calculate*
relating verbs	show relationships between ideas	*is* *as* *have*
thinking verbs	represent thought	*think* *know* *consider*
feeling verbs	represent feelings	*admire* *love* *like*
saying verbs	indicate what someone or something has said	*say* *tell* *ask*

Circumstances

Processes also take place around circumstances (of time, space, conditions, purpose etc.), typically presented in adverbs (e.g., *finally*, *separately*) or prepositional phrases (e.g., *around the corner, with a fork*). Circumstances provide information about time, place, manner, accompaniment, and other meanings. Table 2.5 provides information on some typical meanings expressed in circumstances, the question they typically answer, and some examples.

◆ ***On Mondays*** I go to work.
◆ ***Every afternoon*** we drink tea with lemon.
◆ The cat is sleeping ***on the carpet***.
◆ I usually go ***there***.

Table 2.5: Circumstances, Questions, and Examples

Meaning options	Question it answers	Examples
Time	*When?*	*On the first night, in the afternoon*
Location	*Where?*	*in the train below, on the bed, on the side of the valley, through Seattle, on top of houses, along the cover, outside*
Manner	*How?*	*in these ways* He will die *by the sword* *suddenly* King Phillip started to walk listen *carefully*
Cause	*Why? What for? Who for?*	The king left his home *for the first trip.* *Unable to continue his trip,* he turned around and went back home. It was a place he stayed *for defense*
Accompaniment	*With whom? Who else?*	*with my brother*
Role	*What as?*	*as a child*
Extent	*How far/long/ often?*	*For many years, always, never, sometimes, mostly, only*
Angle	*According to whom?*	*according to…*
Matter	*What about?*	I'm worried *about the fire.* He asked the king *about his intentions.*

Exploring participants, processes, and circumstances in clauses reveals how content is presented.

Enacting Relationships

Enacting relationships explores mood, modality, and evaluative language. We can look at the presence or absence of the subject and finite elements of the clauses and in what order they occur with respect to one another (Halliday & Matthiessen, 2014). These are important because they realize the grammatical choice of the *mood* of a clause: either declarative, interrogative, or imperative. Mood choices help a writer enact a relationship with readers. English has three grammatical moods: declarative, interrogative, and imperative:

> **Declarative**: She is reading the textbook.
> **Interrogative**: Does she want to read the textbook?
> **Imperative**: Read the textbook!

Students can learn to recognize and name these moods and consider how they help an author interact with the reader. These three moods are used to perform four speech functions: statement, question, offer, and command. Declarative mood is typically used for the speech function *statement*, interrogative for the speech function *question*, imperative for the speech function *command*, and various moods for the speech function *offer*, as in these examples:

- ◆ *Statements (giving information)*: The Declaration of Independence was an important document.
- ◆ *Questions (asking for information)*: Why was the Declaration of Independence an important document?
- ◆ *Commands (demanding something)*: Read the Declaration of Independence in your textbook.
- ◆ *Offers (offering something)*: Want to hear the Declaration of Independence? or Let's read the Declaration of Independence!

We interact with each other in different sentence forms, take particular positions, and express points of view. We also have the ability to soften the meaning we make in statements, questions, and commands. A resource for doing this is *modality*, an area which concerns the different ways in which someone expresses evaluation, attitudes, and judgments of various kinds. Modality allows us to express possibility, certainty, normality, usuality, necessity, and obligation. This includes modal verbs (e.g., *should, might, could*), modal adjectives (e.g., *frequent, usual*), modal adverbs (e.g., *probably, certainly, typically*), and modal nouns (e.g., *condition, necessity*). Evaluative vocabulary enables the construction of stance and judgment. Mood, modality, and evaluative vocabulary express meanings that enact a relationship between reader and listener and writer and speaker. Table 2.6 presents some modality examples.

Table 2.6: Modality Examples

Language Structure	Higher Modality	Medium Modality	Lower Modality
Modal Verbs	must, need to, has to, had to, ought to	should, will, would, supposed to	can, could, may, might
Modal Adverbs	certainly, definitely, always, never	probably, usually, likely	possibly, perhaps, maybe
Modal Adjectives	certain, definite, absolute, necessary	probable, usual	Possible
Modal Nouns	certainty, requirement, obligation, need	probability, chance	possibility, likelihood

(based on Humphrey et al., 2015).

Evaluative meanings refer to language choices used to make evaluations. Specifically, they can be expressions of attitude and these expressions can be graded showing strength or force. Attitude can be divided into three categories:

◆ Affect: expressions of feelings to build up empathy and suspense
◆ Judgment: Expressions of moral judgments of people's behavior
◆ Appreciation: Expressions of assessment of the quality of objects

Table 2.7 presents a framework for investigating the processes language employs in evaluation to help teachers identify the ways people pass judgment on other people, events, objects, and, in general, the way they see the world. Following Humphrey et al. (2015), it has probing questions and examples of explicit positive and negative values.

Table 2.7: Type of Attitude with Questions and Examples of Explicit Values

Type of Attitude	Examples of Explicit Values
Affect	
Am I happy/unhappy? Am I secure/insecure? Am I satisfied/dissatisfied?	**Positive** **+ve (feel good)**
	happy, laugh, love, hug
	reassure, trusting, together
	engaged, attentive, impressed
	Negative **−ve (feel bad)**
	sadly, misery, dislike
	frighten, tremble, fearful
	to bore, empty, to engage, embarrassed
Judgment	
Social esteem Is he/she morally and/or legally sound (a good person)?	**Positive** **+ve (admire)**
	special: lucky, fashionable, normal
	capable: powerful, intelligent, skilled
	tenacious: brave, tireless
	Negative **−ve (criticize)**
	unfortunate, odd, weird
	weak, insane, stupid
	rash, cowardly
Social sanction Is he/she morally and/or legally sound (a good person)?	**Positive** **+ve (admire)**
	truthful, genuine, frank, good, just, kind, noble
	Negative **−ve (criticize)**
	dishonest, manipulative, bad, corrupt, cruel, evil

(Continued)

Table 2.7: (Continued)

Type of Attitude	Examples of Explicit Values
Appreciation	
Reaction Did I like it?	**Positive** +ve
	good, lovely, enjoyable, funny, entertaining, beautiful
	Negative −ve
	dull, boring, smelly, weird, ugly
Composition Was it well constructed?	**Positive** +ve
	well-written, well-drawn, imaginative, effective, manicured, clean
	Negative −ve
	simplistic, hard to follow, too detailed, untidy
Valuation Was it worthwhile? Was it significant?	**Positive** +ve
	challenging, profound, meaningful, worthwhile; unique, relevant
	Negative −ve
	shallow, insignificant, irrelevant, worthless

(based on Humphrey et al., 2015).

Constructing a Cohesive Message

Constructing a cohesive message explores Given/New patterns and cohesion. Given/New patterns contribute to building the organization of a text and contribute to the flow of information from sentence to sentence. The Given – or known information – is placed at the beginning of a clause and the New – or unknown information – encompasses the remaining bit of the clause (Halliday & Matthiessen, 2014). Often, new information from one clause is presented as given in the following clause so more information can be added. Tracking Given/New patterns helps us see how the text is organized from clause to clause and paragraph to paragraph. Given choices are important for organizing and moving a text forward. New information can also help with information flow when it is presented as given in a subsequent clause so more information can be added. This New to Given pattern can function for linking with prior discourse so that information can be built up. Let's look at an example, from science, in detail to see how Given/New patterns help organize the text.

> Seeds form after a flower is pollinated. **Pollination** happens when pollen is carried from a stamen to a pistil by wind or animals. For example, bees, birds, and bats feed on nectar, a sweet liquid in some flowers. Pollen sticks to the animals' bodies.
>
> (Harcourt, 2005, p. A85)

Given	New
Seeds	form after a flower *is pollinated*.
Pollination	happens when <u>pollen</u> is carried from a stamen to a pistil by wind or <u>animals</u>.
For example, <u>bees, birds, and bats</u>	feed on nectar, a sweet liquid in some flowers.
<u>Pollen</u>	sticks to the animals' bodies.

This short example shows how several words that appear in the New position are picked up as Given in following clauses. In the first clause, we have a *nominalization*. Nominalization is a language resource for the construction of nominal groups. It refers to the expression as a noun or noun group of what would be presented as a verb, an adjective, or a conjunction in everyday language (de Oliveira, 2010). Typically, in academic discourse, we see the introduction of an idea as a process such as *is pollinated* in the New construction, then this idea is picked up in the Given construction as a nominalization such as *pollination*. Other times words are introduced in the New position then picked up as examples (such as *animals* and *bees, birds, and bats*) or are repeated (such as *pollen* and *pollen*). These moves contribute to the organization of the text and build the flow of information from clause to clause.

Teachers can show students the potential of language to expand and elaborate their ideas. For example, New is a good place to pay attention to, since New helps writers with adding information. If teachers have students break down their texts into Given and New, they can alert students to places where they need to clarify, exemplify, include additional details, and reiterate main points. Then, after students know how a Given/New categorization works, they can focus on developing their ideas themselves by analyzing New patterns to find how they elaborated their ideas and identify places they need to work on. Looking at a text clause by clause can help teachers see how language is construing the meanings students are trying to express. Although an intensive focus is time-consuming, this type of language work, done on a regular basis, can enable teachers and students to talk about text in very concrete ways.

Another important area to explore is **cohesion**, the way a text hangs together with the support of cohesive devices such as pronouns (e.g., *they, that, her*), synonyms and substitutes (e.g., *exemplar-ideal*; *The Declaration of Independence – this document*), and connectors (e.g. *and, despite, if*). Cohesive devices are words or groups of words that create links within the text (Halliday & Matthiessen, 2014). Table 2.8 shows examples of different types of cohesive devices used to construct a message that holds together and builds from clause to clause. These are commonly used across the content areas (notice my use of the demonstrative *these* as a cohesive device itself referring to *cohesive devices* from my previous sentence.) Rather than referring to items by name, cohesive devices are used to construct links between complex and abstract elements.

Connectors are conjunctions and other linking phrases that build the logical development of texts. *Connectors* are words used to explicitly mark the relationship between the information constructed in a text. Other times the relationships are left implicit. In this case, the teacher might need to assist students in figuring out what the connection is between pieces of information.

Text Connectors help authors organize the information in a text by explicitly marking relationships related to time, cause, condition, purpose etc. Text connectors tell the reader how individual statements in a paragraph are connected. To choose connectors that are appropriate, students must first recognize how their ideas are related to each other.

Time and place markers, such as *In* 1850…, *By the end* of the war…, *When* the war finished; or connectors, such as *because, although, however*, provide readers with 'sign-posts' indicating how the text relates the information presented. Text connectors form links between sentences and longer stretches of text. They can be placed at various positions within the sentence. Table 2.9 provides a list of kinds of commonly used connectors organized according to the areas of meaning they contribute to.

◆ **Clause connectors** are used to link different clauses to form sentences.
◆ **Text connectors** function at the text level by linking sentences and paragraphs.

Table 2.8: Cohesive Devices

Cohesive Devices					
Explanation	Reference	Substitution	Ellipsis	Connectors	Lexical Cohesion
	Words that stand for other words in a text. There are different kinds of reference: some that refer back (anaphoric reference) to a noun or noun group used in a previous clause; some that refer forward (cataphoric reference) to a noun or noun group appearing in the next clause; and some that refer to nouns outside of the text (exophoric reference)	Synonyms that appear together with other referrers or as single words that stand for a concept that has been or will be introduced (if substitutes are not used, the text becomes very repetitive).	The omission of a word or words that can be understood from contextual clues.	Linking devices between sentences or clauses in a text. Connectors express the 'logical-semantic' relation between sentences rather than between words and structures.	Choice of vocabulary, concerned with the relationship that exists between lexical items in a text. ◆ **Reiteration** Two items that share the same referent and could either be repeated or have similar meanings in a text. Forms of reiteration: **Repetition, Synonymy, Antonymy, Hyponymy, and Meronymy** ◆ **Collocation** Combination of vocabulary items that co-occur together. It includes combinations of adjectives and nouns and verbs and nouns

Examples	Pronouns / Demonstratives		Addition	Reiteration
	Pronouns *they, their, he, she, his, her, itself, its* **Demonstratives** *this, that, these, those.*	The Declaration of Independence and the U.S. Constitution are key documents in U.S. history. In fact, *both* are studied in history classes. The Declaration of Independence was the statement which announced that the thirteen American colonies were independent from Great Britain. *This document* was a formal explanation needed to declare independence.	**Addition** *and, and then, furthermore* **Time** *when, then* **Comparison/Contrast** *but, for example, instead, in other words, however, in fact* **Cause/Consequence** *because, so, despite, nevertheless, even though, therefore* **Condition** *if, unless* **Purpose** *in order to, so* **Sequence** *first, second, finally* The Declaration of Independence was approved by the Continental Congress on July 4, 1776, *but before* it was adopted, there was a conflict between Britain and the 13 colonies *because* the colonies were fighting for their rights. *Therefore,* the series of events that led to the writing of the Declaration was very important.	**Reiteration** **Repetition**: Restatement of the same lexical item The Declaration of Independence was an important *document*. This *document* is studied in history classes. **Synonymy**: Items of similar meaning The Declaration of Independence was an *important document*. It is *key to* understanding our history. **Antonymy**: Items of opposite meanings Studying the Declaration of Independence in fourth grade is *likely*. It is *unlikely* that it will be the only time you will study it. **Hyponymy**: Items of 'general-specific' or 'an example of' relationship *Birds* are often symbols in history. *The bald eagle* is a symbol of the United States. **Meronymy**: Items of 'whole-part' relationship *The Everglades are part of Florida.* **Collocation** ◆ fast food ◆ weapons of mass destruction ◆ moment of silence ◆ do your homework ◆ give a presentation

Table 2.9: Meaning and Example Connectors

Meaning	Example Connectors
Addition	*and, and then, furthermore, in addition, apart from that, furthermore, besides, along with, again, along with, indeed, apart from that, also*
Cause/consequence	*because, because of this, so, as a result, despite, nevertheless, even though, so, therefore, consequently, due to, for that reason, in that case*
Clarifying	*in other words, to put it another way, for example, for instance, to be more precise, in particular, or rather, in fact, as a matter of fact, that is, namely, to illustrate*
Comparison/contrast	*but, for example, instead, in other words, however, in fact, in that case, while, although, on the other hand, despite*
Condition/	*if, unless*
Concession	*in that case, otherwise, if not, however, nevertheless, despite this, besides, yet, on the other hand, on the contrary, in spite of, instead, still, even so, all the same, in any case, at least, though, despite this*
Purpose	*in order to, so*
Sequence	*first, second, finally, in the first place, to start with, at this point, to get back to the point, in short, all in all, to conclude*
Time	*when, then, next, afterwards, after a while, at the same time, at this moment, meanwhile, previously, before that, finally*

Clause connectors are used to make connections **within** sentences and text connectors are used to make connections **between** sentences and larger portions of text.

Examples

      {Clause 1}   [clause 2]

{*Although* the people overcame many misfortunes}, [their small town continued to struggle].

However, they trusted that hard work and a strong community would help them survive.

Although is a clause connector. *However* is a text connector.

LACI's TLC is meant to enhance the effective instructional practices teachers already use with their MLs. Teachers are encouraged to consider incorporating some of the ideas described in this book into their existing units of study. It is possible to incorporate many of the ideas using the TLC's sequenced process in order to provide high challenge and high support for all students. When teachers start looking closely at texts, they will notice that each text has a configuration of meanings that can lead to many language explorations. One of the teachers featured in this book calls themselves and their students "language detectives"! They are finding out more about a text by exploring it deeply. Another teacher calls this work "language dissection" because teachers and students are dissecting the language like they would do dissection in a science class!

Code-Breaking with *I Hate English!*

This section presents a close examination of language focused on the three areas of meaning *presenting content, enacting relationships*, and *constructing a cohesive message* in the picture book *I Hate English!* (Levine, 1989). Picture books are a common resource in elementary classrooms and an especially useful one to introduce children to language, as they appeal both linguistically and visually. Picture books are a very useful teaching tool for MLs, especially because of the richness in vocabulary and depth in content that they present (Hernández, Montelongo & Herter, 2016; Lado & Hauth, 2022). The visual elements of picture books serve as a key form of scaffolding for MLs as they work to interpret texts and engage in more complex reading skills (Bland, 2013). Picture books may contain characters and events with which MLs can identify, leading to more engagement and positive interactions as a source of enjoyment (Lado, 2012). Because picture books are the primary texts utilized in early childhood education (Arizpe & Styles, 2015), the analysis I present in this chapter focuses on a great picture book about an immigrant girl. The picture book *I Hate English!* describes how Mei Mei, an immigrant child from Hong Kong, changes over time after she immigrates to New York City and learns to love English as much as she loves Chinese.

A strong theme throughout *I Hate English!* is the contrast between Mei Mei's feelings about English and Chinese. Mei Mei is an immigrant child from Hong Kong who has recently moved to New York City. At the beginning of the book, Mei Mei hates English and loves Chinese. As the narrative develops, we can see her feelings about English change, culminating in an appreciation for English and an acknowledgement that she can effectively communicate in both languages without giving up her heritage language.

Presenting Ideas

When we examine texts from the angle of presenting ideas, we focus on content and look at the information that is given through nouns, verbs, adjectives, adverbs, and prepositional phrases. With picture books, we examine components that demonstrate characters, actions, and feelings. The clause constituents *participants*, *processes*, and *circumstances* are analyzed to show how the author presents ideas. By using this functional metalanguage, we are able to look at the different elements of a text as meaningful units, not just individual words. This helps us identify how each unit contributes to the overall meaning of a text (de Oliveira & Schleppegrell, 2015).

Participants

Two main participants, Mei Mei and Nancy, the teacher who came to the Learning Center to help Mei Mei with English, are present in this book (Levine, 1989, p. 14). Participants refer to who or what is participating in the processes, represented as a person or a thing (de Oliveira & Schleppegrell, 2015). Mei Mei is the central participant as the protagonist of the narrative. She is introduced at the very beginning, appearing as the first participant in the text, in "I hate English! Mei Mei said in her head in Chinese" (p. 1). She is also shown as a participant within the images, appearing on nearly every page. Overall, Mei Mei is mentioned 103 times as a participant.

The other main participant is Nancy, the teacher who helps Mei Mei learn to use English. About halfway through the book, "a teacher" is introduced as a participant in the text. "A teacher came to the Learning Center to help Mei Mei in English" (Levine, 1989, p. 14). Readers later find out her name – Nancy. Nancy is depicted in 10 images, and is mentioned 43 times as participant. The participant Nancy has a key role in the narrative because it is through her that Mei Mei comes to appreciate the "present of English" (Levine, 1989, p. 30).

Processes

We illustrate how the picture book utilizes processes, or verbs that show what is going on in the text. I identify the process types *doing, relating, thinking, feeling,* and *saying* to explain how Mei Mei feels and accompanying images that show how her feelings change as the story progresses. We demonstrate how different types of processes highlight Mei Mei's feelings. By identifying *relating* processes, mainly *being* and *having verbs*, readers can see how the book presents descriptions and relationships. *Saying* processes introduce what Mei Mei said in her head or out loud, also making connections to her inner or outer feelings. By identifying *thinking* and *feeling* processes that explain how Mei Mei feels, and by focusing on *doing* processes that explain the actions that occur in different cultural and linguistic settings, readers can better understand how Mei Mei's emotions developed and changed.

These verbal resources are accompanied by visuals that support the presentation of these processes. For example, we can see this clearly demonstrated in two contrasting emotions on pages 1 and 5. On page 1, the text reads "I hate English! Mei Mei said in her head in Chinese" (Levine, 1989). The saying process introduces the message, "I hate English!," which reveals Mei Mei's negative emotion towards English. This text is accompanied by an image of Mei Mei with an angry face, downcast eyes, and crossed arms. Contrasting with this emotion of hate, page 5 depicts love. The text reads, "Mei Mei loved Chinese. Especially writing" (Levine, 1989, p. 5). The feeling process *loved* in the text depicts Mei Mei's positive emotion toward Chinese. After the first sentence on the page, the text lists out all the related objects and actions related to writing in Chinese that Mei Mei loved. "Fast strokes, short strokes, long strokes – the brush, the pen, the pencil – all seemed to fly in her hand. But that was Chinese" (Levine, 1989, p. 5). This emotion is mirrored in the image, which shows Mei Mei sitting at a desk, holding a pen posed above paper, surrounded by Chinese characters, and smiling.

Throughout the rest of the book, we see that the various processes continue to depict Mei Mei's feelings. Altogether, there are several processes that show Mei Mei's emotions: feeling processes such as *hate, loved, felt, don't care*; relating processes such as *is* accompanied by descriptions *too bad*, and saying processes such as *said* accompanied by *"I don't care"*. The images throughout the book are similar to the written words – they provide examples of the feelings depicted through the language presented in the text. Mei Mei is portrayed 25 times in the illustrations throughout the book, and each image portrays emotion through actions. Emotion in action is shown through her eyes (narrowed, downcast, wide), her mouth (downturned, smiling, open), and even her skin color (flushed, pale) (see de Oliveira et al., 2018 for full description of image-text relations in this picture book).

As the story progresses, Mei Mei's feelings toward English are easily visible in both the language and images. The reader can see that her emotions regarding English go through a transformation. The first page shows us Mei Mei's dislike for English. As Mei Mei moves toward an acceptance and appreciation of English (page 30), the reader notices other feelings related to English portrayed throughout, such as loneliness (page 4), fear (pages 14 and 18), interest (page 15), sadness (page 17), and anger (page 20). Processes and related images play a central part in demonstrating all these emotions.

Circumstances

Circumstances help the writer construct events by providing additional information regarding the *when*, *where*, *how*, and *why* of the processes (de Oliveira & Schleppegrell, 2015). In *I Hate English!*, circumstances of place, showing *where*, are particularly relevant. We see the main circumstances of place as Hong Kong and New York, which help construct the contrast between Chinese and English. For example, on the second page, we read, "Mei Mei was smart in school." The participant Mei Mei is shown as *being* smart in school. The circumstance found in the following sentence helps the text provide further information and clarification about *in school* by specifying which school, and in which language. "In *her* school in Hong Kong. In Chinese." Her former school located in Hong Kong is a circumstance of place which helps the author contrast her former (Hong Kong) and current (New York) circumstances of place. She began to hate English when her family moved to New York. As a result, she "wouldn't speak in school… Everything was in English, and Mei Mei would not speak English" (Levine, 1989, p. 6).

By identifying circumstances that are prepositional phrases with an emphasis on languages, we can better understand how Mei Mei's feelings develop from her resistance to speak English to appreciation for and use of the English language. For example, in the beginning, Mei Mei hated English, which she "said in her head, in Chinese" (Levine, 1989, p. 1). Later, English began to seem interesting (Levine, 1989, p. 15); eventually, Mei Mei "talked for twenty-two minutes without stopping. In English" (Levine, 1989, p. 28). While the language resources in *I Hate English!* construct the different circumstances of place, past and present, the accompanying images only show the present circumstances of place. The text might refer to how Mei Mei used to feel in Hong Kong, but all the images depict her in New York. This was an interesting choice perhaps made by the author and illustrator to show Mei Mei in her current place only. Both written text and images present the story of Mei Mei and her transformations.

Enacting a Relationship

Every time we read texts, we employ the language systems and visual components to enact a relationship between the text and ourselves, as readers. When we explore texts from this angle, we focus on how specific language choices and images are used to enact a relationship with the reader. One way that this relationship is often enacted is through processes or qualities that have strong connotations.

I Hate English! constructs a relationship with the reader through verbal and visual resources that show strong emotions through processes or qualities and the mood choices used. Mei Mei, the main participant, has many contrasting feelings throughout the book regarding English and Chinese. The language and image choices used by the author and illustrator cause the reader to empathize with her. The reader is able to go through a process of transformation in their relationship with the language choices and images, aided through the contrast in the processes and qualities as the story progresses that demonstrate Mei Mei's emotional changes towards English. Mood choices include Declarative, Interrogative, and Imperative. The mood system allows us to make statements (typically expressed in declarative mood), ask questions (typically expressed in interrogative mood), and declare commands (typically expressed in imperative mood).

Some of the processes that have a strong connotation in the book are *hate, fight, love, like, laugh, joke, smile, lose, shout, glare, like*. The following evaluative language used as adjectives are employed throughout the book to demonstrate qualities of languages (English or Chinese) or Mei Mei and her feelings about the two languages: *smart, OK, lonely, alone, good, silly, delicious, terrible, afraid, interesting, sad, bad, strange, favorite*, and *invisible*. At the beginning, only the processes or qualities with a negative connotation were used for English and Mei Mei's feelings about English, and those with a positive connotation were used to describe Chinese or Mei Mei's feelings about Chinese. However, as the story progresses, we see that Mei Mei moves from hating English ("I hate English!"; Levine, 1989, p. 1) to being scared to use it ("Mei Mei was afraid."; Levine, 1989, p. 14), to enjoying it ("She talked for twenty-two minutes without stopping. In English… Mei Mei started to smile."; Levine, 1989, pp. 28–29). The relationship enacted with the reader is characterized by the different processes and qualities that have strong connotations.

One specific example in which the language and images demonstrate enacting a relationship with the reader is on a two-page spread about halfway through the book (Levine, 1989, pp. 16–17). At this moment in the narrative, the teacher is reading a book to Mei Mei. At first, Mei Mei is interested in the story when she understands what is happening. However, as the teacher reads on, the book becomes difficult for Mei Mei to understand. "She felt sad, and a tear slid down her cheek" (Levine, 1989, p. 17). *Felt* is a feeling process, and *slid down* is a doing process, but both processes show her emotion. The image reinforces what is presented through the written text. Mei Mei is shown sitting at a table with her head in her hands, eyes downcast, cheeks red, and a tear in the corner of her eye. All of these different processes and qualities help the reader develop a relationship with the participant and become engaged in the text.

Another way that the text enacts a relationship with the reader is through the emphasis of certain words. By italicizing different words in the text, readers are given clues about how Mei Mei feels. These feelings are reaffirmed through the images that demonstrate Mei Mei's emotions. For example, Mei Mei and Nancy are taking a walk, and Nancy is talking non-stop. The text reads, "Nancy didn't *ask* Mei Mei to talk. Nancy didn't *care* if Mei Mei talked. Nancy didn't *want* Mei Mei to talk!" (Levine, 1989, p. 27). On the next page, it reads, "Mei Mei thought about *her* school. She thought about *her* favorite book. She thought about char sui bao, *her* favorite food. And she thought about Siu Fa, *her* cat" (Levine, 1989, p. 28). These emphasized words help the reader empathize with Mei Mei, and further highlight her as a character with feelings. These words also further build a contrast between what Mei Mei feels and Nancy's actions.

Mood choices also enact a relationship. This picture book uses mostly declarative clauses to make statements. Some of the statements are exclamations, such as the very beginning of the book: *I hate English!* The exclamation helps build the emotion that will develop in the rest of the storyline. The story progresses with events constructed in declarative clauses. It is not until page 9 that the first interrogative clause, *Why can't they read Chinese?*, appears. This question was something Mei Mei was struggling to understand at that point in the story. On page 14, there are two more occurrences of interrogative clauses, which follow one after the other: *Who was this person with short hair and blue eyes? And why was she smiling?* This is when the teacher, Nancy, is introduced as a character which made Mei Mei wonder about her. We see several other interrogative clauses later in the book. Once when Mei Mei is questioning Nancy's comment *Why is that too bad?* (p. 21) and on several occasions when Nancy asks Mei Mei several questions: *Don't you want to go to an American movie? Don't you want to ask for pizza? Don't you want to have an ice-cream cone? Don't you want to read the signs at the zoo? Don't you want to talk with me?* (p. 22). The last interrogative clause is at the end of the book, on the last page, when Mei Mei asks *"For what?"* to Nancy after Mei Mei uses English for a while and Nancy thanks Mei Mei for giving her *"the present of English"* (p. 30).

There are four uses of imperative clauses, with three of them being used by the teacher to give directives to Mei Mei and other children at the Learning Center: "Let's sit down" (p. 14); "Let's stop for today" (p. 17); "Get your coat" (p. 24). The last imperative clause used was by Mei Mei when she says "Stop!" (p. 27) after Nancy had been talking for a while and Mei Mei wanted to talk. The use of this imperative clause actually marked a critical part of the storyline which was when Mei Mei started to use English. After that, at the resolution of this narrative, we, the readers, find out that Mei Mei started to use both Chinese and English: *And to this day Mei Mei talks in Chinese and English whenever she wants* (p. 30).

Constructing a Cohesive Message

Constructing a cohesive message builds from clause to clause. One of the ways that language and images can work together is through the different points of departure in clauses and reference ties, combined with the images that are similar to the words in the picture book. This helps readers recognize connections and enables them to see the evolution of meaning throughout the narrative (de Oliveira & Schleppegrell, 2015). At the beginning of *I Hate English!*, the point of departure, the Given (or first element in each clause), for the majority of the clauses is Mei Mei. Once the teacher is introduced, Mei Mei and Nancy both become main points of departure for clauses. Mei Mei appears in almost every image; once Nancy is introduced, she also appears in the remaining images. This helps emphasize meaning among these main elements of the story, both in the images and in the written text.

Another way that cohesion is constructed within the text is through connectors. Connectors are used to demonstrate how clauses are linked and how information flows in a text, and they bring coherence through appropriate selection of logical meaning. They are conjunctions or other linking phrases that help build logical development (de Oliveira & Schleppegrell, 2015). There are two main connectors that we identified in *I Hate English!*: *and* and *but*. *And*, a connector that builds meaning through addition, is the most frequently used. It appears a total of 24 times in the text. The connector *but* builds meaning through comparison and contrast. It is not as common, only appearing eight times in the narrative. There are also a few connectors that create meaning through time, such as *then, at last, and still*, or *as*. We can see an example of two of the most common connectors, *but* and *and*, on the second page.

The text reads, "Mei Mei was smart in school. In *her* school in Hong Kong. In Chinese. But her family moved to New York. She didn't know why. She didn't want to move. And she said all that in Chinese." The connector *but* is used on this page to contrast how the participant Mei Mei feels in New York with how she felt in Hong Kong. In Hong Kong, she was smart. *But* is used to demonstrate a contradiction with that feeling, and the new circumstance in which the participant finds herself. *And* is used to as a way off adding meaning. The participant feels confused and upset about moving. With the connector *and*, the text shows that she verbalized those feelings. The visual resources on this page restate how Mei Mei is feeling. She is shown in New York with her hands in her pocket and her mouth in a straight line, not looking where the rest of her family is looking. All of the verbal and visual elements come together to construct the information, to emphasize the relationship between words and pictures, and to create cohesion.

As we identify language features to be highlighted with MLs, it is important to note that particular texts exemplify only certain features of the range of language features and demands that may be encountered in texts. Other examples would bring other features into focus.

Summary

This chapter introduced LACI's six Cs of support for scaffolding instruction for MLs: 1. Connection; 2. Culture; 3. Code-breaking; 4. Challenge; 5. Community and Collaboration; 6. Classroom Interactions. This chapter showed how a language-based approach allows for a simultaneous focus on content and language. You were also introduced to LACI's Teaching and Learning Cycle (TLC) as a pedagogical framework to provide learners with explicit knowledge about language and application of genre-based pedagogy based on SFL.

The chapter introduced a functional approach to language development showing how teachers can explore language throughout LACI's TLC. The chapter introduced the metalanguage that connects linguistic form with meaning to talk with MLs about the grade-level texts. The language of a functional approach to language development lets us look at whole chunks and label them in ways that relate to their meaning in context. This chapter concluded with an example of how teachers can explore language and meaning, using the picture book *I Hate English!*

Chapters 3, 4, 5, and 6 focus on each one of the content areas: English language arts, social studies, mathematics, and science. They include sections that identify academic language features important for learning that particular subject, sections with examples of LACI implementation in the classroom by teachers and unit plans that incorporate LACI, highlighting different phases of LACI's TLC. At the end of each chapter, you will be engaged in "Putting into Practice" what you have learned and read about.

3

Teaching English Language Arts to Multilingual Learners

Ruby Li, a kindergarten teacher, was working with students on the book *When I Am Old with You*. She led a class discussion about relatives the previous day and then helped students connect to this prior knowledge and experience, as the following excerpt shows:

> Remember how we talked about our relatives yesterday? Not immediate, that immediate family, the really close ones that this boy probably didn't even know right? But they can still talk about grandpa's memories. We can look at old pictures and try to imagine people in them. Let's look at those pictures of your family, a long time ago. Well, it might make us cry but that's ok. Do you ever have your mom look at old pictures of grandma or grandpa and get sad because they miss them? So they are looking at old pictures.
>
> What C of support is prevalent in this excerpt? Why is this C particularly important for MLs learning English language arts?

The teaching of English language arts (ELA) involves language and literacy components, including reading, writing, listening, and speaking. In 2020, in a position paper on the role of English teachers in educating English language learners, the National Council of Teachers of English (NCTE) addressed the need for ELA teachers to develop the knowledge, skills, and practices necessary to support the development of MLs' language, literacy and identity. Acknowledging that "… the majority of multilingual students find themselves in mainstream classrooms taught by teachers with little or no formal

DOI: 10.4324/9781003264927-3

professional preparation for teaching such students" (NCTE, 2020, p. 1). NCTE identified the insufficiency of English teacher candidates' coursework on and preparation with this particular student population and offered recommendations for effective instructional practices for MLs in the ELA classroom.

This chapter provides examples of how LACI has been implemented in the classroom by two teachers to show ways they explored the language of English language arts with MLs. The chapter includes unit plans that show how LACI's six Cs of support have been incorporated. Each unit plan included LACI's TLC phases which were adapted and modified according to the needs of students in each classroom. Examples of classroom instruction show how two teachers' implementation of LACI drew on the six Cs of support to work with all students in the classroom and were particularly helpful for the MLs in general education classrooms.

LACI in the Classroom: Exploring the Language of English Language Arts with MLs

The examples presented in this chapter come from two classrooms, a kindergarten classroom in Indiana and a first-grade classroom in Florida. I worked with both teachers very closely to implement LACI in their classrooms in support of the many MLs. The teachers collaborated with me and my research team at the time to design ELA content-and-language-integrated units. We went to the classroom on multiple occasions to observe the ways in which the teachers implemented LACI. These units differed in length, depending on the nature of the unit (e.g., one to three weeks). ELA instruction included daily blocks. The examples provided here come from audio recordings of classroom observations and corresponding field notes as well as classroom artifacts, such as unit and lesson plans, graphic organizers, assigned worksheets, writing models, and samples of student work.

LACI in a Kindergarten Classroom

Mrs. Ruby Li, whose words opened this chapter, is a kindergarten teacher. Mrs. Li's classroom is in Indiana, which saw a 409% increase in MLs from 2005 to 2014 (Indiana State Department of Education, 2015). At the time of our collaboration, she taught in the Cornfield School District, in a school with a high number of MLs. She is a certified elementary teacher who had just completed a licensure program in English Language Learning (ELL) at Smalltown University. Mrs. Li's school at the time had 30% of students classified as ELLs, mostly from Latino/a backgrounds.

Mrs. Li identifies as a White, monolingual English speaker, though she developed her knowledge of what she termed "classroom Spanish" to be able to provide home language support for her students (see de Oliveira, Gilmetdinova &

Pelaez-Morales, 2015). She typically had 18–24 students in her classroom, about 9–10 of whom would be classified as ELs. At the time of our collaboration, her classroom was composed of 23 students, nine of whom were classified as ELs. The ELs were all Latina/o whose home language background was Spanish. Eight were from Mexico and one was from Guatemala. The nine ELs had different levels of English proficiency with three being fully bilingual and at least three being recent arrivals to the U.S and speaking little to no English.

A Unit Plan with *When I am Old with You*

The unit plan for a series of lessons carried out in Mrs. Li's classroom presents specific information about how she used LACI's six Cs of support within the TLC. Mrs. Li planned various activities focused on the book *When I Am Old with You*, written by Angela Johnson. This book presents a warm intergenerational story portraying an African-American grandfather and grandson spending time together. The boy begins to think and tells his grandfather about the many things that he wants to do with his granddaddy when he gets older. The boy imagines being old with granddaddy and participating in activities together, such as fishing, exploring the attic, playing, cooking breakfast and talking on the porch.

In implementing LACI's TLC, Mrs. Li primarily focused on the Building Shared Knowledge of the Topic and Sustained Reading phases. Mrs. Li planned several interactions that drew upon the different six Cs of support to engage students in understanding the main themes in the book.

Mrs. Li's unit incorporates what the WIDA ELD Standards Framework (WIDA, 2020) describes as some ways that MLs engage in the Key Language Use *Narrate* in kindergarten (p. 42).

◆ Reflect on their lived experiences
◆ Retell personal experiences
◆ Create imaginative new stories through multimodal text, combining drawings and spelling approximations

This unit also addresses some of the language expectations for MLs in kindergarten. Multilingual learners will:

ELD-LA.K.Narrate.Interpretive
Interpret language arts narratives (with prompting and support) by
◆ Identifying key details
◆ Identifying characters, settings, and major events
◆ Asking and answering questions about unknown words in a text

(WIDA, 2020, p. 48).

Table 3.1 presents a unit plan with lessons that took two days in Mrs. Li's classroom.

Table 3.1 Mrs. Li's Unit Plan

Grade Level: Kindergarten
Subject Area: English Language Arts
Lesson Title: *When I am Old with You*
Duration of the Lessons: 2 days

ELD Standard(s)/WIDA Standards e.g., WIDA or state ELPD standard[s] that are the target of student learning. (Note: Please list the **number and text** of each standard that is being addressed.)	English Language Development Standard 2: English language learners communicate information, ideas and concepts necessary for academic success in the content area of Language Arts
CCSS or State Content Standard What CCSS standard(s) are most relevant to the learning goals?	Reading: Literature Learning Outcome K.RL.1 Actively engage in group reading activities with purpose and understanding. Key Ideas and Textual Support K.RL.2.1 With support, ask and answer questions about main topics and key details in a text heard or read. K.RL.2.2 With support, retell familiar stories, poems, and nursery rhymes, including key details. K.RL.2.3 Identify important elements of the text (e.g., characters, settings, or events). K.RL.2.4 Make predictions about what will happen in a story.
Content Objectives (related to the subject matter central focus)	Students will be able to state where the story takes place and answer questions related to the story content.
Language Objectives (related to key language function, task, or skill)	Students will be able to identify the main places that granddaddy and the boy went to in the story, using specific language.

Prior Academic Knowledge and Conceptions What knowledge, skills, and concepts must students already know to be successful with this lesson?	Family, relatives, immediate family, activities to do with family
Instructional Strategies and Learning Tasks *Description of what the teacher (you) will be doing and/or what the students will be doing.*	
Introduction _____ Minutes How will you start the lesson to engage and motivate students in learning?	**LACI's TLC Phase 1: Building Shared Knowledge of the Topic** Mrs. Li had a discussion with students about family and who is part of immediate family members and who is not.
Instruction _____ Minutes **Highlighted LACI's TLC Phase:** Sustained Reading *Procedures:* specific details regarding what the students will do during the lesson (practice/application) **LACI 6 Cs of Support:** *Connection:* What will you do to connect the lesson to students' prior academic learning, backgrounds and experiences?	**LACI's TLC Phase 2: Sustained Reading,** *When I Am Old With You* Mrs. Li does an interactive reading aloud activity along with a discussion of observations about the book content. She asks specific questions about where granddaddy and the boy are to ensure comprehension (*Classroom Interactions*). She connects to students' backgrounds and experiences to recall what they know. She asks students to look at family pictures to connect to students' experiences (*Connection*) Mrs. Li reviews prior knowledge and connects it to new information. Complex concepts such as "relatives" create opportunities for students' output; students are contributing to the discussion. Mrs. Li gives attention to whole-text features. Mrs. Li uses Spanish language to ask questions during interactions and support the culture of her Latino/a MLs (*Culture and Code-Breaking*). She uses Spanish to assist her MLs' understanding of the content she is presenting (*Code-Breaking*). Mrs. Li asks students for vocabulary in Spanish or uses Spanish to help explain the tasks that students are to complete (*Code-Breaking*).

(Continued)

Table 3.1 (Continued)

Culture: How will you link the new content skills and concepts to students' cultural and linguistic resources to support academic learning? *Challenge*: What aspects of disciplinary literacy will you address? Which higher-order thinking and reasoning skills will you focus on? **Code-Breaking**: What will you do to explicitly teach ways of doing school, academic literacy, and disciplinary, linguistic, and cultural codes of content learning? How will you model the language forms/vocabulary/function/skills? **Community and collaboration**: How will you engage students in collaboration and build a community of practice?	The content of the book is challenging for students and requires explanations so they understand main ideas and events (*Challenge*) Mrs. Li uses different participant structures to provide different levels of support for various groups and to encourage students to assume greater responsibility for their learning as the focus of learning shifts between teacher- and student-centered learning (*Community and Collaboration*) Students uses others as language resources (*Code-Breaking and Community and Collaboration*). Students complete a coloring activity identifying where granddaddy and the boy went in the story (*Challenge*) Students complete a drawing and coloring activity with themselves and either their grandpa or grandma.

Classroom interactions: How will you use "interactional scaffolding" in the classroom? Plan for the use of oral discourse to prompt elaboration, build academic literacy, and move discourse and learning forward. **Closure**	
Assessment/Evaluation (Formative and/or Summative)	Formative evaluation was embedded in the lesson as students worked on reading tasks, both individually and collaboratively with peers and Mrs. Li
Extension	Possibility: Teacher may read another book that has relatives and discuss with the class.

LACI's TLC Phase 1: Building Shared Knowledge about the Topic

To introduce the text *When I Am Old with You*, Mrs. Li led a class discussion about relatives. Mrs. Li talks to students about their immediate family – who is included, who is not – and how different families are made up of different members. She tells them that sometimes a grandma and grandpa live with them, and sometimes they live far away. This helps build students' knowledge about the topic of the book.

LACI's TLC Phase 2: Sustained Reading

Mrs. Li used several tasks and activities in which students engaged as part of the longer unit based on the book *When I Am Old with You*. This book was at the core of the unit and was used as a mediational text, or a text around which significant talk occurs and which serves as ways to link prior or future learning, with vocabulary activities coming at the beginning, lots of discussion related to key concepts presented in the book, then reading the book carefully and noting connections between the pictures and the text. Table 3.2 presents the various tasks/activities that Mrs. Li used during the Sustained Reading phase of LACI's TLC.

After building shared knowledge of the topic by discussing relatives and drawing the previous day, on the next day Mrs. Li did an Interactive Reading Aloud with the class. She starts off by saying,

> This is called *When I Am Old with You, Cuando estoy viejo contigo.* When I'm old with you, this is by Angela Johnson. And the pictures are by David Salman. Here goes. I will try to explain this a little bit. Let's read the first page and then I'll explain. {Mrs. Li reading from the book: When I am old with you, granddaddy} What do you think he's saying?

The interactive reading aloud activity offers students opportunities to share their own experiences with family and spending time with their family and at the same time express their understanding of the content. Mrs. Li asks specific questions throughout the reading to help students understand what the book is trying to convey in terms of ideas. Mrs. Li does this by asking, for example,

- ◆ What do you think he's saying?
- ◆ So where are they at?
- ◆ Do you think that's something they've done before?
- ◆ What are they doing here?

Table 3.2: Tasks During Sustained Reading Phase with *When I am Old with You*

Task/Activity	Purpose	LACI's Cs of Support
Interactive Reading Aloud	◆ to model good reading with variation in vocal aspects of delivery (e.g. pitch, tone, pace etc) ◆ to offer students opportunities to express their understanding of the content ◆ to explain the content to students	*Code-Breaking Challenge Connection Culture Classroom Interactions*
Discussion of Observations about Book	◆ to provide opportunities for students to share what they noticed during the interactive read aloud	*Community and Collaboration Code-Breaking Challenge*
Coloring Activity(Review the story)	◆ to review where the main characters have been in the story while coloring the pictures. ◆ to develop a sense of all of the events in the story and the storyline	*Code-Breaking Challenge*
Exploration of Feelings and Sayings	◆ to identify the boy's feelings with evidence from the story about his actions and what he says.	*Code-Breaking Community and Collaboration Connection*
Station Activity	◆ to practice specific skills, such as reading and interpreting a variety of resources ◆ to interact with the material, answer questions or engage in a reflective activity for a specified amount of time.	*Code-Breaking Community and Collaboration Challenge*

◆ Do you think that the boy loves bacon so much? That's the reason he wants to have bacon? Or do you think there's another reason he's telling you this? What's most important to him right now? Eating the bacon or something else?

◆ Why do you think people cut down all the trees?

Mrs. Li uses several Cs during the interactive reading aloud with students. The next example shows her use of the C of *classroom interactions*. Specifically, she uses the interactional scaffolding moves *appropriation*, *recasting*, and *purposeful repetition* that exemplify how Mrs. Li recast their words into more content, language, context appropriate discourse. As explained in Chapter 2, appropriation is when the teacher uses the language previously used by the students, often to connect to what was just said and move the discussion forward. Recasting refers to when the teacher takes what the students say and puts it into academically appropriate discourse. Purposeful repetition is when the teacher repeats what the students say. This move is used for various reasons, including the following: to draw attention to student dialogue, to repeat dialogue so all students can hear, to provide a cue for students to self-correct or extend their thoughts. Elaboration is when the teacher takes the students' contributions and supplements it with additional information.

Example 1

MRS. LI: {Mrs. Li reading from the book: An old dog will sit by my feet, and I will swat flies all afternoon.} So where are they at?

S4: Outside.

MRS. LI: Outside. Maybe at their house, though, at grandpa's house? So the grandpa's sitting there, right? The dog sitting there, they must like to do what?

SS: Flies.

MRS. LI: Swat the flies. {Mrs. Li reading from the book: We'll go fishing too, granddaddy. Down by that old pond, with the flat rocks all around}. Would that be nice to go fishing with your grandpa?

Mrs. Li acknowledges students' contribution by saying "outside", appropriating what students just said, which is also an example of *purposeful repetition*. She goes on to provide a more accurate and precise place "their house" and right after that an even more precise place "grandpa's house" – examples of *recasting*.

Example 2 shows how she used various Cs throughout the activity:

Example 2

MRS. LI: Remember how we talked about relatives yesterday. Yeah, they would talk about not that immediate family, the real close ones, but ones that this boy probably never even knew, right? But they can still talk about grandpa's memories…

> **MRS. LI READING FROM THE BOOK:** {We can look at the old pictures and try to imagine the people in them. Let's look at those old pictures of your family a long time ago. It might make us cry, but that's okay.}
>
> Do you ever have your mom look at old pictures of like her grandma or grandpa gets sad sometimes because they miss them. Yeah, so they're looking at old pictures and it would be sad. Sometimes if I look at pictures of my grandma, grandpa, it makes me sad. Sometimes I love them so much. I miss them. I bet he misses his family.

Mrs. Li uses the C of *connection*, as she links what they are discussing to students' backgrounds and experiences, reminding them about what they discussed the day before. By using "Do you ever have your mom look at old pictures of like her grandma or grandpa gets sad sometimes because they miss them," she *connects* to students' experiences by asking a specific question to relate to perhaps something familiar to students and then continues with "Yeah, so they are looking at old pictures" to connect back to the book and what will be further explored. In "Do you ever have your mom look at old pictures of grandma or grandpa and get sad because they miss them?" Mrs. Li connects language and culture in her classroom through her teaching of the content and the language by means of reviewing prior knowledge and connecting it to new information, teaching complex concepts by means of concrete and abstract linguistic realizations such as the concept of "relatives" in the example, creating opportunities for students' output with students continually contributing to the discussion.

Language and other modes of learning can be provided through a variety of visual, aural, tactile supports: wall charts, graphs, maps, photographs, diagrams, pictures, artifacts with the aim of providing additional media to construct meanings. The use of these additional meaning-making systems is often channeled through multiple systems at the same time to create what is called 'message abundance' and to ensure students' access to information by both language-bound and non-linguistic means. Mrs. Li uses all of the potential meaning-making techniques that she has at her disposal – ranging from technology – use of smartboards, videos, interactive worksheets, on the fly image usage (via Google) – to other multimodal strategies, such as gestures, body language, songs, picture books, among others. Mrs. Li uses illustrative pictures from the book to talk about important concepts and raise students' awareness of the meanings expressed in the book, such as in Example 3:

Example 3

MRS. LI: Do you think the boy loves bacon so much that's the reason he wants to have bacon? Or do you think there is another reason he is telling me this? Chris?

SS: [various answers]

MRS. LI: What's most important to him right now? Eating the bacon or something else?

SS: He's with grandad

MRS. LI: Because he's with his granddaddy, I think so too. It's that LOOK. LOOK how happy that boy looks. I don't think he's that happy because he is eating bacon. I think he is that happy because he is with his granddaddy.

S: The picture is nice

MRS. LI: And I like this picture too. Remember when we talked about relatives? Look at all these people! [Mrs. Li points to the drawings that students did]

Mrs. Li uses the C of *connection* and the C of *culture* consistently in her classroom. In the following example, Mrs. Li talked about one page of the story that shows the grandfather and grandson roasting corn around a campfire with their extended family and friends. Mrs. Li pointed out one student in particular, Guadalupe, and asked her about her family's tradition of roasting corn:

Example 4

MRS. LI: {Reading from the book: In the evening, we can roast corn on a big fire and invite everyone we know and eat it. We can play cards and dance and talk about everything}. Guadalupe I've been to your family's... where you are building the new house. You guys don't roast it over a fire. How do you make corn?

GUADALUPE: Well...we just make fire with, um, dogs and... we can make with marshmallows and chocolate and crackers!"

MRS. LI: That's smores. You roast your marshmallows over a fire don't you? But when you guys make corn don't you have a special oven outside you put it in? It's yummy.

GUADALUPE: Yeah

MRS. LI: It's not a grill, they actually have an oven like in Mexico. They have a really cool oven where they can put the corn in and it tastes yummy. It kinda roasts it like a fire, but it's inside of an oven. We usually in the

> United States, most of us, when we have a fire we roast marshmallows. What else have you roasted over a fire?
>
> SS: Hot dogs!
>
> MRS. LI: Hot dogs.
>
> MRS. LI: Let's think about. He's been to grandpa's house. They have been fishing. They went and sat under the tree.
>
> And now, where are they? [Mrs. Li continues to ask questions about the places that granddaddy and the boy have been]

As Mrs. Li finishes the interactive reading aloud, she asks students if the story made them think of their grandma or grandpa and if they like to spend time with them:

MRS. LI: Give me a thumbs up if that story made you think of your grandma or grandpa… how many of you just like, raise your hand if you really, really like to spend time with your grandma or grandpa. ¿A quien le gusta estar con tus abuelos? [Who likes to spend time with your grandparents?]

This was a great way to move on to the next part of the lesson, a coloring activity about the events of the story.

Example 5

MRS. LI: We're gonna do this paper talking about where they've been. Okay? I will help you with it. That's fine. I'll help you with it. But before we do this, we'll have to get out our crayons.

[and a few minutes later after the kids proceed to stand up and drink some water]

Think and discuss granddaddy and the boy had fun. Where did they go together? Have we ever seen them go to the store together? I don't remember that either. Did we see them sit on the porch together? Yes, we sure did. So let's color that picture up here of the porch where they sat. Does anybody remember what they did on the porch? Yeah, they were swatting the flies. They sat and ate bacon too. That might have been a different porch, but sure enough. Ok, I've got my porch colored. Porches are an important part of people's lives in some places. They sit there and talk with their families… Not as many people sit on their porch with fear. Some people don't have windows like we do and they sit on their porch all day.

Mrs. Li asked questions related to the various pictures that represented the places where granddaddy and the boy went. She asked the students,

"Did you see them go to [place] together?" Students answered yes or no and only colored the pictures of the places that granddaddy and the boy went together.

The class moves to another coloring activity about the events of the story. Mrs. Li asks a series of questions to students about who has a grandma and who has a grandpa:

Example 6

MRS. LI: Who has at least one grandma? ¿Quién tiene una abuela? [Who has a grandma?] Everybody has a grandma? ¿Todos tienen una abuela? [Everyone has a grandma?] ¿Sí? [Yes?] Yes? Or who has a grandpa? Raise your hand if you have a grandpa. ¿Quién tiene un abuelo? [Who has a grandpa?] If you don't have a grandpa, then do this for your grandma. Ok? Si no tienes un abuelo, puedes dibujar tu abuela. [If you don't have a grandpa, you can draw your grandma.] If you have both, you can choose one.

MRS. LI: In this top picture, everybody point to the top picture. It says what? Jocelyn, read out loud.

J: This is me.

MRS. LI: This is me. Good. Draw you in that box. Dibuja tu cara [Draw your face].

In Example 6, Mrs. Li is clearly using the C of *culture* in these examples, asking questions and providing directions in Spanish. Mrs. Li uses "¿Quien tiene una abuela?... ¿Todos tienen una abuela? ¿Si?... ¿Quien tiene un abuelo?... Si no tienes un abuelo, puedes dibuja tu abuela" shows how Mrs. Li uses Spanish to support the culture of her Latino/a MLs. This can also be considered as part of her *code-breaking* because she is using Spanish to assist her MLs' understanding of the content she is presenting – an essential component for Mrs. Li as it is the first experience of her Latino MLs in school, so making these kinds of connections by using Spanish is essential in her view. After this activity, students move to stations and engage in other activities, including learning letters and reading another book with the assistance of a student-teacher that was in Mrs. Li's classroom.

Mrs. Li uses *code-breaking* as she is teaching the content and the language using the following tasks: reviewing prior knowledge and connecting it to new information, teaching complex concepts by means of concrete and abstract linguistic realizations, discussing appropriate language use, creating opportunities for students' output, and attending to textual features. Mrs. Li gives all students the indication of what she is doing and justification for the activities in the classroom.

The choice of tasks as well as the relationship among tasks helps teachers turn students' attention toward more active engagement with the learning material. The step-by-step direction of activities provides a logical sequence where in-depth understanding of challenging concepts occurs within the appropriate context, where other scaffolding techniques, such as support structures, language scaffolds and/or semiotic systems are embedded in such a manner that best fits the needs of that particular group of students. The connection between the tasks prior to the class and in the moment can significantly increase the learning outcome for each task and the entire class unit/goals. Mrs. Li used different participant structures to provide different levels of support for various groups and to encourage students to assume greater responsibility for their learning as the focus of learning shifts between teacher- and student-centered learning. These participant structures helped Mrs. Li focus on *community and collaboration*, from teacher-led discussion so students understand the content of the book to individual work on coloring activities that the grandpa and boy did together, which Mrs. Li did after the book discussion. Shared language learning was often observed in Mrs. Li's classroom, with students using others as language resources, and the teacher herself asking students for vocabulary in Spanish or using Spanish to help explain the tasks that students are to complete, as a key component of *culture* and *code-breaking*.

Mrs. Li makes the appropriate selection of tasks a priority and considers MLs and their language proficiencies in English when planning instruction for them. In the stations activity, students are put into level-appropriate reading groups so they can access the reading materials more easily. Typically, in a stations activity, students are in small groups and rotate around from station to station to complete a series of tasks while the teacher works with small groups or individual students. Students usually rotate to a teacher station as a small group. Mrs. Li typically organizes writing tasks in the classroom to prompt students on the subject of writing, provides appropriate language and structures to give resources to draw upon in their writing tasks, and scaffolds by showing the sample writing structure in whole class examples and/or by reading stories. Many of these activities are done throughout the week, spaced out into reading activities and reviewing vocabulary with short stories.

Mrs. Li used various participant structures to support her MLs in the classroom. Participant structures refer to the variation of organizational structure within a unit of instruction: the nature of the task, the degree and nature of scaffolding within it, as well as changes in grouping. The choice of individual, pair or group work is a decision that is dependent on the learning purposes of the task or activity. Different participant structures also provide different levels of support for various groups and encourage students to assume greater responsibility for their learning as the focus of learning shifts between teacher- and student-centered learning. Various participant structures are used in this unit, from teacher-led discussion so students understand the content of the book to individual work on coloring activities that the grandpa and boy did together. Shared language learning is often observed in the classroom, with students using others as language resources, and the teacher herself asking students for vocabulary in Spanish or using Spanish to help explain the tasks that students are to complete.

The examples used so far show some ways that LACI can be used in the classroom to address the language demands of ELA with MLs. Next are some more examples from a first-grade classroom.

LACI in a First-Grade Classroom

The teacher Mrs. Jana Cabana implemented LACI in her first-grade classroom by incorporating it into LACI's Teaching and Learning Cycle. The school, Sunnyside Elementary School, is self-identified as an "International School of Excellence" which serves an international community of students who come from over 50 countries and speak many languages. The classroom had 23 students, 13 boys and 10 girls, 18 of whom were multilingual learners. Students represented a number of different countries with parents coming from various countries, including the United Arab Emirates, Italy, Brazil, Spain, and several Latin American countries.

A Unit Plan with Last Stop on Market Street

The unit plan for a series of lessons carried out in Mrs. Cabana's classroom presents specific information about how she used LACI's six Cs of support within the TLC. The examples from this section show how Mrs. Cabana *connects* to students' backgrounds and experiences to help them recall what they know. She connects language and *culture* through her teaching of content and language by means of reviewing prior knowledge and connecting it to new information. Mrs. Cabana uses different participant structures to focus on *community and collaboration*, from teacher-led discussion to individual work. Language and other modes of learning are integral parts of *code-break-ing* and are provided through a variety of visual, aural, tactile supports to construct a high-challenge, high-support environment. Mrs. Cabana uses various resources to provide both *challenge* and support for MLs. She uses classroom interactions with various elements of interactional scaffolding to support MLs.

The focal text utilized in this unit, *Last Stop on Market Street* (de la Pena, 2015), was incorporated into the ELA curriculum for the entire first-grade team. This picture book is about a boy named CJ riding the bus with his grandma. The majority of the storyline takes place during a bus ride that the grandmother and her grandson take every Sunday across town. During this specific trip, CJ questions his grandmother about several of their routines and circumstances, often comparing their lives to that of others. CJ's grandmother is able to share her wisdom and provide CJ with a new perspective of their activities and community by answering each of his questions in an encouraging and inspiring manner, helping him appreciate the people and the world around them.

In implementing LACI's TLC, Mrs. Cabana adapted it to this unit by focusing primarily on the Deconstruction and Joint Construction phases. Mrs. Cabana planned several interactions that drew upon the different six Cs of support to engage students in discussions about the book. There are multiple examples of shared experiences in this unit, as a major part of the TLC. For **Sustained Reading**, students shared the experience of discussing visiting family members and reading the book together as a class. For the Joint Construction, Mrs. Cabana brainstormed with students ways that they could help the community, as CJ, the main character, helped at the soup kitchen with his grandma. The students voted and decided that they would collect food items to make Thanksgiving baskets for the "Feed South Florida" initiative which provides food and other resources to those who need it. Students brought in their own donations and solicited donations from other students and staff members at the school. This shared experience was used as a springboard for writing.

Mrs. Cabana's unit incorporates what the WIDA ELD Standards Framework (WIDA, 2020) describe as some ways that MLs engage in the Key Language Use *Narrate* in grade 1 (p. 62).

◆ Begin to develop a sense of story structure
◆ Interpret narratives read aloud with predictable structures and language patterns

This unit also addresses some of the language expectations for MLs in grade 1. Multilingual learners will:

ELD-LA.1.Narrate.Interpretive
Interpret language arts narratives by
◆ Identifying a central message from key details
◆ Identifying how character attributes and actions contribute to an event
◆ Identifying words and phrases that suggest feelings or appeal to the senses

(WIDA, 2020, p. 68)

Table 3.3 presents Mrs. Cabana's unit plan with several lessons that took about 10 days.

The following examples demonstrate specific instances when Mrs. Cabana used the six Cs of support to implement LACI in her classroom within LACI's TLC. *Italics* are used to identify each of the six Cs of support.

LACI's TLC Phase 1: Building Shared Knowledge about the Topic

During this phase, teachers engage MLs in discussion about the topic that will be the focus of various activities, finding out what they know about the topic, and beginning to develop shared understandings. Mrs. Cabana is preparing to read *Last Stop on Market Street* (de la Pena, 2015) to her class. Before reading this new multicultural picture book, Mrs. Cabana uses multiple ways to engage MLs and orient the class towards the main topics and themes from the book, including community, family, and service.

Example 7

MRS. CABANA: The story that we are going to start is *Last Stop on Market Street*. Before we begin, I wanted to ask you some things. First of all, has anyone gone away to visit a family member? Juan, who did you go visit?

JUAN: My grandpa and grandma.

MRS. C: And where do they live?

J: In Argentina. And I am going there this Christmas.

MRS. C: Oh, for the holiday break you will be heading over there? What do you need to take to get there? Because you live here in Florida. So what do you take to get to Argentina?

J: A plane.

MRS. C: A plane. Do you go with your whole family or does mom and dad take you there and you stay with them for a little while by yourself?

J: I go with my whole family.

[AND A LITTLE LATER]

MRS. C: Ok, so Hugo is traveling from Miami, FL, to Brazil, which is in South America, like Nico does, too. And then this time you are not only visiting your grandparents, but also your aunt and uncle. That is his *tio* and his *tia*. And sometimes you stay alone with your grandparents and your parents come back over here to work?

HUGO: Yeah, and my aunts and my uncles.

MRS. C: Ok, so how is that? Because I think you are the first one to say that you spend some time alone with just your grandparents and not your parents, so what was that like?

HUGO: It was fun.

MRS. C: It was fun? Why?

HUGO: Because I slept over with my *primo*.

MRS. C: *Primo* is cousin. So he was able to sleep over with his cousins, that is fun. My daughter stays over at her grandmother's too to sleep over with her cousins a lot and that is sometimes her favorite time. Thank you for sharing!

In Example 7, Mrs. Cabana is *connecting* one of the main topics of the story, family, to students' backgrounds and experiences. This engages their attention and helps them develop a personal connection to *Last Stop on Market Street*. When asking, "Has anyone gone away to visit a family member?" Mrs. Cabana is looking for students to contribute their personal experiences. She gives several students the opportunity to share about their trips to visit family members in various parts of the world. In Example 7, she encourages Juan and Hugo to describe their trips to Argentina and Brazil.

This phase within LACI's TLC presents opportunities for teachers to incorporate the C of *culture*. As this conversation develops, Mrs. Cabana integrated language and *culture* into the discussion by capitalizing on the contributions the students make in their home languages. In her exchange with Hugo, one of her MLs, about his experience in Brazil, she takes advantage of the opportunity to showcase words for family members in Portuguese and English. Mrs. Cabana is also incorporating the C of *code-breaking*. She restates the words for aunt and uncle in Portuguese when she says, "This time you are not only visiting your grandparents, but also your aunt and uncle. That is his *tio* and his *tia*." Then, when Hugo incorporates Portuguese, saying, "I slept over with my *primo*," Mrs. Cabana clarifies that,

Table 3.3 Mrs. Cabana's Unit Plan

Grade Level: 1st grade
Subject Area: English Language Arts
Lesson Title: *Last Stop on Market Street*
Duration of the Lessons: ~10 days

Student Population	23 students – 13 boys, 10 girls; 4 level 4 ESOL students; 12 bilingual students not labeled ESOL. Students represent a number of different countries with parents coming from various countries, including Dubai, Italy, Brazil, Spain, and several Latin American countries.
WIDA Standards (2020)	English Language Development Standard 2: English language learners communicate information, ideas and concepts necessary for academic success in the content area of Language Arts
CCSS Content Standard(s)	<u>CCSS.ELA-Literacy.RL.1.1</u> Ask and answer questions about key details in a text. <u>CCSS.ELA-Literacy.RL.1.2</u> Retell stories, including key details, and demonstrate understanding of their central message or lesson. <u>CCSS.ELA-Literacy.W.1.3</u> Write narratives in which they recount two or more appropriately sequenced events, include some details regarding what happened, use temporal words to signal event order, and provide some sense of closure.
Content Objectives	Students will be able to identify central themes and main events from *Last Stop on Market Street*.
Language Objectives	Students will be able to write a narrative recount based on the steps they completed during their shared experience of collecting and distributing food for the "Feed South Florida" initiative.
Materials	*Last Stop on Market Street* book, smart board and/or overhead projector, *Last Stop on Market Street* mentor text (for purposes of deconstruction), graphic organizer (for joint construction planning)
Desired Outcomes	After completion of this unit, students will have the ability to identify central themes and main events in narratives. Students will also be able to write narrative recounts.

Instructional Strategies and Learning Tasks
Description of what the teacher (you) will be doing and/or what the students will be doing.

Table 3.3 Continued

Introduction	LACI's TLC Phase 1: Building Shared Knowledge of the Topic Mrs. Cabana begins the lesson by asking students, "First of all, has anyone gone away to visit a family member?" This question initiates discussion in which students share their experiences of visiting their grandparents, cousins, aunts/uncles, etc (*Connection and Culture*).
Instruction **Highlighted** **LACI's TLC Phases:** Sustained Reading, Deconstruction, Bridging Reading to Writing, and Joint Construction **Procedures**: specific details regarding what the students will do during the lesson (practice/application) **6 Cs of Support**: *Connection*: What will you do to connect the lesson to students' prior academic learning, backgrounds and experiences?	**LACI's TLC Phase 2: Sustained Reading, *Last Stop on Market Street*** Mrs. Cabana engages the students in a conversation about the front cover of the book. She asks students to make predictions about the content of the book based on the illustration(s) they see and turn to someone near them to share. (*Community and Collaboration*) After discussion about the front cover, they do a picture walk of the book. Mrs. Cabana then tells students that she will read the entire book to them without stopping and encourages them to save their questions for the end. (*Challenge*) After reading the entire book, students share their observations and perceptions about the story with their classmates. They bring up ideas about the characters in the story, the relationship between the two main characters (CJ and Nana), and the way the town looks in the illustrations (*Code-breaking*). Mrs. Cabana begins to discuss the image/text relationship with students in order to talk about the character's feelings. Mrs. Cabana encourages students to pay close attention to both illustrations and text instead of just relying on one or the other (*Code-breaking*). She also relates how the character feels with how they might feel at certain times in their own lives (*Connection and Culture*). Based on this discussion Mrs. Cabana directs students to work together on a graphic organizer to identify the CJ's feelings with evidence from the story about his actions and what he says (*Community and Collaboration*). After completing the graphic organizer with a partner, students come back together as a class to discuss their findings from the story.

(*Continued*)

Table 3.3 Continued

Code-Breaking: What will you do to explicitly teach ways of doing school, academic literacy, and disciplinary, linguistic, and cultural codes of content learning? How will you model the language forms/ vocabulary/function/ skills?	Mrs. Cabana and the students discuss the different parts of the story labeled as, "beginning, middle, end." She informs students that they are identifying the parts of the story so they can write about it the following day (*Code-breaking*). Mrs. Cabana writes the middle part on the board for students to see and think about, "CJ heard the music and it made him happy." She then instructs students to work with a buddy (and their book) to identify the beginning and end parts of the story (*Community and Collaboration*). She circulates around the room to help pairs of students (*Classroom Interactions*)
Collaboration and community: How will you engage students in collaboration and build a community of practice? *Culture:* How will you link the new content skills and concepts to students' cultural and linguistic resources to support academic learning?	**LACI's TLC Phase 3: Deconstruction** Mrs. Cabana begins the deconstruction process by displaying the mentor text on the smart board for everyone to see. She begins by pointing out whole text features. She asks students about the paragraph format and the indent of the first line. She then instructs students to read the text with her out loud. After reading the text, she begins to ask students questions about what they liked from the writing. They provide various responses such as "the rainbow" and "the coin in the man's hat." Mrs. Cabana then starts to point out features of the writing that she believes are important. One of the first items is about the topic sentence. She then points out the transitional words used in the mentor text. She asks students to point out the different transitional words they notice in the mentor text. She asks students to highlight these transitional words on the smart board for everyone to see. Mrs. Cabana then asks students to think of other words they might use in their own writing to transition from one event to the next. She writes their ideas on the smart board next to the mentor text. Mrs. Cabana leads a discussion to review what students learned about "good writing" through the deconstruction process. She encourages students to think of ways they can use these good writing strategies in their own writing.

Challenge: What aspects of disciplinary literacy will you address? Which higher-order thinking and reasoning skills will you focus on? *Classroom interactions:* How will you use "interactional scaffolding" in the classroom? Plan for the use of oral discourse to prompt elaboration, build academic literacy, and move discourse and learning forward. Based on de Oliveira (2016) **Closing**	Mrs. Cabana returns to the mentor text to review the use of common and proper nouns. She instructs students to read through the entire text with her and then asks for volunteers to highlight the proper and common nouns they see in the text. **Added Phase: Bridging Reading to Writing** After going through the deconstruction process, Mrs. Cabana directs students to take their planning sheet that they completed a few days prior and begin their writing about the different events in the story identified as the beginning, middle, and end. Mrs. Cabana asks for volunteers to share their final written product with the classmates. During this sharing period, students and Mrs. Cabana provide feedback to the student sharing their writing by (1) saying something you liked, (2) asking one question, and (3) offering one suggestion to improve the writing. **LACI's TLC Phase 4: Joint Construction** Mrs. Cabana works with students to brainstorm ways to help the community (shared experience) that will influence their joint construction writing piece. As students contribute ideas Mrs. Cabana writes the ideas on the board in a web organizer. Mrs. Cabana and students decide to collect food to make Thanksgiving baskets for people in the community that may not have any. Mrs. Cabana and the students come up with an advertisement to use to make posters to place around the school asking for donations. After collecting items and preparing the baskets, Mrs. Cabana tells students that they need to write a letter together to their principal to let her know about what they have been doing for their community.

(Continued)

Table 3.3 Continued

	Mrs. Cabana types on the smart board for all students to see and instructs them to scribe while she types. The first step is to plan for the writing so she and the students draw 3 boxes to write the 3 main things they did for their community project. Mrs. Cabana asks students to volunteer to talk about the things they did for the project. She helps them put their thoughts into sentences and places emphasis on transitional words that they have been learning throughout the lesson. The final plan is below.
	The next step in the joint construction process is for Mrs. Cabana and the students to write their letter to the principal (based on the plan they wrote the previous day). Mrs. Cabana talks with students to get their input about the best way to write their letter.
	Mrs. Cabana and the students decide on each piece of the letter together and the students write their own letters as Mrs. Cabana types it for them to see on the smart board. Mrs. Cabana and the students deliver the letters to the principal.
Assessment/ Evaluation (Formative and/or Summative)	Formative evaluation was embedded in the lesson as students worked on reading and writing tasks, both individually and collaboratively with peers and Mrs. Cabana.
Extension	Possibility: Students will complete a graphic organizer at home (in collaboration with parents) to identify their Sunday routine. This will be used to compare/contrast with the things that CJ and Nana do on Sunday.

"*Primo* is cousin." Mrs. Cabana provides access to English vocabulary ("*Primo* is cousin.") in a way that keeps the conversation flowing naturally. By translating *primo*, she is able to keep the attention focused on the theme of family and not on language differences. Drawing on students' home languages in the classroom helps promote a sense of belonging and a culture of acceptance, in which all students' *cultural* and linguistic resources through *code-breaking* are valued.

Throughout this example, Mrs. Cabana frequently uses different components of interactional scaffolding to support her students. These *classroom interactions* include *appropriation, recapping, recasting, purposeful repetition*, and *elaboration*. Recapping is when the teacher provides a brief summary of the major points of the interaction. In Example 7, Mrs. Cabana demonstrates recapping and elaboration in the *classroom interaction* with Hugo. She recaps – or sums up – his contribution about visiting his family in Brazil and adds additional information about where Brazil is located with the sentence, "So Hugo is traveling from Miami, FL, to Brazil, which is in South America, like Nico does, too." Another example of elaboration in that same interaction is when she extends the conversation about his sleepover with his *primo*, using elaboration: "So he was able to sleep over with his cousins, that is fun. My daughter stays over at her grandmother's too to sleep over with her cousins a lot and that is sometimes her favorite time."

One of the most significant scaffolds that Mrs. Cabana uses during *classroom interactions* is purposeful repetition. During the exchange with Juan, he describes how he will travel to Argentina, and says, "A plane." Mrs. Cabana uses purposeful repetition, and says, "*A plane. Do you go with your whole family or does mom and dad take you there and you stay with them for a little while by yourself?*" In this instance, she is using purposeful repetition to provide him with a cue to request additional information about his planned trip to Argentina. She also uses this strategy again with Hugo when she is asking him about spending time with his family. Hugo tells her, "It was fun," and she replies, "*It was fun? Why?*" In all of these instances, these uses of purposeful repetition are crucial uses of interactional scaffolding and enable the teacher to ask for elaboration. The *classroom interactions* throughout the lesson provide students with opportunities to engage in conversation about the topic of family which will be the focus of various activities related to the book they will be reading and share their experiences, thoughts, and pending questions.

LACI's TLC Phase 2: Sustained Reading

Mrs. Cabana started the lesson on *Last Stop on Market Street* by asking students to look closely at the cover page and noticing all the details. She begins to focus on the picture book by previewing content through the title, cover illustrations, and page spreads and conducting a picture walk of the book. A picture walk is a wonderful activity to do before the teacher reads a picture book with students in class. In the classroom, it is a shared activity between the teacher and students before they read a new picture book or other stories that contain pictures and visuals. Students can do this by themselves or with teacher guidance by previewing the pictures in a storybook to familiarize students with the story prior to reading the text in detail. In addition, a picture walk serves to stimulate students' interest in the story, allows them to make predictions about the text using visual cues, and think about questions to explore while reading. To start students off with the picture walk, Mrs. Cabana states,

---

Example 8

I want everyone to look at the cover of *Last Stop on Market Street* and I want you to notice all the details you see in this cover. I want you to think "What is going on in this picture?" Now I want you to turn to someone who is near you and tell them what you think is going on in this picture.

This task incorporates the C of *community and collaboration*, as Mrs. Cabana asks students to turn and talk to someone as they are doing the picture walk. Mrs. Cabana creates a classroom environment of high-*challenge*, high-support. She conveys high expectations to all of her students, and consistently employs higher-order thinking activities in order for students to meet the rigorous academic standards. The dialogue depicted below in Example 9 is an illustration of *challenge* and occurs right before they read together as a class, with the teacher reading to students:

Example 9

MRS. C.: Now, I know that this story is going to have some very big words. As a matter of fact, it has very big action words. Action words are called verbs. Everybody say: verbs. And it's going to have a lot of verbs that are big, fancy words. We are going to learn what those words mean.
        [a little bit later, in the same discussion]

> **MRS. C.:** As we read the story we are looking for: *Who are our main characters? Who is this story about?* You had said you weren't sure about the relationship between these two characters, so we want to figure that out this first time around. *What is their relationship? What are they doing?* And I want you to think, "Is there a problem in this story?"

Mrs. Cabana explains to the students that this book will have "a lot of verbs that are big, fancy words." While this implicit *challenge* may appear intimidating at first, she assures the students of her support, continuing with, "We are going to learn what those words mean." A few moments later, immediately before the read aloud, she poses another *challenge* for the students. She provides them with several questions, developed during the picture walk, that she wants them to consider during the first reading of *Last Stop on Market Street*: (1) Who are our main characters? (2) Who is this story about? (3) What is their relationship? (4) What are they doing? and (5) Is there a problem in this story? By providing the students with specific questions for which they need to seek answers, Mrs. Cabana focuses the students' attention and gives them a lens through which they should read the story.

Mrs. Cabana then tells students that she will read the entire book to them without stopping. She encourages them to save their questions for the end. This **reading aloud** activity is another example of the C of *challenge*, as Mrs. Cabana engages students in reading a book that may be challenging for some of them. After reading the entire book, Mrs. Cabana invites students to share their observations and perceptions about the story with their classmates (C of *community and collaboration*). Students bring up ideas about the characters in the story, the relationship between the two main characters (CJ and Nana), and the way the town looks in the illustrations (*code-breaking*). Mrs. Cabana begins to discuss the image/text relationship with students in order to talk about the character's feelings. She also encourages students to pay close attention to both illustrations and text instead of just relying on one or the other. Because images improve student learning when reading a text (Carney & Levin, 2002), it is a powerful multimodal activity for students to connect visual representations and verbal expressions. This is part of the C of *code-breaking*. Because images complement the text in a way that the text becomes more concrete and comprehensible (Carney & Levin, 2002), teachers should explore illustrations, pictures, and other visual resources in texts as these complement the text and enhance it in such a way that it is easier to process, especially for MLs (Humphrey, 2021).

Mrs. Cabana also relates how the character feels with how students might feel at certain times in their own lives which represent the C of *connection* and the C of *culture*. An example of this is when she says: "When you push out of the school doors you are free to do whatever you want. That is how CJ was feeling." Based on this discussion Mrs. Cabana directs students to work together on a graphic organizer to identify CJ's feelings with evidence from the story about his actions and what he says.

CJ:	
Action	Says

After completing the graphic organizer with a partner, students are directed by Mrs. Cabana to come back together as a class to discuss their findings from the story. This enables students to develop a sense of all of the events in the story and the storyline. Mrs. Cabana invites students to participate in a discussion about the different parts of the story labeled as, "beginning, middle, end." She informs students that they are identifying the parts of the story so they can write about it the following day. Mrs. Cabana writes the middle part on the board for students to see and think about, "CJ heard the music and it made him happy." She then instructs students to work with a buddy (and their book) to identify the beginning and end parts of the story (C of *community and collaboration*). She circulates around the room to help pairs of students. Table 3.4 presents the various tasks/activities that Mrs. Cabana used during the Sustained Reading phase of LACI's TLC.

LACI's TLC Phase 3: Deconstruction

Another important part of LACI's TLC is the Deconstruction phase in which the teacher deconstructs a mentor text with students. For this lesson, we collaboratively constructed a mentor text that captured the major events of *Last Stop*. Mrs. Cabana began the deconstruction process by displaying the mentor text on the smart board for everyone to see and used it to discuss different aspects including language used, topic sentence, common and proper nouns, and transitions.

Table 3.4 Tasks During Sustained Reading Phase with *Last Stop on Market Street*

Task/Activity	Purpose	LACI's Cs of Support
Picture Walk	◆ to preview content through the title, cover illustrations, and page spreads as a shared activity between the teacher and students ◆ to familiarize students with the story prior to reading the text in detail and stimulate students' interest in the story ◆ to make predictions about the text using visual cues and consider questions to explore while reading	All Cs are used: *Connection, Culture, Code-Breaking, Challenge, Community and Collaboration, Classroom Interactions*
Reading Aloud	◆ to model good reading with variation in vocal aspects of delivery (e.g. pitch, tone, pace etc) ◆ to focus students' attention on reading as a group	*Code-Breaking Challenge*
Discussion of Observations about Book	◆ to provide opportunities for students to share what they noticed during the Read Aloud	*Community and Collaboration Code-Breaking*
Discussion of Image–Text Relationships	◆ to explore meanings presented in images and meanings presented in the text to better understand story events	*Code-Breaking Challenge*

(Continued)

Table 3.4 (Continued)

Task/Activity	Purpose	LACI's Cs of Support
Exploration of Feelings and Sayings	◆ to identify CJ's feelings with evidence from the story about his actions and what he says. ◆ to develop a sense of all of the events in the story and the storyline.	*Code-Breaking* *Community and* *Collaboration*
Identification of Different Parts of the Story: Beginning, Middle, End.	◆ to identify the parts of the story and label them ◆ to develop a sense of story structure	*Code-Breaking* *Community and* *Collaboration* *Challenge*

CJ had a busy day on Sunday! First, CJ and Nana went to church. After church, CJ and Nana waited for the bus in the rain. When CJ and Nana got on the bus, they saw many different people. CJ listened to the music played by the guitar player. After the song, CJ dropped a coin in the man's hat. Then, CJ heard the bus driver call for the "last stop on Market Street." Soon after, CJ and Nana stepped off the bus and walked down the sidewalk. CJ noticed that it was dirty, but then he saw a perfect rainbow over their soup kitchen. Once CJ saw everyone inside he told Nana that he was glad they came.

She read this text out loud with students and started the discussion by pointing out whole text features. She also asked students about the paragraph format and the indent of the first line. Mrs. Cabana then proceeded to ask students questions about what they liked from the writing. Students provided various responses such as "the rainbow" and "the coin in the man's hat." Mrs. Cabana stressed important features of the writing, highlighting "topic sentence", a concept with which students were already familiar. As shown in Table 3.5, the recount genre has an overall structure of Orientation and Record of Events. Language features include sequences in time, individual nouns, and transition or time phrases to help organize the text (de Oliveira, Jones & Smith, 2020).

Table 3.5 Book Recount and Language Features

Book Recount	Text	Language Features
Orientation	CJ had a busy day on Sunday!	Main Participant: CJ Processes: had (*being*) Evaluative language: a busy day Circumstance: on Sunday
Record of Events	First, CJ and Nana went to church. After church, CJ and Nana waited for the bus in the rain. When CJ and Nana got on the bus, they saw many different people. CJ listened to the music played by the guitar player. After the song, CJ dropped a coin in the man's hat. Then, CJ heard the bus driver call for the "last stop on Market Street." Soon after, CJ and Nana stepped off the bus and walked down the sidewalk. CJ noticed that it was dirty, but then he saw a perfect rainbow over their soup kitchen. Once CJ saw everyone inside he told Nana that he was glad they came.	Time/Sequence Markers/Transitions: First, After church, When, After the song, Then, Soon after, but then, Once Other Participants: Nana, many different people, the guitar player, the bus driver, everyone References: they (CJ and Nana), the man (the guitar player), he (CJ), their (CJ and Nana), he (CJ), they (CJ and Nana) Places: church, on the bus, "last stop on Market Street", sidewalk, soup kitchen Processes: went (*doing*), waited (*doing*), got on (*doing*), saw (*doing*), listened (*doing*), played (*doing*), dropped (*doing*), heard (*doing*), call (*saying*), stepped off (*doing*), walked down (*doing*), noticed (*doing*), saw (*doing*), saw (*doing*), told (*saying*), was (*relating*), came (*doing*)

Example 10

1. Mrs. C: Let's look at some of the great things the author did. Great writing always starts with some sort of topic, some sort of catcher to get us hooked on the reading… All good writing catches a reader's attention… what sentence here catches your attention? Gets you ready to read, makes you ready to read? Where do you find that sentence? Marcos?

2. Marcos: [*reads*] CJ had a busy day on Sunday.

3. Mrs. C: Ok, good, I'm gonna highlight it in yellow. Very good, boys and girls. Notice that first sentence. Let's read it together. Ready, set, go. [*Mrs. Cabana and students read* "CJ had a busy day on Sunday."] What kind of punctuation mark does this sentence end with?

4. Ss: An exclamation mark.

5. Mrs. C: An exclamation mark. There's a lot of feeling in this sentence. Does this sentence hook us? Does it make us wonder… like have a lot of questions?

6. Ss: No.

7. Mrs. C: We know the story about CJ.

8. Student 1: [*reads*] CJ had a busy day on Sunday.

9. Mrs. C: "CJ had a busy day on Sunday". When I read that sentence, that makes me wonder, what did he do? Why was he busy? What happened? Remember when we talked about this too, when we are writing we have to pretend that we've never heard this before… we have to pretend that we've never heard this story before, OK? That way we know that we have all of the important details that we might want to say. This that I highlighted in yellow, what kind of sentence is this? A /t-t-t/. [*Mrs. Cabana says* "/t-t-t/" *to help students think about the kind of sentence it is that starts with the letter t*]

10. Ss: A telling sentence.

11. Mrs. C: It's not a telling sentence.

12. Student 2: Feeling.

13. Mrs. C: There's a lot of feeling in that sentence. Different teachers will call it different sentences. I'm going to call it today a topic sentence. Does it tell you exactly what CJ did?

14. Ss: No.

15. Mrs. C: No. It just gives you the idea that CJ did a lot. It's a sentence that gives us some information but doesn't tell us exactly what happened. Some people in fourth grade might call it a hook. Like a fishing hook? Has anybody gone fishing before? You put a little bait on the end of the fishing rod. This one is called *topic sentence* [*writes* topic *on board*], but some people will call it a hook. It's gonna capture your reader like if you were fishing. They're gonna wonder, what happened next?

We can see in Example 10 a major focus on the C of *classroom interactions.* Mrs. Cabana used several interactional scaffolding moves. With leading students in a discussion about the topic sentence, she asked students questions and they answered as part of the discussion. For example, she used *purposeful repetition* when she repeated with one of the MLs said, "an exclamation mark". She then added an explanation, an example of *elaboration* on what this particular topic sentence was doing. She then continued to ask questions, consistently repeating students' contributions purposefully in order to elaborate on their answers or ask more questions. Within these classroom interactions, Mrs. Cabana is also using the C of *code-breaking* by discussing what a topic sentence is and helping students recognize its function in the text: to orient the reader to what is to come next, the sequence of events. At the end of this example, she was referencing students' out-of-school experiences with fishing, an example of the C of *connection.* She ended by providing an important question for the construction of a recount genre: *What happened next?*

Example 11

1. Mrs. C: I wanna show you something else. This author did something that I really liked. This author used words to help organize our events. We had a lot of events in the story, we know that right? CJ waits in the rain for the bus, CJ listens to the man playing the music, CJ gets to the soup kitchen. But the author didn't just say it like that. The author put some other words in here.
2. Carolina: After.
3. Mrs. C: Ah… I hear something. Ok, what did you see? Carolina, say it again.
4. Carolina: After.
5. Mrs. C: You saw the word *after*? Carolina you saw this one, "after the church"?
6. Carolina: Yeah.
7. Mrs. C: Ok, good. We are highlighting it. Anything else? That was one way to organize it.
8. Sarah: After the song.
9. Mrs. C: Ok, after the song, good. Come here and highlight it *[Sarah proceeds to the board and highlights "after the song"].* Let's see if any of our buddies can find… So far, we see after the church, after the song. So, Carolina is suggesting that these keywords help organize our events. Saying AFTER something… so AFTER church, AFTER the song. That's one way… let's see if there's another one.
10. Isela: Soon after.

11. Mrs. C: Let's see if there is another one. Isela, come on up. What did you find? It might not be after, it might be something else. So, let's see. What do you see? *[Isela goes to board.]*

12. Mrs. C: Let's highlight that "soon after," and there's a comma there. Ok, very good. That one is giving us another way to let us know there's another event coming. *[T and Ss continue discussion and find the word "first" in the second sentence]*

13. Mrs. C: How many of you also agree that *first* is a word that can be used to put things in order? Yeah, I agree too. Highlight it. Very good. Highlight *first* with the comma behind it.

Mrs. Cabana continued the Deconstruction of the mentor text by asking students to focus on a key aspect of the recount genre: *words to help organize our events.* She used the C of *code-breaking* to help students develop a sense of story structure and recognize some language patterns present in recounts. She continued to use interactional scaffolding moves through the C of *classroom interactions.* In turn 2, one student, Carolina, identified *after* as one word that helps organize events. Mrs. Cabana used *cued elicitation* when asking Carolina to repeat so all could hear. In turn 7, Mrs. Cabana made sure students know what they are doing and asked *anything else* to continue the exploration, an example of *moving the discourse forward.* In turn 9, Mrs. Cabana continued the exploration and then summarized *So far, we see after the church, after the song* while continuing to affirm Carolina's answer and summarizing what they have done so far. This is a clear example of *recapping*, briefly summarizing the major points of the interaction. In turn 12, Mrs. Cabana ended this extended discussion with another affirmation, *Ok, very good*, and a summary *That one is giving us another way to let us know there's another event coming.* The identification of these "words that organize events" is helping students develop a sense of story structure.

Mrs. Cabana then engages in a discussion of the transitional words used in the mentor text. She asks students to point out the different transitional words they notice in the mentor text. As they identify the transitional words she asks students to highlight them on the smart board for everyone to see. Mrs. Cabana then asks students to think of other words they might use in their own writing to transition from one event to the next. She writes their ideas on the smart board next to the mentor text.

Example 12 starts out with Mrs. Cabana's "summing up" of the series of exchanges, *recapping* what they had been discussing. In turn 1, Mrs. Cabana offered a definition for *phrase* ("remember, phrase is a group of words"), part of the metalanguage that she was introducing to students. In turn 2,

Example 12

1. Mrs. C: So, let's take a look, so far, we have *first, after church, after the song, soon after*. Was there anybody else that noticed another phrase, remember, phrase is a group of words. *[Sarah raises her hand.]* Sarah, do you want to come and whisper to Mrs. Cabana? *[Sarah goes to the front and whispers to the teacher.]*

2. Mrs. C: She's looking at this part, right here *[Mrs. C reads]* "but then he saw a perfect rainbow over their soup kitchen". There is a little word there that she's looking at. Who can guess? Paulo?

3. Paulo: Then.

4. Mrs. C: There you go! *Then*. So highlight it. Then, are there any other *thens* in this writing? Miguel, come on up, any other *thens* that you see? Then is another great word to organize writing. Do you see one more? This is fun. We are writing detectives. *[Teacher and students read paragraph again.]*

5. Miguel: *[reads]* Then, CJ heard the bus driver. *[Mrs. Cabana brainstorms with students other words that can be used to organize information]*

6. Mrs. C: What do these words help us do? They help us put those things in what?

7. Miguel: Put in order.

8. Mrs. C: Say it again, Miguel, shout it from the rooftop!

9. Ss: *[loudly]* Put those things in order.

10. Mrs. C: The things that he means are the events. It helps us put the events in order. So, we can call these *time order words*. You wanna learn the fourth-grade fancy word for it? In fourth grade, they call them transitional words, everybody say *transitional words*. *[Students repeat, "Transitional words."]* Sometimes they call them phrases because it's more than one word. A phrase is more than one word… that's in fourth grade.

Mrs. Cabana used the move *clarification* to explain what Sarah was doing so all students could understand. In turn 4, Mrs. Cabana asked questions to one of the students, Miguel, which served the function of *moving the discourse* and work *forward*. She ended the extended discussion with an IRF sequence with the Initiation as the question (turn 6) *What do these words help us do? They help us put those things in what?*, a Response from Miguel (turn 7) *put in order*, and Feedback from Mrs. Cabana (turn 8) *Say it again, Miguel, shout it from the rooftop!* which students responded (turn 9) *Put those things in order*. In turn 10, Mrs. Cabana provided *elaboration* by further explaining what *things* Miguel was referring to, *events*, and reminded students that those words help *us put the events in order.* By asking *What do these words help us do? They help us put those things in what?*, Mrs. Cabana is also using the C of *code-breaking* since she is asking students to identify the **function** of these words in writing. When Miguel, one of the MLs in the classroom, says *"Put those things in order"*, Mrs. Cabana confirms that is the purpose of the words they had been discussing. In turn 10, Mrs. Cabana uses *recasting* for what Miguel said *"those things"* to *"The things that he means are the events"* and elaborates on the purpose of the words: "It helps us put the events in order." She then names them, adding to the metalanguage that students are learning "So, we can call these *time order words*." Then she proceeds to ask students "You wanna learn the fourth-grade fancy word for it?" which is a clear example of the C of *challenge*. Mrs. Cabana adds to the metalanguage by saying, *"In fourth grade, they call them transitional words, everybody say* **transitional words**.*"* She proceeds to further explain that these transitions can be more than one word: *"Sometimes they call them phrases because it's more than one word. A phrase is more than one word…"*

Mrs. Cabana then leads a discussion to review what students learned about "good writing" through the deconstruction process. She encourages students to think of ways they can use these good writing strategies in their own writing. Mrs. Cabana returns to the mentor text to review the use of common and proper nouns. She instructs students to read through the entire text with her and then asks for volunteers to highlight the proper and common nouns they see in the text.

While Mrs. Cabana selected transitions and common and proper nouns to highlight with students, there are many other important language features in the mentor text that could be the focus. For example, Table 3.3 showed some of the main language features from the mentor text. Identifying the participants, processes, and circumstances in the mentor text also helps students see how the events are structured, who is participating in them, and the circumstances surrounding the events. As is typical of recounts, doing processes are prevalent in the text and could show students all of the different actions present in the text, just as a discussion of actions and sayings during Sustained Reading helped students identify various events in *Last Stop*. Several cohesive devices such as references are also used in their mentor text and could be a focus of discussion.

Added Phase: Bridging Reading to Writing

In Mrs. Cabana's adaptation of LACI's TLC, she noticed that her first-grade students would need additional practice that bridged the reading and writing components. She, therefore, added a phase to the TLC that we call *Bridging reading and writing* so first-graders would be more prepared for the other phases of the TLC. After going through the deconstruction process, Mrs.

Cabana directed students to take their planning sheet that they completed a few days prior and begin their writing about the different events in the story identified as the beginning, middle, and end. Mrs. Cabana asked for volunteers to share their final written product with the classmates. During this sharing period, students and Mrs. Cabana provide feedback to the student sharing their writing by (1) saying something you liked, (2) asking one question, and (3) offering one suggestion to improve the writing.

LACI's TLC Phase 3: Joint Construction

A major part of the TLC is a **shared experience**, and Mrs. Cabana worked with students to brainstorm ways to help the community, as CJ, the main character, helped at the soup kitchen with his grandma. As students contributed ideas Mrs. Cabana wrote the ideas on the board in a web organizer. The students voted and decided that they would collect food items to make Thanksgiving baskets for the "Feed South Florida" initiative which provides food and other resources to those who need it. Mrs. Cabana and the students came up with an advertisement to use to make posters to place around the school asking for donations. Students brought in their own donations and solicited donations from other students and staff members at the school. This **shared experience** was used as a springboard for joint construction.

For the Joint Construction phase, Mrs. Cabana told students that she had not been able to speak with the principal but would like to let her know about what they are doing:

> Mrs. Cabana has not been able to speak to Dr. Pearson about the project we're doing, so what we need to do is that we're going to have to write to her a letter telling her what we've done because if today she walks around the school and sees these posters up, she's gonna say, what is this?

The teacher and students proceed to plan and do the Joint Construction.

After collecting items and preparing the baskets, Mrs. Cabana and the students proceeded with writing a letter together for the Joint Construction phase. Mrs. Cabana typed on the smart board for all students to see and instructed them to scribe while she typed. The first step was to plan for the writing so she and the students drew three boxes to write the three main things they did for their community project. Mrs. Cabana asked students to volunteer to talk about the things they did for the project. She helped them put their thoughts into sentences and placed emphasis on transitional words that they had been learning throughout the lesson.

The next step in the Joint Construction was for Mrs. Cabana and the students to write their letter to the principal, based on the plan they wrote the previous day. Mrs. Cabana talked with students to get their input about the best way to write their letter. Mrs. Cabana and the students decided on each piece of the letter together and the students wrote their own letters as Mrs. Cabana typed it for them to see on the smart board.

The next step in the Joint Construction was for Mrs. Cabana and the students to write their letter to the principal, based on the plan they wrote the previous day. Mrs. Cabana talked with students to get their input about the best way to write their letter. Mrs. Cabana and the students decided on each piece of the letter together and the students wrote their own letters as Mrs. Cabana typed it for them to see on the smart board.

Example 13

1. Mrs. C: What were we planning? A way to do what? We were planning a way to help…
2. Sts: The community!
3. Mrs. C: Okay? So… we… [Writing on computer.] OK, I'm going to do this. I'm just gonna put the word in here… First…
4. Student 1: But we have to write *first*?
5. Mrs. C: So we're gonna write together now… yes! First, [Typing on the computer.] we planned, or we thought?
6. Ss: we thought!
7. Mrs. C: We thought about ways to help the community [Mrs. C starts writing on computer.] Should we say the community or our community?
8. Ss: Our community!
9. Mrs. C: So, I'm going to change this word… take out the and put our community. Perfect! OK, put this in your planner! [Continues after answering a question about formatting from a student.]
10. Mrs. C: What transition words did we use here? What time order word did we use? We talked about this… Which of these words lets us know…
11. Student 2: Oh, *first*!
12. Mrs. C: First, good! [Mrs. C gives directions to individual students and works with their spelling.]
13. Mrs. C: Boys and girls, when you're copying a long word, here is what Mrs. Cabana likes to do, I like to look up at the word and pick three or four letters—T-H-O—and then I look down—T-H-O… U-G-H, like that! [Mrs. C continues working with individual students. Students are writing in their planners what she is writing on the computer and projecting on the screen]

14. Mrs. C: OK! Back together now! Boys and girls, let's go ahead and focus on what we did next! So, the first thing we did was we thought about ways to help our community. What happened after that? What happened after we thought about ways to help our community?
15. Mrs. C: [*After a brief discussion about the different ways they thought about helping the community*] What were we making? You wrote it on your poster! What were we making?
16. Ss: Thanksgiving baskets!

This example shows how the Joint Construction phase took place in the classroom and provides several instances of application of various Cs of support. The C of *classroom interactions* was again prevalent throughout. Mrs. Cabana started out by using *cued elicitation* with "*What were we planning? A way to do what? We were planning a way to help…*" She engaged students in conversation by offering a strong verbal hint about expected responses. In turn 10, Mrs. Cabana asked students about transition words/time order words, referring back to the Deconstruction that happened a few days before this, using the interactional scaffolding move *linking to prior experiences and pointing to new experiences*. This is also a strong example of the C of *connection*, as she was connecting to a previous lesson and discussion. In turn 12, Mrs. Cabana repeats *first*, an example of *purposeful repetition*. After a brief discussion about the various ways to help the community that they had brainstormed, in turn 15 Mrs. Cabana asked questions to remind students about what they were making, another example of *cued elicitation*. The Joint Construction continued for another 20 minutes, with similar moves to the ones in Example 13. Mrs. Cabana ends this with the following:

Example 14

1. Mrs. C: Alright, let me have… Sit… 5, 4, 3, 2, 1. Before we leave, let's read our planner together. Mrs. C is not going to read this time, just you all. I'll point. Ready, set, go!
2. ALL: [*reading from planners*] Dear Dr. Pearson, First, we thought about ways to help our community. Next, we decided to collect food to make Thanksgiving baskets to give to the people that need it. Lastly, we made posters to tell the other first-graders to bring in food for our baskets.
3. Mrs. C: Round of applause! This is a beautiful piece of writing [*Proceeds to ask students to give planners to the student teacher*] Fantastic!

The finished product is read out loud by all of the students together. In turn 3, Mrs. Cabana affirmed everyone's work with *"Round of applause! This is a beautiful piece of writing... Fantastic!"* Mrs. Cabana and the students then delivered the letters to the principal.

These examples show Mrs. Cabana's use of LACI's six Cs of support in several instances of her classroom instruction. Mrs. Cabana consistently tries to *connect* to students' background and experience, values their different *cultures*, provides *code-breaking* in support of content and language development, incorporates different participant structures to facilitate *community and collaboration* in the classroom, *challenges* her students with higher-order thinking tasks, and encourages *classroom interactions* through her use of interactional scaffolding strategies.

This chapter focused on examples of the implementation of LACI in two classrooms, a kindergarten and a first-grade classroom. Both Mrs. Li and Mrs. Cabana incorporated LACI's six Cs of support and adapted LACI's TLC phases according to the needs of students in each classroom. Examples of classroom instruction bring the approach to life in actual classroom situations with students.

Putting into Practice

Planning a Unit with I Hate English!

In Chapter 2, you were introduced to the picture book *I Hate English!* We identified language resources for *presenting content, enacting relationships,* and *constructing a cohesive message*. You were introduced to the theme of contrast between Mei Mei's feelings about English and Chinese which appears throughout the picture book.

For this practice, using a similar format as the unit plans presented in this chapter from Mrs. Li and Mrs. Cabana, start planning a unit of instruction with *I Hate English!* for your elementary classroom.

1. Consider which aspects of the code-breaking section presented in Chapter 2 you would incorporate into your unit. Why would you focus on those areas?
2. How do you plan to incorporate LACI's six Cs of support throughout this unit? Which Cs would you use at the beginning, in the middle, and at the end of the unit? Why? Use the questions in the unit plans for planning with the six Cs of support.
3. How do you plan to incorporate LACI's TLC in the unit? Will you incorporate all five phases of the TLC as described in Chapter 2? If not, why not? Which activities would be best suited for each phase?

4

Teaching Social Studies to Multilingual Learners

Social studies is an umbrella term for several school subjects that represent social sciences: history, geography, economics, civics, sociology, psychology, philosophy, among others. Each of these school subjects has its own ways of presenting information and constructing knowledge. Learning social studies is highly dependent on reading and writing texts, especially at the intermediate elementary grades and beyond.

Social studies has its own expectations and typical discipline-specific linguistic choices that present and re-present interpretations and perspectives (de Oliveira, 2011; Schleppegrell & de Oliveira, 2006). A focus on these specialized ways of presenting and constructing social studies content helps MLs see how language is used to construe particular contexts in this content area. Because of MLs' language needs, they need language support in social studies in order to be successful in the reading and writing tasks that require them to build connections, relationships, and interpretations.

Every text a social studies writer writes is an interpretation in itself (Martin, 2003). The social studies texts that MLs are expected to read in school are a compilation of explanations. Historians interpret and explain what happened; they do not just record what happened. Interpretations and explanations involve the presentation of social values and different points of view (Martin & Wodak, 2003) which need to be recognized and understood. While social studies discourse is functional for its purposes, it also presents particular language demands for MLs.

DOI: 10.4324/9781003264927-4

Multilingual learners need to gain access to specialized social studies content which involves the use of academic language. Focusing on academic language in social studies requires a focus on meaning. Social studies teachers need to develop understanding of how the discourse of social studies is constructed so they can identify ways to address the linguistic needs of their MLs so that they can access discipline-specific meaning-making resources.

This chapter starts by identifying some academic language demands of social studies, specifically focusing on dense definitions, descriptions, and explanations, mood choices to connect with the reader, and cohesive devices that create links within the text. It presents a sample unit plan to address these demands and to explore the language of social studies. The chapter then shows applications of LACI in the classroom, exploring the language of social studies with MLs, with examples from a second-grade classroom and a fifth-grade classroom.

Content-Specific Language in Social Studies

Previous work on social studies discourse demonstrates that disciplinary knowledge in social studies is presented very differently from the ways in which meanings are constructed in students' everyday language (de Oliveira, 2010, 2011; Schleppegrell & de Oliveira, 2006). A close look at the language choices used in academic texts enables social studies teachers and students to see the differences between language used at school and the English language that students use every day in their lives outside of school. The concepts students must learn at higher levels at school increasingly become more difficult. In addition, the grammar that constructs these concepts becomes more distinctive and specialized. Knowledge about how academic language differs from everyday language is critical for social studies teachers who are preparing MLs for higher levels of schooling.

Social studies has expectations for the way that it uses language to express interpretations of experience. These expectations include: displaying knowledge by presenting and interpreting historical events; being authoritative by recording, interpreting, and judging; and organizing text in ways that enable explanation and interpretation (Schleppegrell, 2004). These expectations are seen in the combination of language features that the historian uses when writing about the past.

My work in K-12 classrooms has demonstrated that, as MLs progress at school, they need to understand how social studies authors construct the abstract discourse of school social studies (de Oliveira, 2011), typically presented in social studies textbooks. Drawing on linguistic features of academic registers, the language of social studies textbooks has been described as dense and packed with information (Beck & McKeown, 1994). While recent work has attempted to produce more interesting social studies textbooks by adding vivid language and captivating details to make content more readily available to students, these additions did not necessarily lead to superior text comprehension (Paxton, 1999). Textbooks are a widely used resource in social studies classes (Ravitch & Finn, 1987; Thornton, 1991), so students need to be able to read and understand them to be successful in school social studies. The goal of social studies teaching in developing students' content knowledge and understanding has been linked to being able to access the language used by textbook authors and historians (Harniss, Dickson, Kinder & Hollenbeck, 2001).

Many content area teachers of MLs draw on a variety of strategies and techniques to simplify the language of textbooks and to dilute textbook content in order to make textbook content comprehensible to MLs. While these strategies and techniques may be helpful for MLs at the beginning levels of language proficiency, they are not appropriate for MLs at intermediate to advanced levels, especially as they progress through the elementary grades and beyond and move out of special bilingual or ESL programs into mainstream classes. Under a watered-down curriculum, MLs may never learn to read textbooks without modifications or adaptations if not taught how to deconstruct the language of textbooks (Gibbons, 2006). At intermediate-advanced levels MLs commonly read content area texts and so need to have additional strategies and be able to access difficult content (de Oliveira & Dodds, 2010). Social studies teachers, then, have the dual responsibility of facilitating MLs' learning of events and concepts while also supporting their ongoing English language development.

The Language of History-Social Studies

Understanding the ways in which language constructs historical meanings enables teachers to anticipate potential challenges that MLs may encounter when reading social studies. This is an essential element of the C of code-breaking. Social studies teachers need to understand how language works in social studies while remaining experts in their content area.

Social studies teachers are typically experts in their content area and often read texts without much difficulty as they are familiar with the textual constructions of social studies. To incorporate code-breaking in their teaching, social studies teachers need to develop knowledge about how to make content *accessible* to MLs by giving them *access* to the ways in which knowledge is constructed in social studies, not by simplifying the texts, but by keeping a focus on functions and meanings present in these texts. Code-breaking involves developing knowledge about how to engage MLs to help them learn the content better. In general content area classes, mere exposure to academic language is not enough to help MLs develop their content knowledge. The challenge for MLs is to have their language needs explicitly addressed. The challenge for social studies teachers of MLs is to ensure access to grade-level content and materials by addressing these language needs.

Developing their knowledge about how language works in social studies enables teachers to address MLs' language and content needs simultaneously. The situational context of social studies teaching and learning uses language in particular ways. Analysis of the language of a particular text can help teachers see the potential demands and characteristics of academic language for MLs so they can understand what they read and learn content more effectively. For social studies teachers, this is a tall order. They may feel uncomfortable seeing themselves as responsible for addressing the linguistic needs of the MLs in their classes. But social studies teachers are in the best position to do so. They often know about their disciplinary practices and would be best able to develop MLs' ability to read and write the texts in social studies.

The knowledge about language that social studies teachers need to develop in order to teach academic language to MLs includes knowledge about how abstractions are defined or described, how dense definitions and explanations are constructed, how mood choices help authors connect with the reader, and how cohesive devices work to organize historical meanings. These are only some features of the academic language of social studies highlighted here as potential challenges for MLs (for more information about social studies discourse, see Coffin, 2006; de Oliveira, 2010, 2011; Fang & Schleppegrell, 2008; Martin, 2002, 2003).

Developing social studies teachers' knowledge about language requires consistent and focused professional learning opportunities such as the ones offered through the literacy work by The California History-Social Science Project. By making visible and explicit the literacy demands of social studies, teachers can learn how to focus on language while still teaching social studies content in a meaningful way.

Potential Demands of the Language of Social Studies

Multilingual learners need to access specialized social studies content. They need to gain access to and participate in experiences involving the use of academic language. Although the academic language of social studies may present several challenges for MLs, it is functional for historians to present interpretations and generalizations through linguistic choices for expressing the historical content.

The social studies texts analyzed in this chapter are from a third-grade textbook published by McGraw Hill and used in many classrooms in Florida (see Figure 4.1). Though this textbook is specific to Florida, similar textbooks are widely used throughout the United States. I analyzed several

1   Text 1: One Country, Five Regions

2   The United States is divided into five regions. A region is an area on Earth with common

3   features that set it apart from other areas. The five geographic regions of the United States are the

4   Southeast, the Northeast, the Midwest, the Southwest, and the West.

5   Areas within a region usually share similar types of landforms. They share a common

6   climate, too. Climate is the weather in a certain area over a period of time. Regions also have

7   their own types of vegetation. Vegetation is the kinds of plants that grow in an area. Regions

8   have landmarks, which are important places or objects. Landmarks can be natural or man-made.

9   In this lesson, you will learn about the climate, vegetation, landmarks, and other physical

10   features of each region of the United States.

(a)

Text 2: The Southeast

Let's begin our journey in the Southeast. You probably know a lot about this region already,

since this is where you live. What is your climate like? Is it warm and humid? Does it sometimes

rain? In Florida and the rest of the Southeast, the climate includes mild winters and hot, humid

summers. There is a lot of sunshine, but the region also gets quite a bit of rain. Did you know

that a region's climate affects its vegetation? That's because different types of vegetation have

different needs. In the Southeast, the mild climate is perfect for growing crops like oranges,

peanuts, rice, and cotton. In fact, Florida has thousands of orange and grapefruit farms! These

fruits grow well in the region's mild climate. What other vegetation have you seen in the

Southeast?

(Only the first paragraph is included here, but the analysis includes two paragraphs)

(b)

Figure 4.1 Texts 1 and 2: Passages from The United States: Its Regions and Neighbors. (Bank 2013, pp. 21–23).

passages from similar textbooks when I was a linguistics researcher for the History Project at the University of California, Davis (http://historyproject. ucdavis.edu/), and also observed social studies teachers' applications of activities to help students develop their academic literacy skills in social studies.

The area of meaning we are focusing on, the questions to guide analysis, potential academic language focus, and what to analyze to identify them are presented in Table 4.1.

More than Concrete Entities: Dense Definitions, Descriptions, and Explanations

Social studies uses both concrete entities in the form of individuals or groups, and abstract entities in the form of things, places, or ideas. This makes social studies often difficult to understand. These appear as participants in the

Table 4.1: Areas of Meaning, Questions, Academic Language Focus, and Focus of Analysis

Area of Meaning	Question to Guide Analysis	Academic Language Focus	Focus of Analysis
Presenting content	What is going on in the text?	*More than Concrete Entities: Dense Definitions, Descriptions, and Explanations*	Sentence Constituents: ◆ Participants ◆ Processes ◆ Circumstances Definitions and explanations
Enacting a relationship with the reader	What is the perspective of the author?	*More than Statements: Mood Choices to Connect with the Reader*	Mood choices: ◆ Declarative ◆ Interrogative ◆ Imperative Use of second-person pronoun *you* in declarative sentences
Constructing a cohesive message	How is the text organized?	*More than Naming: Cohesive Devices that Create Links within the Text*	Cohesive devices and links to construct a message that holds together and builds from clause to clause

processes – who or what is presented as *doing, thinking, feeling,* or *saying,* or what is being *defined* or *described* (Fang & Schleppegrell, 2008). For instance, in *The United States is divided into five regions, The United States* is a participant in the *relating* process *is*. In text 1, many abstractions are present as participants in different processes. Processes in this passage mostly show definitions and descriptions: *is, is, are, have, can be*. The participants that occur before the processes are abstractions realized in nominal groups: *The United States; A region; The five geographic regions of the United States; Areas within a region; Climate; Regions; Vegetation; Regions; Landmarks*.

Most of these abstractions are either defined or described in the text. The entire text selection is about definitions or descriptions. These sequences of definitions and descriptions may cause difficulty for students who are not familiar with academic language used in historical texts. To focus on the meanings in the passage, MLs would need to recognize these sequences and the abstractions, which pack a lot of information into this short text. These are discussed next.

Dense definitions and explanations are common features of the discourse of social studies. In text 1, several definitions occur within two short paragraphs:

A region is *an area on Earth with common features that set it apart from other areas.*
Definition 1
The five geographic regions of the United States are *the Southeast, the Northeast, the Midwest, the Southwest, and the West.*
Explanation 1
Climate is *the weather in a certain area over a period of time.*
Definition 2
Vegetation is *the kinds of plants that grow in an area.*
Definition 3
Regions have landmarks, *which are important places or objects.*
Definition 4

The term *a region* is defined with the sentence structure "Participant + *being* process + definition" which also occurs in definitions 2 and 3. Definition 4, introduced by the pronoun *which*, may not be as clearly understood as definitions 1, 2, and 3. The definitions occurring so close to each other may be challenging for MLs.

In text 2, we find another definition:

Phosphate is *a mineral that farmers use to help crops grow.*
Definition 5

This sentence follows the same sentence structure as the sentences where definitions 1, 2, and 3 appeared.

More than Statements: Mood Choices to Connect with the Reader

Mood choices help a writer enact a relationship with readers. Remember that English has three grammatical moods – declarative, interrogative, and imperative – as described in Chapter 2. The typical mood choice in academic subject area texts is declarative, with writers presenting themselves as knowledgeable providers of information. Unlike conversational interaction, where interrogative and imperative forms are frequent, school-based texts typically present information in precise ways. In social studies, because authors are presenting information authoritatively, mood choices are often declarative, with little use of interrogative and imperative forms, especially as we move from elementary to secondary levels. In addition, social studies authors do not often use the second-person pronoun *you* to connect with the readers.

At the elementary level, mood choices may vary according to the various texts presented in social studies textbooks. In Texts 1 and 2, for example, we see more than declarative sentences. The social studies author connects with readers through the use of both interrogative and imperative sentences as well as use of the second-person pronoun *you* in declarative sentences.

In Text 1, most sentences are declarative because they are introducing readers to the topic of the unit. The last sentence of the paragraph is a declarative sentence in which the social studies author uses the second-person pronoun *you* to state what readers can expect in the lesson: *In this lesson, **you** will learn about the climate, vegetation, landmarks, and other physical features of each region of the United States.*

Text 2 uses all of the mood choices. The most prevalent is still declarative, but interrogative and imperative moods are used in the first paragraph of the text. The social studies author is connecting with the reader through the use of these mood choices. The second and third paragraphs, part of the section entitled "Natural Resources and Landmarks" uses only declarative mood. The text starts with the imperative mood choice in *let's begin: Let's begin our journey in the Southeast.* Table 4.2 shows the mood choice in each sentence from the first paragraph of Text 2.

Table 4.2 Mood Choices in Text 2

Let's **begin** **our** journey in the Southeast.	Imperative with first-person pronoun *us* in *Let's* (Let us) and *our*
You probably *know* a lot about this region already, since this *is* where you live.	Declarative with second-person pronoun *you*
What *is* **your** climate like?	Interrogative
Is it warm and humid?	Interrogative
Does it sometimes *rain*?	Interrogative
In Florida and the rest of the Southeast, the climate *includes* mild winters and hot, humid summers.	Declarative
There is a lot of sunshine, but the region also *gets* quite a bit of rain.	Declarative
Did you know that a region's climate affects its vegetation?	Interrogative
That's because different types of vegetation *have* different needs.	Declarative
In the Southeast, the mild climate *is* perfect for growing crops like oranges, peanuts, rice, and cotton.	Declarative
In fact, Florida *has* thousands of orange and grapefruit farms!	Declarative
These fruits *grow* well in the region's mild climate.	Declarative
What other vegetation *have you seen* in the Southeast?	Interrogative

Through these mood choices, we can see how the social studies author is enacting a relationship with readers by connecting with them. Particular language choices enable the social studies author to move between stating ideas and interaction with the reader. First is the choice of imperative mood with first-person pronouns *us* and *our* to start the text: *Let's begin our journey in the Southeast.* The second mood choice, declarative, shows the second-person pronoun *you* that talks directly to the reader, construing interaction in declarative sentences. The third relevant mood selection, interrogative, relates to the author's choices in the moments of moving between statements and interaction. The questions that follow present build the context as one of interaction and engagement with the reader. The use of these mood choices makes this text somewhat unique as the social studies author is connecting with the reader at a personal level. These choices change when we move from elementary to secondary grade levels, with texts that mostly use declarative mood at the secondary levels.

More than Naming: Cohesive Devices that Create Links within the Text

Cohesive devices are words or groups of words that create links within the text (Halliday & Matthiessen, 2014). As explained in Chapter 2, different types of cohesive devices can be used to construct a message that holds together and builds from clause to clause. These are commonly used in social studies discourse. Cohesive devices are used to construct links between complex and abstract elements.

In Text 1, the pronoun *it* functions as a cohesive device to connect back to *A region* in *A region is an area on Earth with common features that set it apart from other areas*. Figure 4.2 shows the cohesive devices connected to the parts of the text to which they refer.

- Personal pronouns (*it, they*), possessive pronouns (*their*), and relative pronouns (*which*) refer back to different Participants (anaphoric reference);
- Personal pronoun (*you*) refers to the reader as someone outside of the text (exophoric reference);
- Repetition is used throughout this text to introduce different features that will be the focus of the following pages of the textbook. Repeated words are marked by different kinds of underline: region, area, climate, vegetation, and landmarks.

Text 1: **One Country, Five Regions**

The United States is divided into five regions. **A region** is an area on Earth with common features that set it apart from other areas. The five geographic regions of the United States are the Southeast, the Northeast, the Midwest, the Southwest, and the West.

Areas within a region usually share similar types of landforms. **They** share a common climate, too. Climate is the weather in a certain area over a period of time. **Regions** also have **their** own types of vegetation. Vegetation is **the kinds of plants that** grow in an area. Regions have **landmarks, which** are important places or objects. Landmarks can be natural or man-made. In this lesson, you will learn about the climate, vegetation, landmarks, and other physical features of each region of the United States.

Figure 4.2 Cohesive Devices in Text 1.

Cohesive devices are pervasive in Text 2. A range of cohesive devices is found:

◆ Demonstratives (*this, these*) occurring with substitutes (*region, fruits*) – or words that stand for other words – refer back to things or ideas already named.

◆ Two examples of exophoric references (outside of the text) are used: *our country, our new nation.*

◆ Demonstratives occurring with substitutes (*this coal*) refer back to entire clauses (e.g. *this coal* refers back to the clause *Coal mined in the Southeast is used in power plants.*)

◆ Ellipsis is used after naming (e.g. *The Cape Henry Lighthouse*) when information can be retrieved from a previous clause (e.g. *The Cape Henry Lighthouse* is referred to as *the lighthouse; lighthouse* is used with lower case as readers are supposed to know which *lighthouse* it is)

◆ Repetition is also common in Text 2: region, climate, vegetation, natural resources, phosphate, and landmarks are common repeated words. These repeated words were underlined in Figure 4.3.

◆ Several examples of lexical cohesion occur in this text, shaded in Figure 4.3:
  ▪ Hyponymy:
    ▪ *crops – oranges, peanuts, rice, and cotton*
    ▪ *orange and grapefruit – fruits*
    ▪ *natural resources – coal*
    ▪ *natural resources – phosphate*
    ▪ *Trees – cedar trees*

Figure 4.3 shows the cohesive devices in Text 2. The arrows show the connections between the cohesive devices and previous discourse, especially the words, groups of words, or full sentences to which they refer. The cohesive devices are in italics and the words and groups of words to which they refer are in bold.

Cohesive devices help identify and keep track of what or who is being discussed in a particular text. They have an important function in social studies, constructing links between complex and abstract elements that need to be understood in the context of a passage.

Focusing on *dense definitions, descriptions, and explanations; mood choices to connect with the reader;* and *cohesive devices that create links within the text* in these texts illustrates some of the features of academic language and exemplifies how explicit discussion of language-meaning connections can help MLs read for deeper understanding.

Text 2: **The Southeast**

Let's begin our journey in **the Southeast**. You probably know a lot about this region already, since this is where you live. What is your climate like? Is it warm and humid? Does it sometimes rain? In **Florida and the rest of the Southeast**, the climate includes mild winters and hot, humid summers. There is a lot of sunshine, but the region also gets quite a bit of rain. Did you know that a region's climate affects its vegetation? That's because different types of vegetation have different needs. In the Southeast, the mild climate is perfect for growing crops like oranges, peanuts, rice, and cotton. In fact, Florida has thousands of **orange and grapefruit** farms! These fruits grow well in the region's mild climate. What other vegetation have you seen in the Southeast?

Natural Resources and Landmarks

The Southeast has many natural resources. A natural resource is found in nature and is used by people. **Coal** mined in the Southeast is used in power plants. This coal helps create half of our country's electricity! Trees found in the Southeast are an important natural resource, too. Cedar trees are used to make fences. Phosphate is also found in the Southeast. Phosphate is a mineral that farmers use to help crops grow. Florida is one of the world's largest producers of phosphate.

The Southeast has landmarks, too. Landmarks can be natural or man-made. One natural landmark in the region is **the Florida Everglades**. The Everglades is one of the largest wetland areas on Earth. **The Cape Henry Lighthouse** is an example of a man-made landmark. This lighthouse was built along the Atlantic Coast in Virginia over 200 years ago. Its light helped guide ships along the coast of our new nation! The United States

Figure 4.3 Cohesive Devices in Text 2

LACI Unit Plan for Exploring Language and Addressing Language Demands

A possible unit plan to apply LACI in addressing these language demands can be found in Table 4.3.

This unit plan incorporates LACI's six Cs of support. The unit plan also includes LACI's TLC with a focus on deconstruction of the two texts that students are reading. The teacher, Ms. Williams, works through the language demands identified in the analysis of the two texts. Ms. Williams incorporates

Table 4.3 Unit Plan by Ms. Williams

Teacher: Ms. Williams
Grade Level: Third grade
Subject Area: Social Studies
Lesson Title: *Conserving Resources*
Duration of the Lesson: ~ 5 days, 60 minutes each

Student Population	25 students – 13 boys, 12 girls; 9 students receive ESOL services, 2 students with limited formal education; 12 bilingual students not receiving ESOL services. Students represent a number of different countries with parents coming from Puerto Rico, Cuba, Guatemala, Honduras, El Salvador and other South American Countries.
WIDA Standards (2020)	WIDA ELD STANDARD 5 Language for Social Studies: ELD-SS.2-3. Explain. **Interpretive** Multilingual learners will interpret social studies explanations by evaluating disciplinary concepts and ideas associated with a compelling or supporting question. ELD-SS.2-3. Explain. **Expressive** Multilingual learners will construct social studies explanations that describe components, order, causes, or cycles.
CCSS Content Standard(s)	Florida Social Studies, 3rd Grade, Standard 2, Places and Regions SS.3.G.3.2 Describe the natural resources in the United States, Canada, Mexico, and the Caribbean.
Content Objectives	Students will be able to determine what natural resources are, in which regions they are more commonly found, and why they are important to know and protect.
Language Objectives	Students will be able to gather multimodal information from provided texts, conversations and group internet research to read and understand renewable and nonrenewable natural resources. Students will produce, categorize, and present examples of natural resources and write persuasive texts to protect and conserve natural resources from regions in the United States, Canada, Mexico, and the Caribbean.

(*Continued*)

Table 4.3 (Continued)

Materials	*Conserving Resources* text with four different lessons from Harcourt School Publishers. Smart board for multimodal projections, bilingual Spanish vocabulary in written and oral forms, and student technology devices. Different colored pens and highlighters. Graphic organizers for sorting information – paper and digital formats for student choice. Google Earth, Timelapse (interactive map to Earth change over time) and National Geographic will be resources for their final products. Classroom accounts in a digital sharing platform such as Flipgrid or Seesaw.
Desired Outcomes	After these lessons, students will be able to share and communicate their understanding of renewable and nonrenewable natural resources, types of soil, how people impact the environment, and how to use resources carefully with their teacher and peers. Future lessons they will produce persuasive texts/multimodal resources to advocate for environmental conservation.
Instructional Strategies and Learning Tasks *Description of what the teacher (you) will be doing and/or what the students will be doing.*	
Introduction	**LACI's TLC Phase 1: Building Shared Knowledge of the Topic** **These opening activities, introductions, sustained readings, deconstructions, bridgings, and constructions are repeated for each text within the Conserving Resources Unit Text:** Day 1: What are Some Types of Resources? Day 2: What are Some Types of Soil? Day 3: How do People Use and Impact the Environment? Day 4 How Can Resources be Used Wisely? Ms. Williams introduces the lesson with a slide show of images on the smart board using English and Spanish, checking for student understanding. The first slide has four squares with four different images and asks the students "Which one doesn't belong and why?" This is an activity the students have practiced before in other content areas. The first slide contains four squares: three natural resources and one manmade resource. Some of the pictures include familiar images from student's native countries and the county they are currently in (*Culture* and *Connection*).

	Ms. Williams directs the class to have one minute of silent, independent thinking and then one minute of group sharing before one member from each group shares with the class. Ms. Williams encourages conversation with sentence starters, and student language preferences. The next slide has four squares again, this time with three manmade resources and one natural resource. The same procedure for independent thinking and sharing occurs. No correction or redirection is given at this point by the teacher, but she repeats students' answers for clarification and validates their thinking and reasoning (*Classroom Interactions*).
Highlighted Strategies: Sustained Reading, Deconstruction, Bridging Reading to Writing, and Joint Construction **Procedures:** specific details regarding what the students will do during the lesson (practice/application) **6 Cs of Support:** *Connection:* What will you do to connect the lesson to students' prior academic learning, backgrounds and experiences?	**LACI's TLC Phase 2: Sustained Reading,** *Conserving Resources* After the brief picture slide show of resources, Ms. Williams projects the selected text for Sustained Reading, first showing only the cover and introduces the vocabulary terms: Resource, reusable, renewable, and nonrenewable. Ms. Williams provides a graphic organizer that outlines different columns for the different types of resources. Students work in groups to quickly brainstorm what they think some examples of these could be in a black pen. Even though each student has their own copy of the organizer, they can help each other fill in their group's choices (*Community and Collaboration, Classroom Interactions*). Ms. Williams walks around the room to check for students' understanding, seeing areas of misconceptions to address when they return to read the rest of the text (*Challenge*). She then reads the whole text out loud with a reading aloud activity, modeling fluency, tone, and skips the designated questions for this round, but pointing to the words as she reads. **LACI's TLC Phase 2: Deconstruction** Ms. Williams then directs the class back to the smart board to reread the text, but this time, stopping at the designated sections to ask questions, and repeatedly checks for understanding in group responses. Then she instructs students to use a blue pen to quickly add examples or ideas to their graphic organizer. While reading, Ms. Williams models using the highlighter tool on the smart board when she sees repeating words, such as verbs and nouns that students will be expected to use in their final writing product. For example, verbs *are, can be, is, and use* with the nouns such as "*Reusable resources are resources that can*

(Continued)

Table 4.3 (Continued)

Code-breaking: What will you do to explicitly teach ways of doing school, academic literacy, and disciplinary, linguistic, and cultural codes of content learning? How will you model the language forms/vocabulary/function/skills? *Collaboration and community:* How will you engage students in collaboration and build a community of practice?	*be used again and again"* (p. 3). She especially calls students' attention to *dense definitions, descriptions, and explanations.* Phonetic spelling in English or Spanish is encouraged, this organizer will be edited later as a group to use for their final product in the next lesson (*Code-Breaking*). She then directs students to see how the texts *connects with the reader* by examining mood choices (she uses the terminology *questions, statements,* and *commands* to help third grades identify mood choices) and *cohesive devices that create links within the text* (which Ms. Williams identified as *referrers* such as pronouns and demonstratives) After the text is completed, Ms. Williams switches the groups so that new members share what their previous groups talked about and add new ideas in their organizers with a red pen (*Community and Collaboration*).
Culture: How will you link the new content skills and concepts to students' cultural and linguistic resources to support academic learning? *Challenge:* What aspects of disciplinary literacy will you address? Which higher-order thinking and reasoning skills will you focus on?	**Added Phase: Bridging Reading to Writing** Students return to their independent areas and Ms. Williams hands out a sentence making graphic organizer, scaffolded for varied writing supports, and pulls a small group of students to a side table to develop their writing in a more supported approach, with teacher-directed discourse (*Challenge, Classroom Interactions*). Students take their graphic organizer full of examples and different colored writing to develop initial sentences to express their understanding of the text, the vocabulary, and the main ideas. They can use Google docs to use voice typing features and then scribe them to their paper.

Classroom interactions: How will you use "interactional scaffolding" in the classroom? Plan for the use of oral discourse to prompt elaboration, build academic literacy, and move discourse and learning forward. Based on de Oliveira (2016) **Closing**	**LACI's TLC Phase 3: Joint Construction** After completing the 4 lessons for the shared readings, Ms. Williams models the creation of a short video clip. Using students' graphic organizers, Ms. Williams asks students to develop final products to represent their understandings. She then engages students to use their writings to help them create a short video clip in their classroom's Seesaw account which is also printed to share with their families at home through a QR code (*Culture, Connection*). They can recite their writings, ask a partner to join them to record a dialogue, and offer their opinions on what they learned. Part of their digital sharing routine is commenting on each other's videos. Ms. Williams opens up discussions afterwards and discovers that the students want to find a way to share information to the public on how to preserve the resources in their native countries. (*Community and Collaboration, Code-Breaking, Culture, Challenge, Classroom Interactions*). **LACI's TLC Phase 4: Collaborative Construction** Ms. Williams allows the students to group themselves to work on specific projects based on common problems they want to address or common native countries/regions. Some developed digital advertisement videos, paper pamphlets, learning videos, bilingual resources, and posters to share around the school, and also submitted them to the community resources in the county and their native countries. Ms. Williams helped to find newspapers and digital media that have sections for youth submissions (*Community and Collaboration, Code-Breaking, Culture, Challenge*).
Assessment/Evaluation (Formative and/or Summative)	Formative evaluations were completed during the consistent routine by Ms. Williams when she checks for understandings, assessed group participation and individual products on the graphic organizers, and watched digital classroom clips and comment threads.
Extension	Students have the opportunities to develop their projects as a group or independently and seek feedback from their peers or Ms. Williams. They can follow up with the effect of their product sharing in the community and develop learning further to help their cause.

a focus on the highlighted language demands in the analysis presented in this chapter, including dense definitions, descriptions, and explanations as well as mood choices (which she explains to students as *questions, statements,* and *commands*) and cohesive devices that create links within the text which Ms. Williams identifies as *referrers* such as pronouns and demonstratives. The unit plan shows how a teacher might explore the language of social studies with students and build in lots of collaboration opportunities for MLs to comprehend the content necessary and then apply that knowledge in multimodal activities, including videos.

LACI in the Classroom: Exploring the Language of Social Studies with MLs

The examples presented in this chapter come from a second-grade classroom in Indiana and a fifth-grade classroom in Florida. I worked with the second-grade teacher to implement LACI in integrated English language arts and social studies lessons in support of MLs. The fifth-grade examples come from Mrs. Cabana, already introduced in Chapter 2 as a first-grade teacher. We worked with Mrs. Cabana for multiple years and she moved to teaching fifth-grade after our initial collaboration.

LACI in a Second-Grade Classroom

At the time of this project, Mrs. Lillian Martin was a second-grade teacher with five years of teaching experience at Aciwi Elementary School in the Lenaswa School District. The school had approximately 1,000 students, situated in a highly industrial city in Indiana. Mrs. Martin used many instructional strategies to focus on literacy development with her students, and was particularly interested in how teachers can incorporate reading and writing in the content areas. Mrs. Martin taught first grade the previous year and then moved to second grade with the same students. This is commonly referred to as looping. Eighteen students participated in this project. Reading and writing activities, with a focus on research and inquiry, were daily components of her classroom.

The social studies topic selected by the teacher was Ancient Egypt, a very interesting and relevant topic that usually is very popular in elementary classrooms. In writing about this experience, the process that the teacher and students went through in reading and writing about Ancient Egypt is described, along with the Cs of support that she incorporated into the activities.

The literacy activities in Mrs. Martin's classroom consisted of a two-and-a-half- to three-hour block of time every morning. During this time, students participated in reading activities, writing activities, and word study. Content area studies took place in the afternoon and included mathematics, science, and social studies. Lessons in the content areas were often integrated into the literacy block, which provided an additional opportunity for students to explore topics in greater depth.

Author studies are often utilized in classrooms as a way for students to study the craft of specific authors and the decisions they make as they write books. In Mrs. Martin's second-grade classroom, students were engaged in an author study of Judith Schachner. The study began as a time to enjoy Schachner's books for children. The class read multiple books by Schachner, in the form of read alouds, and were making connections among the books and forming hypotheses about her intentions as a writer.

Schachner has created a series of books about a Siamese cat named Skippyjon Jones. Skippyjon does not want to be a cat, but rather a chihuahua who has all kinds of adventures when he is in his room. One such adventure was when he was sent to his room as a punishment and pretended to be in Egypt. While reading the book *Skippyjon Jones in Mummy Trouble*, it was evident that the students did not understand the book because none of the jokes seemed to be funny to them. Mrs. Martin thought her students needed more background knowledge on Ancient Egypt. She reported that they had loved the two other Skippyjon Jones books that were read previously and their interest was sparked because they began asking questions to better understand this story. Because of the interest demonstrated by the students, Mrs. Martin decided to spend time on an in-depth study of Ancient Egypt to combine reading and writing activities and social studies content.

LACI's TLC Phase 1: Building Shared Knowledge of the Topic

Mrs. Martin engaged students in a discussion about what they already knew about Ancient Egypt. Students shared that they knew about mummies and pyramids. This is an example of how Mrs. Martin used the C of *connection*. Mrs. Martin used a word wall and added the following words divided up into categories. Word walls, when used with discussions and interactive activities, can support teachers' use of the C of *code-breaking*. She engaged students in a discussion about where they thought the words should go, asking questions such as "Do you think this is a person, a place, or a thing? Why do you think so?" Students provided different answers. It was important for Mrs. Martin to engage students in discussion, using the C of *classroom interactions* to support them, instead of providing them with definitions of words out of context. Instead, Mrs. Martin had various images that showed students what the words referred to and they discussed how interesting the images were. The use of multimodal activities to build shared knowledge of the topic can be very useful for all students, and especially MLs, as they can better connect what the images show and what the vocabulary words express.

Ancient Egypt

People
- ◆ Egyptian
- ◆ pharaoh
- ◆ mummy
- ◆ Cleopatra
- ◆ Ramses the Great
- ◆ archaeologist
- ◆ Tutankhamun

Things
- ◆ papyrus
- ◆ hieroglyph
- ◆ scarab
- ◆ silt
- ◆ linen
- ◆ artefact

Places
- ◆ pyramid
- ◆ Sphinx
- ◆ Giza
- ◆ Great Pyramid
- ◆ Obelisk
- ◆ Cairo
- ◆ temple
- ◆ sarcophagus
- ◆ tomb
- ◆ Red Sea
- ◆ Nile River
- ◆ Sahara Desert
- ◆ Thebes
- ◆ Valley of the Kings
- ◆ Mediterranean Sea
- ◆ oasis

Mrs. Martin explained to students that they would be seeing some of these words in the books they were going to read. They would revisit this list once they were done with the reading alouds.

LACI's TLC Phase 2: Sustained Reading

Mrs. Martin immersed students in many types of books through reading alouds and independent reading on the topic of Ancient Egypt during daily afternoon social studies time. Her rationale and purpose in doing this was clear and focused: To build the background knowledge of students in the area of Ancient Egypt in order to build accessibility for students as they read more complex texts and to introduce students to the concept of research. This is a focus on the C of *challenge*.

Students were introduced to what we have termed "genre studies" focusing on moving from reading to writing in social studies. These genre studies were structured as reading and writing activities and started by providing students with information about a specific social studies topic, Ancient Egypt, and the different ways to deliver information about the topic to readers. Using the C of *code-breaking*, Mrs. Martin introduced different texts via reading alouds to students who gained experience reading different texts and finding specific language features that constitute these texts. Students then chose which genre they would like to further study and use in their own writing. They created charts about the specific components of their chosen genre to draw out unique features that they could later utilize. Through genre studies, students also have opportunities to see how language is used in texts and how texts are structured to make meaning, also an important part of the C of *code-breaking* (de Oliveira et al., 2020).

Mrs. Martin was going to move students toward independence by gradually releasing responsibility to enable them to independently research their own topics of interest. For three weeks the class read, watched, and discussed Ancient Egyptian culture. Discussions were sparked by information learned during reading-aloud experiences of many types of texts, Internet and recorded media presentations, and small-group study students conducted when wanting to learn more about one specific aspect of Ancient Egyptian culture. Mrs. Martin engaged students in *classroom interactions* about the books, their content, organizational structures, and language features, all part of the C of *code-breaking*. We recorded information and new understandings on charts for reference.

As we observed students, we discovered that they were using content language to speak to each other, to write, and to come to new understandings within books. Mrs. Martin's teacher notes from writing conferences and field notes about student conversations in group discussions showed that the discussions in class became more detailed and complex; students were experimenting with content-specific language and voicing understandings (and more than a few misconceptions) with the teacher and each other.

They had gained the background knowledge required to understand references to Ancient Egypt in the books they read independently; and they had taken part in authentic learning, not failure or success in academic tasks, that they could engage in independently outside the classroom setting.

Some students had already started writing on Egyptian topics because of their new learning. Mrs. Martin started to wonder if the students could transfer this new content language into their own writing. Mrs. Martin consistently looked at how books are organized, including their genre and organizational structure. During the Ancient Egypt study, students were exposed to several types of non-fiction text and some fiction text. Some books were organized by a table of contents and each section started with a specific title and gave facts on that topic. Mrs. Martin referred to these books as "all-about" books. They represented the genre of Reports whose goal was to provide information about a topic. Some other books taught the process of how to make something such as a mummy. Mrs. Martin called these books "how-to" books. They represent the genre of Procedures. Other genres included Biographical Recount and Stories (some being Historical Stories). Table 4.4 shows the different books available for students categorized in terms of their genres, their characteristics, purposes, and typical stages. We wondered if they would be able to use their knowledge of these structures and their new knowledge of Ancient Egypt to create their own books with purposeful structure, content vocabulary, and genre-specific language features.

As students and teacher engaged in these activities, Mrs. Martin made sure that students were familiar with fiction and non-fiction aspects of Ancient Egypt. It was important to highlight that books may use fictional elements to make stories more interesting, but it was also important to focus on the social studies content of the texts.

LACI's TLC Phase 3: Deconstruction

All units of study in the classroom writing activities followed a similar framework. Through an inquiry approach, the students were immersed in books which were the best examples of the genres the students would soon write. During close study of these texts and how they are written, the writers develop an understanding of how that particular genre works so that they can begin envisioning what they will try writing.

The students chose the genre and topic for their books that they would write. Mrs. Martin told the students that the topic and genre had to 'fit together'. An example presented to students was: 'If you were going to write about King Tut's life, what genre would you choose?' She was surprised to hear students discuss the possibility of different structures with sound reasoning; for example, King Tut's life could be written as a historical story with elements of

Table 4.4 Genres used in Genre Studies

Genre	Description	Purpose	Typical Stages/ Text Structures	Books Used in the Classroom
Reports ('all about books')	Informational books that were about one topic	To provide information about a topic	◆ Classification or Positioning ◆ Description	◆ *Mummies Unwrapped* ◆ *Egypt* ◆ *Tutankhamen's Tomb* ◆ *Who Built the Pyramid?* ◆ *The Best Book of Mummies* ◆ *Ancient Egypt Revealed* ◆ *100 Things You Should Know About Egypt* ◆ *I Wonder Why the Pyramids Were Built* ◆ *Mummy* ◆ *Pyramid*
Biographical Recount	A written account of a person's life	To chronicle others' significant life events	◆ Orientation ◆ Record of stages	◆ *Tutankhamen's Gift*
Stories (Historical)	Imaginative stories with fictional characters and events in a historical setting	To engage readers in a problem/complication and resolving it (Based on a historical event)	◆ Orientation ◆ Complication ◆ Resolution	◆ *Magic Tree House: Mummies in the Morning* ◆ *Ghosts of the Nile* ◆ *Skippyjon Jones in Mummy Trouble*
Procedure ('how-to')	Written instructions to complete a task	To instruct someone how to do experiments, observations, and other tasks	◆ Materials ◆ Instructions	◆ *Tut's Mummy... Lost and Found* ◆ *The Best Book of Mummies*

mystery because his death was mysterious, but it could also be a biographical recount, a written account about his life. If students selected to write a historical story, they could use fictional elements. However, if they chose to write a biographical recount, they should only use factual information.

After students chose the genre, they were divided into groups to begin close study of the books to see commonalities in the organizational structure and chart their findings. The first time they encountered these books was for the purpose of enjoying and learning about Ancient Egypt. But this time, they were reading them with a new goal: To understand their purpose, organization, and the language choices made by the author. These are also elements of the C of *code-breaking*. The students were being asked to read these books as writers. The teacher modeled how students were supposed to create a chart with the characteristics, stages, and language features of the books, a process of Deconstruction of a genre. Students then created charts about the characteristics of the books. Working in heterogeneous groups allowed the students to support one another and explain complex ideas, an important element of the C of *community and collaboration*. The students collaboratively developed strong beliefs as to how they could use what they saw in these books. They then incorporated that knowledge into their own writing. After three to four days of careful examination of these texts, students began to envision how they would take their chosen Ancient Egypt topic and write a book following the genre they had studied.

LACI's TLC Phase 5: Collaborative Writing
Students worked in genre groups the entire time they worked on collaboratively constructing their books, part of the C of *community and collaboration*. The classroom was filled with an exciting buzz as students stapled together blank pieces of paper to begin writing. Though students had done significant research on their own, they still needed the support and guidance of how to go about using their newly acquired knowledge of Ancient Egypt, genres, and organizational structures.

Mrs. Martin met with various groups for short mini-lessons that were focused on helping students organize their ideas. It became evident that some groups could use an organizer to plan their books. The group studying Reports/'all about books' could do this through the use of a table of contents page. The Biographical Recount group found it useful to make a timeline of the person's life they would be writing about and put key events on their timeline that would make up the pages of the book. Those students studying 'how-to'/Procedures writing also utilized a table of contents to put each step in order with additional information pages. Students who were writing Historical Stories struggled the most with how to organize their writing before they began. Some chose to use a table of contents and make chapters like a fiction book. Others wrote lists on paper of the major events in the story. Mrs. Martin realized they had difficulty because they were not only just beginning to read chapter books but also mixing fictional and historical events together. Therefore, they had to be crafted in an intertwined way. To support these writers, Mrs. Martin spent extra time closely looking at how other familiar books had done this such as *The Magic Tree House* series (Osborne, 2002). In these books, fictional characters travel to far-off lands to solve mysteries. Within the story are many true facts about that land. These books were a perfect scaffold because the class had read many of them together.

Throughout the unit of study on genres and organizational structures, Mrs. Martin reported finding it essential to constantly be aware of what decisions the writers were making and how she could support them in crafting their books. Individual writing conferences gave us the opportunity to better understand the attempts they made in their writing. We also found it useful to pull the students in particular genre groups to provide extra support.

Mrs. Martin noticed students were supporting one another in new ways. Prior to the genre study, they consulted with their friends about their writing. But now, it seemed they were relying more on the members of their genre groups. Students chose to sit near their group members as they wrote for additional support in the task at hand. This showed that students found peer mentors to help them in the writing.

Students successfully used large amounts of content language, defined as language patterns including vocabulary terms learned when studying Ancient Egypt, and added to the word wall that Mrs. Martin initially started when writing 'all-about'/Reports and 'how-to'/Procedures and language features that helped them provide information about the topic (for Reports) and instruct someone how to do something (for Procedures):

- ◆ "Scientists think that Eye shot the back of his head but the **'newest' theory** is that he was hunting and driving his **chariot** at the same time and something scared the horses and ran away and **King Tut** fell over and died."
- ◆ "**Hieroglyphics** are a type of writing in which represents picture or sound. And, it is writing in **Egyptian** style. Like these letters."
- ◆ "**Pyramids** look like mountains. They stopped making them because people would know the gold would be in there so the robbers would go get the gold. The **pharaoh** would create the **pyramid**. He would make it in the 1300's **BC**. The **pyramid** is for the **pharaoh** when he dies."
- ◆ "The tools you need are a hook to take out the brain out the nose. They have **canopic jars** to put the body parts in."

Though Mrs. Martin did not jointly construct a text (Phase 4 of LACI's TLC) with students, she provided them with multiple opportunities to understand the genres. We highly recommend spending time on joint construction with the classroom, even if multiple genres are involved. Joint Construction is a critical phase in genre-based writing instruction and provides students with guidance through interactions with the teacher and other students.

LACI in a Fifth-Grade Classroom

The examples used in this section come from two fifth-grade classes at Sunnyside Elementary School in Florida. This school houses an International Studies Magnet Program that provides instruction in two languages (e.g., English/Spanish, English/French, or English/German), with a clear focus on bilingual and biliteracy development. With over 50 countries and numerous languages represented in the student body, this school has been nicknamed a "mini United Nations". The classes were taught by Mrs. Cabana. Together, the classes were comprised of 44 students, 40 of whom spoke a language other than English at home. In the United States, the great majority (3.6 million) of MLs speak Spanish at home (National Center for Education Statistics, 2020), and this was reflected in Mrs. Cabana's fifth-grade classrooms, where most of the bilingual students spoke Spanish and English. As part of the Spanish pathway in the international studies magnet program, many students were bilingual English/Spanish speakers; however, there were a number of other languages present as well, including French, German, Arabic, Russian, Mandarin, among others. The MLs' language proficiencies in English ranged from Level 2 to Level 6 (in a 6-point scale).

Students had been studying Christopher Columbus as part of the social studies content. They had studied what Columbus had done when he arrived in the Americas. Specifically, they were discussing the settlement of Spanish colonists in what was named La Isla Española (Hispaniola in its Anglicized form) in 1492. Mrs. Cabana assigned an Argument genre for students to argue whether they thought that Columbus was a hero or a villain. Students read and discussed several sources about Columbus. They used a handout to summarize the sources, shown in Figure 4.4.

Example 1 shows Mrs. Cabana leading the class in identifying main ideas and summarizing information from sources. She asks students to open the Journal Entry from the Columbus journal. Mrs. Cabana teaches students how to find details and turn them into evidence using their own words for writing a summary. In the process of addressing the question "Is Columbus a villain or hero?" Mrs. Cabana highlights how to find details and recognize facts by eliciting and discussing with students. In finding the details from the journal,

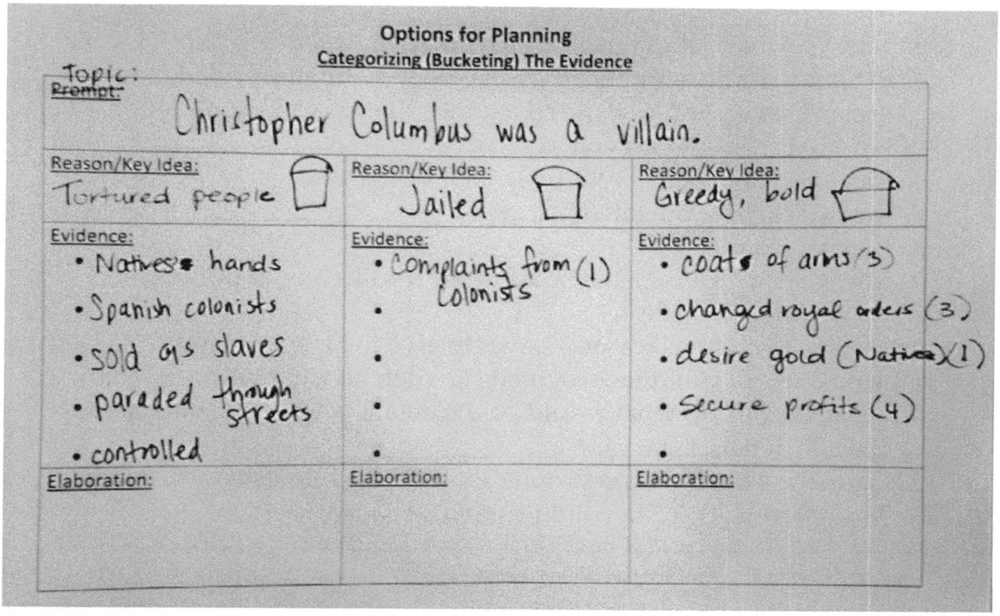

Options for Planning
Categorizing (Bucketing) The Evidence

~~Prompt:~~ Topic: Christopher Columbus was a villain.

Reason/Key Idea: Tortured people	Reason/Key Idea: Jailed	Reason/Key Idea: Greedy, bold
Evidence: • Natives hands • Spanish colonists • sold as slaves • paraded through streets • controlled	Evidence: • Complaints from colonists (1) • • • •	Evidence: • coats of arms (3) • changed royal orders (3) • desire gold (Natives)(1) • Secure profits (4) •
Elaboration:	Elaboration:	Elaboration:

Figure 4.4 Handout for Planning Used by Mrs. Cabana's Students.

there is some new language for students. Mrs. Cabana took this opportunity to practice new words that students encountered. To make sure students use correct terminology to describe details, Mrs. Cabana spent some time clarifying the process *rules over* with students.

Example 1

1. Mrs. Cabana: All right. The first one, the first source talk to me about, I know you did it. This was a journal entry. This was a journal entry from Columbus's journal, right? Basically, what was the main idea of this one? On the first one? So what did you put in your chart? What was the main idea here? Did anybody else have another main idea sentence? Obviously it might be similar because they may be about wording a little differently. Jules.
2. Jules: Columbus enslaved the natives to give the queen and king.
3. Mrs. Cabana: Okay. Very good. Bruna.
4. Bruna: Columbus rules over Native Americans to bring back to Spain.

5. Mrs. Cabana: Columbus rules over Native Americans to bring back to Spain. And it's not that they maybe something he ruled over, because when you rule over, it sounds like he's a king. But more like he, what word would you say?
6. Ricardo: Subjugate
7. Mrs. Cabana: Subjugated?
8. Lorena: Dominated
9. Mrs. Cabana: Dominated? Captured? It's like any of those would work. Any other ideas?
10. Lorena: Columbus wanted slaves to give to his queen and king.
11. Mrs. Cabana: Columbus wanted slaves to give to his queen. That all works out. So what would be the details? What are some of the specific details, Gabriela?
12. Gabriela: That there are? I don't know, they didn't stand a chance?
13. Mrs. Cabana: OK. They didn't stand a chance.

In this example, we see Mrs. Cabana helping students identify main ideas in the documents they had read. In turn 5, we see an example of the C of *code-breaking*, with Mrs. Cabana helping Bruna understand the meaning of *"rules over"* as having to do with what a king does. Then she uses the C of *classroom interactions* with the interactional scaffolding move *moving the discourse forward* asking "What would you say?" and students provide some possible words that could be used. In turn 11, she moves on to ask students "So what would be the details?" These exchanges continue for a few more minutes. Then Mrs. Cabana asks students about how the document answers the question of whether Columbus was a hero or a villain:

Example 2

14. Now, the next part, this is the one that you have to be more careful with. How does this document answer the question? Go back. What is the question?
15. Ricardo: Was Christopher Columbus a hero or a villain?
16. Mrs. Cabana: So from this one, you have to decide on the information. This is really your opinion. In the information that's given. Is this heroic? Or is he a villain? Now, the first thing I'm gonna tell you is, I know we are practicing this document, blah, blah, blah, right? But I'm gonna challenge you now again. What kind of document is this? What is this?
17. Students: informative

18. Mrs. Cabana: No, what kind of document like… It's an excerpt and an excerpt of what?

19. Students: of a journal

20. Mrs. Cabana: of a journal. So that's one way to up your language, to be more specific, to create that language that when you're writing that makes us all wanna read. So right now, if you have the word document, I want you to erase it and put journal, this journal, you could even say this excerpt. I know you don't have a lot of space, but this excerpt from Columbus's journal if you wanted. But journal will just work fine right now. So in this document, in this journal, let's change that. Let's start working on that kind of very precise language that makes us sound smart over here. In this journal or this journal. Now, what does this journal do? What is the action word you're going to use? So I want to just hear your action words. What were your verbs?

21. Student: proves?

22. Student: I put

23. Mrs. Cabana: What is the verb you're using? What is this journal doing? Tells?

24. Student: […]

25. Mrs. Cabana: But how did you start that sentence?

26. Student: I said from Columbus… But when you just said this excerpt and then I don't know.

27. Mrs. Cabana: So where's the verb? The excerpt from this journal…

28. Students: shows me, tells me, helps me, states

29. Mrs. Cabana: proves me, helps me, supports… it's not gonna state that he's a hero. Is that stating that he is a villain or hero, right? Like this journal didn't say Columbus is a hero. You're making that inference, you're making that guess. So here it's not that it's stating it. But it's helping you infer, helps me infer, helps me determine, supports my idea that… Yeah, what is he? So let me hear, look at yours, reread it for just a second. See if you want to edit, edit it, make any changes. And then let me hear it out. What did you say? Lucas.

30. Lucas: this journal tells…

31. Mrs. Cabana: How about instead of "tells"… Because Columbus is not saying, hey, guys, I'm a villain, dear journal, I am a villain. Right? It shows me, it proves to me, maybe it proves to you. How does it prove to you? You can make sense of your answer. How does it prove to you?

32. Marcus: This journal proves to me that Columbus is a villain.

33. Larisa: It has information like how he enslaved people.

> 34. Mrs. Cabana: How he enslaved people. Yeah. I like that. That combination together, Larisa and Marcus, that collaboration you just did would be a perfect, solid, sixth-grade response. This journal proves to me that Columbus was a villain because he enslaved natives. Through the details that show me and he enslaved natives that would be six grade writing. You would be super set… Anybody else want to share that explanation part? Pedro?
>
> 35. Pedro: This excerpt supports the question, because it gives the reason why he is a villain.
>
> 36. Mrs. Cabana: Very good because it gives the reason why he's a villain. So if you use this sentence in writing, then it would be the same thing. I would say, like a collaboration with Marcus's idea. To add, because the reason why he's villain. And then if you were writing this in a summary down here [pointing to handout], you tell me what it is that you saw. You tell me what those details were from that second box. Does that make sense? OK Good job, guys. I'm really proud of you.

This example shows the use of many Cs of support for scaffolding. There is clear integration of content and language, as Mrs. Cabana guides students to find details from the source to justify their claims. Mrs. Cabana uses the C of *classroom interactions* throughout this example. Turn 16 is a clear example of the C of *challenge* – Mrs. Cabana even uses the word *challenge* here when she says "But I'm gonna challenge you now again. What kind of document is this?" which does present a challenge for students. At first, they answer *informative* (turn 17). Mrs. Cabana probes students using both the interactional scaffolding move *probing* as well as *cued elicitation* when she asks: "No, what kind of document like… It's an excerpt and an excerpt of what?" emphasizing the word *kind*. In turn 20, she further elaborates, using the interactional scaffolding move *elaboration*, when she says "So that's one way to up your language, to be more specific, to create that language that when you're writing that makes us all wanna read. So right now, if you have the word document, I want you to erase it and put journal, this journal, you could even say this excerpt." She emphasizes the word *document* in the exchange. Here there is also clear use of the C of *code-breaking* as she is guiding students to be more precise and *specific* in their use of language to describe the document they are analyzing. Code-breaking continues as Mrs. Cabana tells students "Let's start working on that kind of very precise language that makes us sound smart over here. In this journal or this journal." And continues to ask a question using the interactional scaffolding move *moving the discourse forward*: "Now, what does this journal do? What is the action word you're going to use? So I want to just hear your action words. What were your verbs?" Here we see Mrs. Cabana's use of the metalanguage that students are already familiar with *action words and verbs*. Mrs. Cabana continues to guide students to think of the verbs that they are using in turns 21–27. In turn 28, several students provide answers: *shows me, tells me, helps me, states.* In turn 29, Mrs. Cabana affirms what students said by repeating "proves me, helps me, supports" and then clarifies why *state* is not an appropriate choice of verb:

> it's not gonna state that he's a hero. It that stating? that he is a villain or hero, right? Like this journal didn't say Columbus is a hero. You're making that inference, you're making that guess. So here it's not that it's stating it. But it's helping you infer, helps me infer, helps me determine, supports my idea that… Yeah, what is he?

All of these explanations are critical components of the C of *code-breaking*, as Mrs. Cabana continuously explains why a certain verb is not an appropriate word choice for this particular instance. These explanations continue in turn 31 when one of the MLs in the class, Lucas, suggests the use of the verb *tells* (turn 30):

> How about instead of tells… Because Columbus is not saying, hey, guys, I'm a villain.
> Dear journal, I am a villain. Right? It shows me, it proves to me, maybe it proves to you. How does it prove to you? You can make sense of your answer. How does it prove to you?

These continued explanations and engagement with students to explore these language choices are critical for developing their knowledge about language, given also that the majority of the class (40 out of 44 students) are multilingual learners. This language exploration plays a critical role in language development for all students but is particularly important for the MLs in the classroom. In turns 32 and 33, Marcus and Larisa, two MLs, contribute two pieces of a response that they included in their handouts:

> 32. Marcus: This journal proves to me that Columbus is a villain.
> 33. Larisa: It has information like how he enslaved people.

Notice here the use of the verb *enslaved* instead of the noun *slaves*. Mrs. Cabana had been using this verb instead of the noun throughout the lesson, even when students used the noun *slave*, she typically recast their answer and used *enslaved*. *Slave* is a dehumanizing word whereas *enslaved* emphasizes circumstances, conditions, and a person's experiences (de Oliveira & Beatty, 2023). In turn 34, Mrs. Cabana reacts to what Larisa and Marcus said with:

> how he enslaved people. Yeah. I like that. That combination together, Larisa and Marcus, that collaboration you just did would be a perfect, solid, sixth-grade grade response. This journal proves to me that Columbus was a villain because he enslaved natives. Through the details that show me and he enslaved natives that would be sixth-grade writing. You would be super set…

Mrs. Cabana affirms students' answers enthusiastically saying "Yeah. I like that" and emphasizing the collaboration that the students did in their contribution to the discussion; this also shows the C of *community and collaboration* as students are engaged with each other in responding to Mrs. Cabana. Mrs. Cabana uses the interactional scaffolding move *purposeful repetition* when she repeats the combined response by Marcus and Larisa, saying "This journal proves to me that Columbus was a villain because he enslaved natives". In this turn, we also see how she uses the verb *enslaved* and not *slaves* as a static attribute. At the end of turn 34, she asks for Pedro to contribute his response (turn 35): "This excerpt supports the question because it gives the reason why he is a villain." In turn 36, Mrs. Cabana again affirms Pedro's contribution with "Very good" and uses the interactional scaffolding move *purposeful repetition* when she repeats "because it gives the reason why he's a villain."

> Very good because it gives the reason why he's a villain. So if you use this sentence in writing, then it would be the same thing. I would say, like a collaboration with Marcus's idea. To add, because the reason why he's a villain. And then if you were writing this in a summary down here [pointing to handout], you tell me what it is that you saw. You tell me what those details were from that second box. Does that make sense? OK Good job, guys. I'm really proud of you.

She ends turn 36 with an affirmation to the entire class on a job well done and shows how proud she is of what they have done. Example 3 continues the examination of sources and we see how Mrs. Cabana clarifies some of the social studies content on which students need clarification.

Example 3

37. Mrs. Cabana: OK so over here, this journal, this journal proves. Source 2, this is a good one. Source 2 is a what?
38. Laura: a picture?
39. Mrs. Cabana: It's a photograph
40. Bruna: of him in jail.
41. Mrs. Cabana: It's a photograph.
42. Andres: Wait.
43. Laura: and he has chains.
44. Mrs. Cabana: so in the photograph. You're seeing Columbus in chains. You're seeing him. Obviously, he has chains, he is locked up. He is in jail. What do we see in the reading? Is that in I want you back in your reading. Now I want to see everyone in source 2.
45. Alex: Did he eat in jail?
46. Mrs. Cabana: Yeah, they'll feed them. You're not gonna get a five-course meal. Lucas, what do you see? Where is this is? Sure. If anything, we didn't mention in the photograph or what do you see in the text?
47. Lucas: That in the... amount of tools. And if they didn't connect enough to go that their hands will be cut off. They rebel against Spanish.
48. Mrs. Cabana: Excuse me [students were talking loudly].
49. Lucas: Spanish will be executed at the gallows.
50. Mrs. Cabana: OK. Let me stop there for a second. Let's just highlight the key words, hands cut off, right? Executed. So that person, that person that first sentence is that person's opinion, right? The person is saying, he's Columbus, he could be brutal and tyrannical, like he was a tyrant. He was a leader. And if you didn't follow what he did, he would kill you like kill the people. So that is the person who wrote this caption, that is their opinion. But with supporting their opinion, with the facts, that's what you want. Those are the details you want. When you are looking for information, you don't want to just to say someone else's opinion. You want to pull out the pieces that are facts. What are the facts here? The facts are if you didn't collect enough gold and you were a native, then your hands were cut off. If you rebelled, if you went against, if you went against the Spanish explorers, the Spanish colonists that were living on that land, you were getting executed this up. So the gallow is what they call the wooden structure where they would hang people. Yeah, BUT this shows us what happened, what was happening in Europe. This is how rulers rule in Europe. Right? Maybe not all of them to the

extreme, but some of them just did it because they felt like, you went against me and my opinion, gone. It looks like that's what's happening here. Then look, the colonists. So now, not only once they come to the land, there's people who stay behind. They become colonists, they're living in a colony, they're living in the place. When they stay there, when they are there, they're saying now that the colonists complained to the monarchy, to the king and queen. Who did they complain to? And they complained to the royal commissioner who was dispatched – that means that commissioner was a person that was sent from the king and queen to come to Española and see what was happening. They come. Exactly. Do you think, do you think that King Ferdinand and Queen Isabela that they only sent Columbus there? No, I mean that they only jailed Columbus because of how he was treating the natives? Why would the king and queen? Do you think that the king and queen would decide to jail Columbus because of his treatment of the natives? Or do you think it's because of his…

51. Ricardo: he didn't bring enough gold
52. Louise: protesting the natives
53. Mrs. Cabana: Who was protesting? The colonists, the Spanish citizens that stayed on the colony. The Spanish citizens that stayed on the colony were the ones that were protesting.
54. Felipe: and then they got killed.
55. Mrs. Cabana: No, guys hold on. Wait.
56. Felipe: It says and the rebel Spanish colonists were executed at the gallows. So like if you're a Spanish colonist and you complain to Columbus, then it I just like…
57. Mrs. Cabana: Yeah, yes, you're right. So if you were a rebel Spanish colonist, a colonist who was going against Columbus, they were being executed. But do you think… that's what I'm saying? Is it do you think Queen Isabela and King Ferdinand stepped in because of the natives or because of what was happening to the Spanish colonists?
58. Mauricio: Because of what happened to Spanish colonists. Those are Spanish… OK so like…
59. Mrs. Cabana: Yes, I agree, but I agree with you, Mauricio. And I think that's what he was doing. I'm sure that there were people who saw and were upset or bothered by what he was doing to the natives. And that's why they were rebelling against Columbus, but that's exactly what's going on. So he was arrested in August 1500 and brought back to Spain in chains.

In turn 50, Mrs. Cabana uses *code-breaking* to provide extended explanations that connect language and content explicitly. She explains that the caption is that person's opinion and asks students to highlight key words *hands cut off* and *executed*. She explains that the first sentence is that person's opinion. She further elaborates "The person is saying, he's Columbus, he could be brutal and tyrannical, like he was a tyrant. He was a leader. And if you didn't follow what he did, he would kill you like kill the people. So that is the person who wrote this caption, that is their opinion." Mrs. Cabana then clarifies to students that this is their opinion and what they want is the facts: "When you are looking for information, you don't want to just to say someone else's opinion. You want to pull out the pieces that are facts. What are the facts here?" She continues to explain that the facts are: "if you didn't collect enough gold and you were a native, then your hands were cut off. If you rebelled, if you went against, if you went against the Spanish explorers, the Spanish colonists that were living on that land, you were getting executed up." Here we also see Mrs. Cabana using a synonym for *rebelled – went against –* in the context of her explanation. This is a critical part of *code-breaking* and an effective way of defining key vocabulary for students, in the context of content-area discussions, not as isolated terms before they build shared knowledge of the topic or read more extensively. Mrs. Cabana does this again when she says "So the gallows is what they call the wooden structure where they would hang people." Again, using discussions for integrated content and language development, including vocabulary development, provides unique opportunities for teachers to highlight key language patterns and terms for students while simultaneously building their content knowledge (Molle et al., 2021). This discussion also serves to continue to build shared knowledge of the topic.

Mrs. Cabana keeps on defining key language: "Then look, the colonists. So now, not only once they come to the land, there's people who stay behind. They become colonists, they're living in a colony, they're living in the place." She is explaining to students that colonists are those who "come to the land" and "who stay behind" and "they become colonists, they're living in a colony". She explains that the colonists complained to the monarchy ("to the king and queen") and to the "royal commissioner who was dispatched", describing the role of this person to students as "that means that commissioner was a person that was sent from the king and queen to come to Española and see what was happening," another example of language development in the context of content instruction. She proceeds to ask students:

Do you think, do you think that King Ferdinand and Queen Isabela that they only sent Columbus there? No, I mean that they only jailed

Columbus because of how he was treating the natives? Why would the king and queen? Do you think that the king and queen would decide to jail Columbus because of his treatment of the natives? Or do you think it's because of his...

This is an example of how Mrs. Cabana was guiding students to think critically about the content they were learning. She ends turn 50 with the use of the interactional scaffolding move *cued elicitation*, involving students in the learning as they engage with the critical content in social studies. In turns 51 and 52, two students, Ricardo and Louise, reply, respectively: "he didn't bring enough gold" and "protesting the natives." In turn 53, Mrs. Cabana asks the question using the interactional scaffolding move *probing*: "Who was protesting?" and answering it right after: "The colonists, the Spanish citizens that stayed on the colony. The Spanish citizens that stayed on the colony were the ones that were protesting." This clarified for students who was doing the protesting. In turn 54, Felipe says "and then they got killed" to which Mrs. Cabana replies "No, guys hold on. Wait." Felipe continues to explain what he meant in turn 56, "It says and the rebel Spanish colonists were executed at the gallows. So like if you're a Spanish colonist and you complain to Columbus, then it I just like..." Mrs. Cabana acknowledges that Felipe is right and continues to clarify "So if you were a rebel Spanish colonist, a colonist who was going against Columbus, they were being executed." Right after this clarification, she asks, continuing asking students to think critically about the social studies content, using the interactional scaffolding move *moving the discourse forward*: "But do you think... that's what I'm saying? Is it do you think Queen Isabela and King Ferdinand stepped in because of the natives or because of what was happening to the Spanish colonists?" to which Mauricio answered in turn 58 "Because of what happened to Spanish colonists. Those are Spanish... OK so like..." In turn 59, Mrs. Cabana reaffirms Mauricio's answer and further clarifies:

> And I think that's what he was doing. I'm sure that there were people who saw and were upset or bothered by what he was doing to the natives. And that's why they were rebelling against Columbus, but that's exactly what's going on. So he was arrested in August 1500 and brought back to Spain in chains.

This last exchange finalizes this particular part of the dialogue with the class in which she explained many key concepts in the context of the discussion, clarified ideas, and supported students' critical thinking in integrated language and content ways.

Mrs. Cabana goes back to asking students about the main idea of the document, who it is about, and instructing students to write on their charts. Students continue working on their charts writing main idea sentences and adding details to their charts as small bullet points. Mrs. Cabana continues to integrate language and content to help students understand what Columbus was doing, coming from Spain and setting up a colony.

The Cs in focus in these examples were *code-breaking, classroom interactions*, and *challenge*. Mrs. Cabana continuously clarified the social studies language she was using, providing definitions and explanations in the context of the discussion, highlighting the C of *code-breaking*. She used several interactional scaffolding moves, part of the C of *classroom interactions*, as responsive support for students to continuously engage with the social studies content. This is a powerful example of a high-challenge, high-support classroom, offering prime opportunities for MLs to develop their language and content knowledge with the appropriate level of scaffolding. Mrs. Cabana set high expectations and standards for all her students and engaged them in challenging social studies content.

Putting into Practice

Analyzing a Case Study: Fourth-Grade History Lesson in California

Case Studies can help us prepare for and consider issues we have yet to come across in our own teaching. We will consider issues for MLs in a mainstream classroom to help us reflect about what is happening in the classroom and how we might act in a determined situation. We will also consider what each teacher is doing and what issues come up based on her actions. Specifically, we want to focus on how the teacher might address the needs of MLs in her classroom. We will consider all sides to the problems and try to see beyond this particular example.

The example for an implementation of LACI in history comes from a fourth-grade classroom in California. The teacher, Jane Smith, taught in the Urban School District, in a school with a high number of MLs. She typically had 25–27 students in her classroom, about 9–10 of whom would be classified as MLs. The following case study depicts a general education classroom in a school district in California. As you read the case study, consider some of the variables at play here. At this time, this approach was just developing and focused primarily on the C of *code-breaking*, as the following lesson demonstrates. It shows how Mrs. Smith planned a focus on language for her classroom. As you read the lesson and consider LACI's six Cs of support, think about how you could adapt the lesson to implement the other Cs – *connection, culture, challenge, community and collaboration*, and *classroom interactions*.

Mrs. Smith has 20 students in the classroom, many of whom are classified as English language learners (ELLs). All of the ELLs need to work on a variety of issues as developing users of English, even though they are all at intermediate to advanced levels of language proficiency. The teacher prepared a history lesson for the class that also focused on important aspects of the English language. The teacher asked students to read the text "Settling Alta California," part of a unit about California history. She developed students' background by doing several activities that led to this close focus on language in history, so students were prepared for the work ahead. The lesson plan that Mrs. Smith created appears next.

Explanation, References, and Connectors

Newcomers to California: Settling Alta California (Fourth Grade)
California (Boehm et al., 2000, pp. 142–143)

California History – Social Science Standards:

1. Students describe the social, political, cultural, and economic life and interactions among people of California from the pre-Columbian societies to the Spanish mission and Mexican rancho periods.
2. Describe the Spanish exploration and colonization of California, including the relationships among soldiers, missionaries, and Indians (e.g., Juan Crespi, Junipero Serra, Gaspar de Portola).

Guiding Questions:

1. Why did the Spanish king build settlements in Alta California?
2. Why did the Spanish build missions? What did missions do?

1. **Directions**: The cohesive devices have been italicized. Draw an arrow from the cohesive device to who or what it refers to.
2. Key terms have been highlighted. Underline the definition of that term.

Settling Alta California

Spain paid little attention to Alta California until the 1760s. Then King Carlos III of Spain heard that other countries, such as Russia, had started to explore the Pacific coast of North America. To protect Spanish claims, King Carlos ordered that settlements be built in Alta California.

The Spanish Return

King Carlos gave *this order* after *he* heard that Russia had set up a colony in Alaska. *The king* worried that Russian fur traders would move south from Alaska. *They* might try to set up a colony in California.

Starting *a Spanish colony in Alta California* was not easy, however. Travel to California was difficult, and few people wanted to move so far away. Spain decided that the best way to start a colony was to build missions, or religious settlements.

Missions were run by missionaries. A missionary is a person who teaches his or her religion to others. In California the missionaries were Catholic priests or other church workers *who* believed it was *their* duty to teach the Native Californians about Christianity.

The missions had many uses. *Their* main goals were to convert the Indians to Christianity and to teach them Spanish ways. But the missions also brought in people for the new colony in Alta California. Spain hoped the missions would raise crops and make money for the colony, too.

Historical Questions:

1. In this reading, what is another term (a synonym) for *settlement* found on paragraph 3??
2. What were the Russians doing on the Pacific coast of North America and in Alaska?
3. What synonym for Native Californians is used?
4. Why did King Carlos want to start a Spanish colony in Alta California?
5. What was a mission? What were their goals?
6. What role did missions play in settling Alta California?

Mrs. Smith italicized many words in this text to help ELLs understand the text better. Mrs. Smith also wrote historical questions for students to focus on in this text.

Discussion Questions:

1. Which area of language did Mrs. Smith find important to focus on with her students? Notice the italicized words in the text.
2. Why do you think the teacher found that to be an important area to address?
3. Now look at the historical questions, what language issues do some of these questions address? Explain.
4. Are there other language issues that this text could help the teacher address?
5. Based on your developing knowledge of LACI, what advice would you give the teacher working with this text and these students?

Below are some issues you may have discussed as possible additional ideas for this teacher. This text uses many **connectors**. After students read the text and complete the cohesive device activity, you could go through the text and identify the connectors being used and explain their function to students. The following are a few points you can bring up with students (as you feel appropriate).

On line 2, the connector (also called *time marker*) "**until the 1760s**" is used to introduce the time period prior to the time period that is the focus of this text. We know that because the connector "**then**" implies that it was after the 1760s that King Carlos III of Spain heard of other explorations in the Pacific coast of North America. This connector "**then**" also shows that Spain would now pay attention to Alta California, as it is seen in the text. On line 2, the connector "such as" is used to introduce an example of "other countries."

On line 6, in the sentence **"King Carlos gave this order *after* he heard that Russia had set up a colony in Alaska,"** the connector "**after**" marks the time when King Carlos gave the order of building settlements in Alta California. But this connector "**after**" has an even more important function in this sentence: it also functions as a causal marker. In other words, it was because he heard that Russia had set up a colony in Alaska that King Carlos gave the order (he felt the need to do so, as the next two sentences explain: **The king worried that Russian fur traders would move south from Alaska. They might try to set up a colony in California**.)

On line 8, the connector "**however**" establishes a relationship of contrast with the previous sentences. The next sentences explain why building a colony in Alta California was not easy. On line 14, the connector "**and**" is used to show the two main goals of missions. Then the connectors "**but ... also**" on line 15 establish a contrast between the two main goals and what else the missions brought. The connector "**too**" on line 16 is used to show the addition of one more thing the king hoped the missions would do.

Connectors in the History Text

Settling Alta California

Spain paid little attention to Alta California **until the 1760s. Then** King Carlos III of Spain heard that other countries, **such as** Russia, had started to explore the Pacific coast of North America. To protect Spanish claims, King Carlos ordered that settlements be built in Alta California.

The Spanish Return

King Carlos gave this order **after** he heard that Russia had set up a colony in Alaska. The king worried that Russian fur traders would move south from Alaska. They might try to set up a colony in California.

Starting a Spanish colony in Alta California was not easy, **however**. Travel to California difficult, and few people wanted to move so far away. Spain decided that the best way to start a colony was to build missions, or religious settlements.

Missions were run by missionaries. A missionary is a person who teaches his or her religion to others. In California the missionaries were Catholic priests or other church workers who believed it was their duty to teach the Native Californians about Christianity.

The missions had many uses. Their main goals were to convert the Indians to Christianity **and** to teach them Spanish ways. **But** the missions **also** brought in people for the new colony in Alta California. Spain hoped the missions would raise crops and make money for the colony**, too**.

Cohesive Devices in the History Text

Settling Alta California

    Spain paid little attention to Alta California until the 1760s. Then King Carlos III of Spain heard that other countries, such as Russia, had started to explore the Pacific coast of North America. To protect Spanish claims, King Carlos ordered that settlements be built in Alta California.

The Spanish Return

    King Carlos gave *this order* after *he* heard that Russia had set up a colony in Alaska. *The king* worried that Russian fur traders would move south from Alaska. *They* might try to set up a colony in California.

    Starting a *Spanish colony in Alta California* was not easy, however. Travel to California was difficult, and few people wanted to move so far away. Spain decided that the best way to start a colony was to build missions, or religious settlements.

    Missions were run by missionaries. A missionary is a person who teaches *his or her* religion to others. In California the missionaries were Catholic priests or other church workers *who* believed it was *their* duty to teach the Native Californians about Christianity.

    The missions had many uses. *Their* main goals were to convert the Indians to Christianity and to teach *them* Spanish ways. But the missions also brought in people for the new colony in Alta California. Spain hoped the missions would raise crops and make money for the colony, too.

5

Teaching Mathematics to Multilingual Learners

Jason Ware, at the time a second-grade teacher at a school with 90% students classified as MLs, came to talk with me after a professional development session in which he participated at his school district. He came to tell me that Gabriela, a ML in his classroom, was having some difficulties understanding word problems from the math textbook when asked to read on her own. She asked him what *the sum of* meant in a math word problem, after they had done several activities and exercises to practice addition. I had been in his classroom just the week before and noticed that, instead of using the word problem from the math textbook, Mr. Ware explained things orally to his students and never addressed the language of word problems, as they were written. He used the question *"How many are there altogether?"* and used gestures to help students understand what *altogether* meant, since students already knew *how many* was typically asking about a quantity. I asked him what he thought the issue was with Gabriela's question and why she was unable to understand the nominal group *the sum of* in the word problem. He replied that he really wasn't sure because he had been using the same pattern, the question *"How many are there altogether?"* so they would know how to do additions. We then talked about how the word problem "question" was structured. The word problem is the following:

Lily planted 5 trees this morning and 6 trees this afternoon. Calculate the sum of the number of trees Lily planted today.

DOI: 10.4324/9781003264927-5

Mr. Ware and I talked about how the "question" was structured as a command, asking students to do something, *calculate*, and establishing what they needed to calculate – *the sum of the number of trees Lily planted today*. The math textbook had used these words before – *the sum of…* – but Mr. Ware had not called his students' attention to how different this nominal group was from the question that he was always using with students. Gabriela – and many other MLs in Mr. Ware's class – was not familiar with this academic language feature in mathematics, so she had difficulty understanding what she was supposed to do. When Mr. Ware told her that she has to answer the question *"How many are there altogether?,"* Gabriela's expression was one of surprise, saying *"Awwwww, I know how to do that, teacher!"* Mr. Ware, of course, knew that Gabriela could do the word problem, but her lack of understanding of what the "question" asked prevented her from being successful on this word problem. Mr. Ware and I went on to discuss what strategies he could use to make sure he was exposing his students to the academic language of mathematics in word problems.

What could Mr. Ware have done differently in his classroom? Why did Gabriela have difficulty understanding what she was supposed to do in the word problem? How can teachers identify the language demands of word problems and help multilingual learners understand what they have to do? This chapter addresses these and other questions about the content area of mathematics.

Language and mathematics are intrinsically connected in mathematics teaching and learning. As in the other content areas, mathematics draws on everyday uses of language but also uses language in new ways to construct mathematical knowledge. Mathematics is constructed in different ways from other school subjects. This discipline-specific nature of language in mathematics is an important consideration for mathematics learning.

The Multisemiotic Nature of Mathematics

The mathematics register has been described as *multisemiotic* because there are multiple meaning-making systems that work together in the construction of mathematics: language, symbols, and visual images (O'Halloran, 2005). The combination of various meaning-making systems is part of the discipline-specific structure of mathematics as a content area. What gives mathematics its discipline-specific nature relates to the notion of a *mathematics register*, a set of meanings appropriate to particular functions of language along with words and structures which express these meanings. A mathematics register refers to the meanings associated with the language of mathematics used for mathematical purposes (Halliday, 1978).

In mathematics teaching, language is used in written and spoken forms, presenting particular challenges for MLs, as we have the spoken language used by the teacher in the classroom, the written language of a textbook or other written material, symbols and visual images used all interacting together within a math lesson. Because of the ways in which these meaning-making systems interact in the construction of mathematics content, teachers need to engage in analysis of the demands of mathematics discourse and address these demands with MLs, enabling them to access the content knowledge of mathematics.

Perhaps you have heard that mathematics does not draw on language like the other content areas do. Actually, this is a common misconception about the role of language in mathematics learning. As with the other content areas, mathematics is constructed in language and through language and its language challenges go beyond vocabulary. The metaphor that *mathematics is a language* was used by Pimm (1987) in his seminal work to describe the language of mathematics, including its usage of everyday words with different meanings (*difference, table*) and technical terms used only in mathematics.

In terms of presenting content, the language in mathematics is characterized by the dominance of *relational processes* realized through verbs setting up relations, such as *be, have,* and *represent,* and a new process type used in mathematics only, *operative processes,* processes that establish operations – processes of addition, multiplication and other computations (O'Halloran, 2005). Numbers and variables occur as *participants* and nominalizations such as *the sum of the number of trees* (which comes from the verb *add up the number of trees*), as in the word problem shown at the beginning of this chapter, are used frequently. Enacting a relationship in mathematics features a monologic voice of the author or writer as the primary knower. The absence of words of modality, such as *might* and *could,* other features indicating probability, such as *possibly* and *perhaps,* and vocabulary that shows expressive or evaluative meanings, all make mathematics appear objective, rational, and factual. In terms of constructing a cohesive message, connections within clauses and across clauses typically involve complex chains of reasoning focusing typically on relations of purpose, condition, consequence, concession, and manner (O'Halloran, 2005).

This chapter provides a close look at some potential language demands of the language of mathematics for MLs. The chapter presents a framework for analyzing word problems at the elementary level to help teachers draw MLs' attention to the multisemiotic nature of mathematics and its particular language as well as engage them with mathematical texts. Language-based mathematics instruction is more than just vocabulary and should draw on other aspects of school mathematics language. The chapter then discusses the application of LACI in the classroom, using examples from a kindergarten teacher of how to infuse language in mathematics teaching. It concludes with a "Putting into Practice" section to help teachers consider how to apply LACI in mathematics teaching and learning.

Potential Demands of the Language of Mathematics

Teachers need to enhance their ability to make content *accessible* to MLs. As with the other chapters in this book, the word *accessible* takes a different connotation than in recent literature on modifying the language of texts to help MLs learn better from them. Making content accessible to MLs means providing them *access* to the ways in which knowledge is constructed in the content areas, as they are written, by not simplifying the texts, but by developing teachers' understanding about how mathematical disciplinary discourse is constructed.

Word Problems in Mathematics

Word problems present significant comprehension difficulties and are particularly challenging for MLs (Martiniello, 2008). These comprehension difficulties have to do with both vocabulary and sentence complexity (Abedi & Lord, 2001). The complexity of the vocabulary words that appear in mathematics tasks is significant, but the demands go beyond vocabulary. Word problems permeate mathematics textbooks, tasks, and standardized tests and often are seen as important measures of mathematical understanding.

One key point that must be highlighted is that particular word problems exemplify only certain features of the range of language demands that may be encountered in word problems. Other examples would bring other demands into focus. However, the word problems presented here illustrate some key language challenges with which MLs would have to deal in performing these tasks.

Word Problems as a Genre

Word problems can be seen as a specific *genre* of traditional mathematical pedagogy (Gerofsky, 2004). As any other genre, word problems can be characterized as "staged, goal-oriented social processes" (Martin & Rose, 2008, p. 6). They follow specific stages to reach goals, have specific purposes, and are written for specific audiences. The goal of this genre is to relate mathematical problems to real-life situations and to apply mathematical concepts into solving the word problems. My previous work has shown that the typical organization of word problems consists of three essential components or stages:

Orientation, Information Sequence, and Query (de Oliveira et al., 2018). Table 5.1 illustrates the typical stages of word problems with an example.

Table 5.1: Word Problem Typical Stages and Example

Word Problem Stage	Example
Orientation	Three sisters attended a movie that cost $5 per person.
Information Sequence	Each sister spent $2 on popcorn. Their mother gave them $30 to spend for all three.
Query	How much money was left?

The *Orientation* typically establishes the situation, and introduces the participants and location. In the example, we know who is doing what and for which purposes. The first sentence introduces the context of the word problem: *Three sisters attended a movie that cost $5 per person*. It also introduces a participant *three sisters* and a situation *attended a movie*. This sentence is part of the *Orientation* which often includes a mathematical reference that is often needed to answer the problem satisfactorily. The second sentence introduces another participant, *their mother*, and is part of the *Information Sequence* Stage, presenting information needed to solve the problem. In this example, the relevant information includes *spent $2 on popcorn* and *gave them $30 to spend for all three*. Finally, the *Query* contains the question or information that needs to be answered to solve the problem. The *Query* in the example includes a question that starts with *how much*: *How much money was left?*

A Framework for Analyzing Word Problems

The framework presented in Table 5.2 presents a set of five questions to help teachers identify the language demands of word problems so they can then help their students work through them. This framework is designed to guide teachers to analyze the word problem *before* they present it to students. By focusing on each question, teachers will get a better sense of the structure of the word problem and the language demands it may present for MLs.

Each question helps teachers to focus on the mathematical concepts integrated in the word problem at the same time they are identifying aspects of language with which MLs may have difficulty. The "Guiding Questions" column presents the questions that will guide teachers' analysis of the word problems. The "Language Demands to Identify" column leads teachers in focusing specifically on the language used in the word problems in order to address each guiding question. The language demands provided in this column are some examples of what teachers can focus on to address the guiding

Table 5.2: Framework for Analyzing Word Problems: Guiding Questions, Language Demands, and Tasks for Teachers

Guiding Questions to Ask				
1. What task is the student asked to perform?	2. What relevant information is presented in the word problem?	3. Which mathematical concepts are presented in the information?	4. What mathematical representations and procedures can students use to solve the problem based on the information presented and the mathematical concepts identified?	5. What additional language demands exist in this problem?
Language Demands to Identify				
Type of questions and their structure – e.g. *how many, how much*	Overall clause construction – the processes and participants (*who, what, to whom*)	Specific clause construction – numerical information presented in different parts of the clause	Question + overall clause structure + specific clause structure	Language "chunks" within clauses – not as isolated elements:- participants- processes- circumstances Connections between clauses to determine how different parts are connected.

(*Continued*)

Table 5.2 (Continued)

Tasks for Teachers to Perform				
To analyze the question in the Query stage by identifying what it is asking	To break down the clause by finding what information is presented in the Orientation, Information Sequence, and Query stages	To connect the mathematical concepts needed by looking for specific numerical information presented in the clauses of each stage	To connect all previously analyzed pieces to determine a variety of mathematical representations and procedures that can be used to solve the problem	To identify any aspect of language that seems problematic not recognized through the previous guiding questions

(based on de Oliveira, 2012).

questions; however, this is not an exhaustive list, so teachers may find other areas that will help them address the guiding questions. The "Tasks for Teachers to Perform" column provides an explanation for teachers in terms of what it is that they are doing when they are analyzing each word problem.

The example word problem is from a fifth-grade mathematics textbook (Charles et al., 2005). This word problem is demanding because of the way each clause is structured and how the mathematical information is presented.

Example 1   Word Problem 1

Three sisters attended a movie that cost $5 per person. Each sister spent $2 on popcorn. Their mother gave them $30 to spend for all three. How much money was left?
    This word problem can be divided into four clauses:

Clause 1: Three sisters attended a movie that cost $5 per person.

Clause 2: Each sister spent $2 on popcorn.

Clause 3: Their mother gave them $30 to spend for all three.

Clause 4: How much money was left?

Next, I explain how teachers can analyze the language demands of the word problem by focusing on each guiding question.

1. *What task is the student asked to perform?*

To help MLs solve a word problem, teachers need to identify what task the problem is asking students to perform. To answer this question, teachers can look at the word problem and identify the *question* being asked in the Query stage. To identify the question, teachers can look at the word problem and find the question mark (?) and look closely at what that question asks students to do. Typically, word problems use the *interrogative mood*, that is, they ask a question. If a question mark is not found, another possibility is finding a statement in the *imperative mood*, such as in *Find the perimeter, in meters, of the triangle*. The process *find* is in the imperative mood and implies the question, *What is the perimeter, in meters, of the triangle?*

To recognize what task the problem is asking students to perform, teachers will identify the *question* being asked in the word problem. We first find the question mark (?) and look closely at what that question asks students to do. Word Problem 1 identifies *"How much money was left?"* This question is requesting particular information from students. Yet, there are several language demands within this question that need to be highlighted and further examined. The expression *how much* is used in the question and will involve a **quantity**. This expression is accompanied by the participant *money*, so we know the question is specifically asking for a sum of money. The main language demand of this question appears in the process *was left*. MLs may consider *left* as the process, which in its everyday sense means "to go away from somewhere." This interpretation would not help MLs to solve the problem. With the sense of *remain*, the entire process *was left* may be particularly challenging for MLs. Therefore, it will be very important for teachers to focus on what the question is asking to help MLs understand what task they are asked to perform. Recognizing the type of question with the construction *how much* and the structure of the question with its potential linguistic challenges can help teachers answer the question, *What task is the student asked to perform?*

2. *What relevant information is presented in the word problem?*

To help teachers recognize the relevant information presented in the word problem, we can identify *different important aspects of the text*, or what is being presented in terms of the content of the problem in all stages of the word problem: Orientation, Information Sequence, and Query. For example, in Clause 1, *"Three sisters attended a movie that cost $5 per person,"* we see the *human participants* – who? – identified as *three sisters*. The three sisters did something, what did they do? They *attended a movie*. The process *attended* here is an unusual choice because typically in everyday language we do not use this verb to describe the process of going to the movies. We already see the word *three* which will be an important piece of information to solve the problem. Yet this information is not presented in numerical form (3) but as a lexical item, i.e. a word. This clause contains an embedded clause – *that cost $5 per person* – which is additional information about the *movie*, also key information for solving the problem. We know now how much *attending* the *movie cost* the *three sisters* – *$5 for each*. But this is not the *total* amount spent. The prepositional phrase *per person* needs to be translated to refer to the number one, as the preposition *per* implies a single one, which may pose additional challenges for MLs. In addition, the noun *person* needs to be connected to *sister*; the cost of the movie was $5 per sister.

Clause 2 – *Each sister spent $2 on popcorn* – also has key mathematical information that students need to recognize. Like in Clause 1, a construction with the word *each* is present. *Each sister* is a complex construction for MLs because they need to make the connection between the word *each* and the number *1* – *each* is equivalent to *1*. We see the process *spent* with the numeral amount *$2* and what each sister spent that amount on – *on popcorn*.

The third clause – *Their mother gave them $30 to spend for all three* – presents additional important information that is key for solving the problem. Another *human participant* – *their mother* – is suddenly introduced to the word problem. The pronouns *their* and *them* refer back to *three sisters* that appeared in Clause 1. Typically, pronouns are used to link discourse that is immediately preceding, but in this case, readers have to recover the reference from two clauses before. The doing process *gave* is commonly used in everyday language; most importantly in this clause is the prepositional phrase *for all three*. Because this is crucial information in this problem, MLs need to realize that this means that the sisters had a total of 30 dollars to spend. Table 5.3 presents the clauses and relevant information presented in each clause.

Recognizing the different parts of the clauses and breaking each clause into its different parts with its potential linguistic challenges can help teachers answer the question, *What relevant information is presented in the word problem?*

3. *Which mathematical concepts are presented in the information?*

To help teachers recognize the mathematical concepts presented in the information, we can connect the information analyzed in Guiding Question 2 with the mathematics concepts needed to solve the problem. Based on the analysis, we know which information is presented and what the question is asking.

Table 5.3: Clauses and Relevant Information Provided in Word Problem 1

Clause	Relevant Information Provided
Three sisters attended a movie that cost $5 per person.	Who? = Three sisters What did they do? = attended What? = a movie Other information = that cost $5 per person.
Each sister spent $2 on popcorn.	Who? = Each sister What did they do? = spent How much? = $2 On what? = on popcorn
Their mother gave them $30 to spend for all three.	Who? = Their [the three sisters'] mother What did she do? = gave Whom? = them [the three sisters] What did their mother give them? $30 For what? = to spend for all three

Table 5.4 helps teachers connect the mathematical concepts with the language that presents these concepts.

Table 5.4: Information Provided and Mathematical Concepts in Word Problem 1

Information Provided	Mathematical Concepts
Clause 1: Three sisters attended a movie that cost $5 per person.	Number of sisters = 3 Price of movie per person = $5 Number of persons = 3* This is important here because students need to make the connection between *"per person"* and the number 3.
Clause 2: Each sister spent $2 on popcorn.	Each sister = 1 Money spent on popcorn for each sister = $2
Clause 3: Their mother gave them $30 to spend for all three.	Total money they had = $30

First, Clause 1 has two important mathematical concepts: three sisters *(3)* attended a movie and how much the movie cost per person *($5)*. Clause 2 provides further information about how much money each sister spent on popcorn *($2)*. Clause 3 presents the total money that the sisters had *($30)*. The question, *How much money was left?*, involves the mathematical concept of an **unknown** that directly connects to **quantities**. Even though we see the numbers 5, 2 and 30, MLs must understand *per person* and *each sister* to be able to accomplish the mathematical task. To be able to figure out how much money was left, students need to make the connections between the language of the word problem and the mathematical concepts they represent. Teachers can make these connections explicit to MLs so they will be better able to solve word problems on their own. Connecting the information analyzed with the mathematics concepts needed to solve the problem can help teachers answer the question, *Which mathematical concepts are presented in the information?*

4. *What mathematical representations and procedures can be used to solve the problem based on the information presented and the mathematical concepts identified?*

To determine the mathematical representations and procedures that can be used to solve the problem, teachers can connect all of the different guiding questions. The information presented identifies how much money each sister spent on the movie ($5) and on popcorn ($2). We know that the three sisters had $30 total to spend, which is important information presented in the problem. First, one can calculate how much money the three sisters spent out of the total money they had. The mathematical procedure could be: $5 plus $2 equals $7. Each sister then spent $7. Since there were three sisters, we can calculate how much they spent altogether by multiplying $7 by 3 which gives us $21. We know the total amount that the three sisters spent. Then the amount left can be calculated by subtracting $21 from $30, which gives us $9. The answer to the question *How much money was left?* is $9. Table 5.5 helps the teacher draw on the crucial mathematical language and ideas inherent in the construction of the word problem to plan lessons that enhance MLs' access to the problem.

In order to determine the mathematical representations and procedures that need to be highlighted for MLs, we can use the crucial mathematical information identified through the construction of the word problem and the mathematical concepts presented in the information. This will help teachers work through the problem with MLs as they simultaneously analyze the language and make connections with the mathematical concepts and procedures. Connecting all of the different guiding questions presented can help teachers answer the question, *What mathematical representations and procedures can be used to solve the problem based on the information presented and the mathematical concepts identified?*

Table 5.5: Information Provided, Mathematical Concepts, and Mathematical Representations and Procedures in Word Problem 1

Information Provided	Mathematical Concepts	Mathematical Representations and Procedures
Clause 1: Three sisters attended a movie that cost $5 per person.	Number of sisters = 3 Price of movie per person = $5	$5 + $2 = $7 $7 × 3 = $21 Clause 1 Representation
Clause 2: Each sister spent $2 on popcorn.	Each sister = 1 Money spent on popcorn for each sister = $2	Sister 1 $5 Sister 2 — $15 on movies $5 Sister 3 $5 Clause 2 Representation movie popcorn Sister 1 $5 $2 — $21 on movie and popcorn Sister 2 $5 $2 Sister 3 $5 $2
Clause 3: Their mother gave them $30 to spend for all three.	Total money they had = $30	$30 − $21 = $9 money the mother gave $30 $21 $9 money sisters spent

5. *What additional language demands exist in this problem?*

To help teachers identify any other aspect of language that seems problematic for MLs, we can identify language "chunks" within clauses that may be difficult for MLs to comprehend and recognize the relationships of these language chunks to other parts of the word problem. One of the major challenges of this word problem is the *reference devices* used. *Reference devices* "are words that stand for other words in a text" (Schleppegrell & de Oliveira, 2006, p. 263). For example, the human participant Denise is first introduced as *Denise* in Clause 1, then is referred to as *She* in Clause 2. The noun group *3 of her friends* is introduced in Clause 1 then these participants are picked up in Clause 2 as *each friend* and in Clause 4 as *her friends*. Teachers have to notice that mathematically there's no one-to-one correspondence between *each friend* and *3 of her friends*. This means that each friend means one friend, but *3 of her friends* and *her friends* refer to the same participants. As previously mentioned, the numeral 3 used when this participant is first introduced may also cause confusion. In word problem 1, the main difficulty is how the different human participants are introduced and tracked within the word problem. Several other language demands were identified as we addressed other guiding questions, all of which could be pointed out to MLs. Identifying language "chunks" that may be difficult for MLs to comprehend can help teachers answer the question, *What additional language demands exist in this problem?*

The guiding questions presented in this framework provide a way for teachers to connect language and mathematics content for MLs. To make content accessible to MLs, teachers can look at the construction of word problems without modification or simplification. This framework can enable teachers to enhance their understanding about how mathematical disciplinary discourse is constructed in language.

This close look at the language of these word problems shows how teachers can analyze the construction of word problems by following the guiding questions presented. The goal of this framework is to make content accessible to MLs by providing them *access* to the ways in which knowledge is constructed in mathematics word problems, **as they are written**. The goal is not to simplify these word problems but to enhance teachers' understanding about how mathematical disciplinary discourse is constructed in them.

LACI in mathematics provides a simultaneous focus on mathematics language and mathematics content. In order to address mathematics content, teachers must attend to the language of mathematics. This involves meaning-making of mathematical concepts that goes beyond vocabulary (Celedon-Pattichis & Ramirez, 2012). As the framework presented in this chapter shows, just addressing vocabulary is not enough to help MLs understand and solve a word problem. Next, I turn to an example of LACI in a kindergarten classroom and how the teacher, Mrs. Li, helped MLs understand important mathematical concepts and language.

LACI in the Classroom: Exploring the Language of Mathematics with Multilingual Learners

The example for the implementation of LACI in mathematics comes from Ruby Li's kindergarten classroom. She was introduced in Chapter 3. The following example shows how Mrs. Li used the six Cs of support to implement LACI in her classroom. The Cs are highlighted by using *italics* to identify each C of support. The excerpt comes from a mathematics lesson. In this class, Mrs. Li is giving a demonstration about weighing to scaffold for measuring and weighing different objects in the classroom. All of these exchanges occur within the first 10 minutes of the mathematics lesson.

1. Mrs. Li: We used cubes the other day to find out how... tall something was right? The length of something? How long it was or how tall it was? Is that correct?
2. Students Yes [Students answer in unison]
3. Mrs. Li: How many of your moms and dads use one of these? [Holds up a yardstick]
4. Guadalupe: Me!
5. Mrs. Li: ... or they use a tape measure, it goes out and then it pops back in, Se parece com cita [looks like a tape], does that make sense? You can measure a pencil like this! It's six inches long. [Teacher measures the pencil against Unifix cubes] But there's another way. Do you remember with the panda? We talked about that you could weigh her or measure her... We measured our what?
6. Students: Feet
7. Mrs. Li: Daniel! We also stood up and we figured out who was taller, do you remember that?
8. Daniel: [Student nods]
9. Mrs. Li: If I pick up this thing of blocks... it is heavy. Pesado. My pencil – do you think my pencil is heavy or light?
10. Students: Heavy! Light!! [Students answer in unison]
11. Students: I don't know!
12. Mrs. Li: Jessica is honest, she said I don't know Mrs. Li. When you use the scales... You use a ruler if you want to measure how long something is, if you want to weigh how heavy it is, you use scales.

13. [after a few seconds, Mrs. Li picks up two objects]
14. Can you tell me, which thing is heavier? Ah – Kay!
15. Kay: Big!
16. Mrs. Li: The book is big. Okay now listen, the book is big, big is… big is like talla [size] like the size, ok? But the WEIGHT. Okay, the book is HEAVY. Because this book is not a big book, THIS BOOK is a big book right? [Mrs. Li alternates holding up a small and a big book] What is heavy? Why do think that book is heavy? [Teo, a ML]
17. Teo: Because it's too big, because a pencil, it's like, it's like little, and then the book is big.
18. Mrs. Li: Well, it's not that it's bigger, I could have something smaller… something small. No, I want you to understand the concept. Look. Pencil! Boat. Which do you think is heavier?

This classroom example shows that the concepts that Mrs. Li was teaching were challenging for students, including her MLs, emphasizing the C of *challenge*. In turns 1 through 5, Mrs. Li is using the C of *connection* to ask students to recall what they know, which is very helpful for MLs. She also connects language with the C of *culture* in her classroom through her teaching of the content and the language by means of reviewing prior knowledge and connecting it to new information as well as experiences students may have in their home lives. She also uses the C of classroom interactions in this example by employing several interactional scaffolding moves. In turn 1, she *links to prior experience and points to new experiences*. In turn 5, Mrs. Li shows how they measured the length in a previous class in the same way, by placing a number of cubes alongside an object, and counting how many cubes it took to match the length. She also asks another way to measure something, referencing a common experience within the classroom – when they had read a story about a panda and watched a video, as well as when they had measured their own feet as the panda did in the video. In turn 7, Mrs. Li asks a specific question to an ML, who gives a nod in response, helping him to connect the present lesson to the past lesson that involved measuring.

Turns 5, 9, and 14 shows how Mrs. Li uses Spanish to support the *culture* of her Latino/a MLs. This can also be considered as part of her *code-breaking* because she is using Spanish to assist her MLs' understanding of the content she is presenting – an essential component for Mrs. Li as it is the first experience of her Latino MLs in school, so making these kinds of connections by using Spanish is essential in her view.

Turns 9–14 show how multisemiotic resources are being used to communicate abstract concepts, with concrete objects being used along to demonstrate the difference between weight and size, and what means are used to measure weight as opposed to height. Turns 12–14 show Mrs. Li eliciting from Kay her current understanding of height and size. These turns are examples of the C of *classroom interactions* and the use of several interactional scaffolding moves: Mrs. Li uses *recasting* and *appropriation* with Teo's response and *elaboration* to further expand on the critical concept of something heavy – that something small can be heavy, with the use of a toy boat and pencil. Unfortunately, the toy boat and pencil have similar sizes, and the point is somewhat lost for the students. In turns 12–14, Mrs. Li asks a question, Kay answers *big* and Mrs. Li uses *purposeful repetition* with *the book is big*. Mrs. Li continues with further elaboration on what they had discussed because students were still confused about this concept. Turn 16 is an example of Mrs. Li using *clarification* and *moving the discourse forward*, clarifying the concepts of heavy and big and asking an additional question to continue to help students understand the concepts. Mrs. Li used exchanges like this to build on, and extend, students' discourse.

Mrs. Li used different participant structures to provide different levels of support for various groups and to encourage students to assume greater responsibility for their learning as the focus of learning shifts between teacher- and student-centered learning. These participant structures helped Mrs. Li focus on the C of *community and collaboration*, from teacher-led discussion which the example shows so students understand the mathematics content to individual work which she did after the discussion. Shared language learning was often observed in Mrs. Li's classroom, with students using others as language resources, and the teacher herself asking students for vocabulary in Spanish or using Spanish to help explain the tasks that students are to complete, as a key component of the C of *code-breaking*.

Through these examples from Mrs. Li's classroom instruction, we see her use of LACI's six Cs of support in her integration of language and content for MLs. Mrs. Li *connects* to students' backgrounds and experiences, uses *culture* as an asset, provides *code-breaking* in support of language development and use of Spanish, draws on various participant structures to support *community and collaboration*, *challenges* while also supporting students, and employs *classroom interactions* that support interactional scaffolding through the use of clarification, recasting, elaboration, purposeful repetition, and moving the discourse forward.

Table 5.6 presents a possible lesson plan to continue covering the concepts heavy and light as well as introduce *heavier than* and *lighter than* to further support Mrs. Li's classroom example.

Table 5.6: Unit Plan for Heavy and Light Concepts

Grade Level: Kindergarten
Subject Area: Mathematics
Unit Title: Heavy and Light and Balancing Weights
Duration of the Unit: 1 day

ELD Standard(s)/WIDA Standards e.g., WIDA or state ELPD standard[s] that are the target of student learning. (Note: Please list the **number and text** of each standard that is being addressed.)	English Language Development Standard 2: English language learners communicate information, ideas and concepts necessary for academic success in the content area of Mathematics
CCSS or State Content Standard What CCSS standard(s) are most relevant to the learning goals?	K.M.1 Make direct comparisons of the length, capacity, weight, and temperature of objects, and recognize which object is shorter, longer, taller, lighter, heavier, warmer, cooler, or holds more.
Content Objectives (related to the subject matter central focus)	Students will understand how a balance works to compare weights. They will practice balancing objects of different weights.
Language Objectives (related to key language function, task, or skill)	Students will practice comparison and contrast language patterns *heavier than, lighter than, weighs more, and weighs less.*
Prior Academic Knowledge and Concepts What knowledge, skills, and concepts must students already know to be successful with this lesson?	Students need to understand the concepts of heavy and light and how different weights connect to these concepts. They need to understand that something small can be heavy and something big can be light. That way they can compare and contrast objects. Materials needed: balance, manipulatives of different weights (paper clips, pennies, pens, books)

(Continued)

Table 5.6 (Continued)

Instructional Strategies and Learning Tasks	
Description of what the teacher (you) will be doing and/or what the students will be doing.	
Introduction _____ Minutes	**LACI's TLC Phase 1: Building Shared Knowledge of the Topic**
How will you start the lesson to engage and motivate students in learning?	Teacher distributes handout with examples:
	Visit this hyperlink: https://www.embibe.com/exams/heavy-and-light-objects/ Teacher explains that some objects are heavy and some are light. There are also objects that are heavier or lighter than other objects. Teacher says: From all of these heavy objects, which one do you think is the heaviest? From all of these light objects, which one do you think is the lightest?
	Explain to students that today they are going to be exploring weight and a special tool used to measure weight, a balance. Show students the balance (as a visual and realia). Explain that a balance can help compare the weights of different objects. Have a conversation with the students about the weight of different things, for example, a pen and a book and show students a pen and a book. Ask them to name some heavy things or things that weigh a lot (help if needed). Then ask them to name some light things, or things that do not weigh much or are easy to pick up (help if needed) (*Connection*)
Instruction _____ Minutes	1. Show the diagrams of the different balances. Explain that a balance compares the object's weight on one side to the object's weight on the other side. Point to the objects on the diagrams and tell what they are (show them the real objects too)
Highlighted LACI's TLC Phase: Sustained Reading	2. Throughout the visual aids, ask questions (*Code-Breaking* and *Classroom Interactions*) such as:
Procedures: specific details regarding what the students will do during the lesson (practice/ application)	◆ Which side do you think weighs more or is heavier? ◆ Which side weighs less or is lighter? etc.
LACI 6 Cs of Support: *Connection:* What will you do to connect the lesson to students' prior academic learning, backgrounds and experiences?	(Teacher follows up with "why" questions and explains as needed) (*Challenge*) Explain that more than one object can equal the weight of one different object. Make sure students understand all of these concepts.

Culture: How will you link the new content skills and concepts to students' cultural and linguistic resources to support academic learning?	To involve MLs at lower proficiency levels, show them which side is heavier on one picture, then ask them "Is this side heavier?" for the other picture (this will provide an opportunity for them to see the teacher modeling first, then answer the question with a Yes or No or nodding their head). Repeat this with the question "Is this side lighter?"
Challenge: What aspects of disciplinary literacy will you address? Which higher-order thinking and reasoning skills will you focus on?	To involve MLs at intermediate proficiency levels, show the picture and ask "Which side weighs more, the side with 3 pennies or the side with one penny?" Ask MLs at higher proficiency levels to answer "How many pennies do you think we need to balance the scale?" Based on this picture, "When do you know when the objects weigh the same?" What does the balance look like?
Code-Breaking: What will you do to explicitly teach ways of doing school, academic literacy, and disciplinary, linguistic, and cultural codes of content learning? How will you model the language forms/vocabulary/function/skills?	3. After the lesson, ask students to think about the animals in nature, which they think weigh more or less. Give an example, which animal is heavier: an elephant or a bumble bee? Make connections to their field trip to the Lafayette Zoo during the Boo at the Zoo event from the week before. Students could also investigate why they think animals that fly are light (extension to science). Have students draw their own balance and draw two animals, one heavy and one light and appropriately place them on the balance (model if needed) Put the pennies on the balance.
Community and collaboration: How will you engage students in collaboration and build a community of practice?	4. Show students the actual balance. Let them explore it for a moment. Then work together with the students to balance out the different manipulatives that are provided.
Classroom interactions: How will you use "interactional scaffolding" in the classroom? Plan for the use of oral discourse to prompt elaboration, build academic literacy, and move discourse and learning forward.	**LACI's TLC Phase 1: Sustained Reading** 5. Teacher shows the video Story Monster Presents: *So Light, So Heavy* https://www.youtube.com/watch?v=gMKs-GAP37U This is an Interactive Reading Aloud activity because the Story Monster interacts with the viewers and asks them to make animal sounds and asks questions. 6. Teacher shows video with concepts lighter and heavier and does this together with students, asking questions to accompany the video (*Community and Collaboration*): https://www.youtube.com/watch?v=c3cmm_c6vyE
Closure	

(Continued)

Table 5.6 (Continued)

Assessment/Evaluation (Formative and/or Summative)	Teacher distributes handout and asks students to circle the lighter or heavier object. Assists as needed.
	Handout Circle the lighter object. Circle the heavier object. Circle the lighter object. Circle the heavier object.
Extension	Students could read and/or watch a video of a reading aloud for the book: On The Scale, A Weighty Tale https://www.youtube.com/watch?v=eXbsmsaTEOY

Language in Mathematics Teaching and Learning

Language plays a key role in mathematics teaching and learning. MLs need to have experiences with content expressed in grade-level mathematical language and structure. To provide such experiences, the language demands of mathematics need to be clearly considered. Understanding the language demands of mathematics for MLs is a critical component of planning instruction.

Both teachers and students of school mathematics can develop language awareness of some typical features of mathematics. To be able to read mathematics word problems effectively, MLs need to be able to engage with the meanings presented. Learning mathematics means learning the language that expresses mathematics. The language demands this chapter addresses highlight the kind of discipline-specific academic support in language and literacy development that would enable MLs to be more successful in their mathematics learning.

One of the main goals of this work is to enable teachers to be more proactive in helping MLs learn the ways language is used to construct mathematical knowledge. Efforts to change the language of the content areas are counterproductive, as *all* students will need to deal with the specialized knowledge presented in the disciplines to fully participate in school.

Teachers can better understand the language demands of mathematics and address them in their curriculum and instruction. The framework presented here suggests the need for an explicit attention to mathematics language in classrooms. This could include a close look at language from the perspective of identifying some potential language challenges for MLs. For example, teachers can select passages from mathematics textbooks and identify some of the features described in this chapter. This is a helpful activity in which teachers could engage to further develop their knowledge about mathematics language. Teachers can then plan instruction to not only teach particular mathematical concepts but also work on the language of mathematics with MLs.

Putting into Practice

Applying the Framework

This chapter provided a framework for analyzing word problems in mathematics. Analyze the following word problems from a fourth-grade textbook

(Fuson, 2009) using the framework to identify some potential challenges for MLs.

> Lesson 10: Group and Array Word Problems (Big Idea: Consolidation) – p. 33
>
> Latisha's uncle gave her 32 stamps and a new stamp book. The book has 8 pages, and she put the same number of stamps on each page. How many stamps did she put on each page?
>
> Lesson 12: Multiply and Divide with 8 and 7 (Big Idea: Fluency with Basic Multiplication and Division) – p. 40
>
> Julian arranged his swimming trophies on the 8 shelves above his dresser. He put 7 trophies on each shelf. How many trophies does he have?
>
> Kyle has 8 friends who would like to start an ant farm like his. He took 64 ants from his farm and divided them equally into 8 containers for his friends. How many ants will each friend receive?
>
> Lesson 7: Solve Multistep Word Problems (Big Idea: Comparison Problems) – p. 77
>
> In art class, Ernesto made some fruit bowls for his mother and brother. Nine apples can be placed in each bowl. Ernesto's brother placed 18 apples in the bowls he was given, and Ernesto's mother placed 36 apples in the bowls she was given. How many fruit bowls did Ernesto make?

Analyzing a Case Study

The following case study depicts a mainstream third-grade classroom in a school district in the United States. There are 25 students in Ms. Brady's third-grade math classroom. All students sit in small groups and around tables; there are 5 students in each group. Four students face each other; the fifth student sits somewhat separately from others because the tables are large. There are 12 girls and 13 boys in the classroom. There is one female ML from Taiwan, Sha. The student's English language proficiency Level is 4 (on a 6-point scale). The girl sits at the side of the table and is a member of one of the groups. One of the students sits near the computer. As the teacher uses the projector to show problems on the screen, this student serves as an assistant to the teacher helping her with technology. The topic of the lesson is "Writing Rules"; the date and the topic are written on the blackboard.

As you read the case study, consider some of the variables at play here. Try to imagine yourself serving the role of the teacher. Are there specific things you would do differently?

Lesson Procedures

Activity 1: After the students have taken their seats, Ms. Brady asks one of the students to read the problem projected on the screen out loud:

> 1 cup = 2 pints
> 2 pints (pt) = 1 quart (qt)
> 4 quarts (qt) = 1 gallon (gal)
> 32 qt = ? (gal)
> How many gallons are in thirty-two quarts?

Ms. Brady gives the students about 5 minutes to solve the problem. She walks around the classroom and comes up to individual students answering their questions and guiding them through the problem if necessary. The teacher comes up to Sha and asks her if everything is clear. Then, the teacher asks students to check their responses with their student neighbors. As there are some students who do not have partners (these students sit at the side of the table), the teacher asks them to pair with a student from another group. For example, Sha is paired with a male student who sits at the next table and has special needs. After that, the teacher asks some students to share the answers out loud. The ML student gives the wrong answer and the teacher corrects her.

Activity 2: The teacher explains that students will work in small groups. They will have to find "a pattern" in the problem. The teacher provides each student with a handout on which the problem is written and projects the problem on the screen. The problem is presented in the form of a chart and has gaps in some places that the students have to fill out looking for "a pattern." One of the students reads the problem out loud. The teacher asks, "What is the pattern? What is the rule?" The problem includes the following terminology, "Total cost of item and shipping; price of item, 'in and out'." Some students, who sit at the side of the table farther away from their group members, work on the problem individually. Ms. Brady asks some students to give her the answers and then she fills out the gaps in the chart on the blackboard. Some students copy the answers. Sha did not have enough time to copy the answers because the teacher erased the chart.

Activity 3: The teacher says, "We are going to revisit our practice today. You will watch the Vision Math video. Try to find a pattern in the problem presented in this video." The problem includes subtraction and division, and requires that students know the multiplication table. The teacher asks individual students to give her the right answer. If the student is right, the teacher says, "Thank you, Diane. Nice job!" If the student is wrong, the teacher says, "Thank you. You need to think a little bit more." The teacher subtracts, divides, and multiplies on the blackboard, and explains each step. The students copy the answers from the blackboard.

Closure: At the end of the lesson, Ms. Brady tells her students that they are going to write a Reflective Journal. She says, "The topic for your journal today is, 'What are you going to do nice for the holiday season?'" The students start writing journals in their notebooks.

Discussion Questions:

1. Considering that there is a ML in the classroom, what strategies did the teacher use to build this student's conceptual understanding?
2. The ML's English language proficiency level was identified as Level 4 (on a 6-point scale). How did the teacher work with the language to help the student understand the content material?
3. What strategies did the teacher use to assess the ML's understanding of the content material? How did the teacher assess the ML's understanding of the English language in the problem?
4. What kind of adjustments could the teacher make for a ML in this lesson? Consider groupings and supportive feedback.
5. What kind of *code-breaking* could the teacher provide for the student? Consider academic language needs of an ML student.
6. Overall, what are potential issues for a ML in this lesson? Based on these issues, how could the lesson be improved?
7. Based on your answer above, how would you incorporate LACI in this lesson?

6

Teaching Science to Multilingual Learners

Science presents disciplinary knowledge very differently from the ways in which meanings are constructed in students' everyday language (Fang, 2006; Fang & Schleppegrell, 2008). To learn about science, MLs need to be able to understand the language of science. My work in K-12 classrooms has demonstrated that, as MLs progress at school, they need to understand how authors construct the technical discourse of school science.

During the upper elementary grades (Grades 4–5, ages 9–11), where literacy plays a key role in communicating and conveying content area knowledge, beyond students' familiar genres such as story or personal narrative, there is an increasing focus on disciplinary-based written tasks and genres, including procedural recounts, procedures, reports, and explanations. In these grades, the content areas become more specialized, and disciplinary-based written tasks and texts become more linguistically complex.

Research has demonstrated that upper elementary school literacy instruction places new demands on teachers who are called to provide the kinds of instructional support necessary for students to succeed in the content areas (Carrasquillo et al., 2004). In addition, there has been increasing attention to teaching genres for upper elementary MLs (Brisk, 2015; Gebhard, 2019). Writing in science, for example, is a critical skill to be learned for *all* elementary school students, including MLs, who are suddenly confronted with more specialized content-area literacy tasks. Learning to write scientifically further highlights the need for students to learn not only a technical language but a set of written genres characteristic of school science. Students,

DOI: 10.4324/9781003264927-6

therefore, need to be able to read science textbooks to understand scientific content and write in genres that become more specialized as students move through the years of schooling.

This chapter identifies some academic language demands in science, specifically highlighting the content-specific language of science textbooks and writing in science at the elementary school level. The chapter then shows applications of LACI in the classroom, exploring the language of science with MLs, with examples from a fourth-grade classroom. This chapter shows a unit plan which contains how the teacher used LACI's TLC to plan instruction applying LACI's six Cs of support. Two writing samples from a ML are used to show what he was able to do before the implementation of genre-based writing pedagogy in the classroom, and a writing sample after the implementation.

Content-Specific Language in Science Textbooks

A close look at science textbooks reveals that textbook authors present disciplinary knowledge very differently from the ways in which meanings are constructed in students' everyday language (Fang, 2006; Fang et al., 2010; Fang & Schleppegrell, 2008). To learn about science, MLs need to be able to understand the language of science. The difficulty found among MLs in comprehending textbooks has been connected to their need to develop vocabulary knowledge in the content areas. But the language of science is much more than vocabulary, specifically technical terms in science. Technical terms are a vital part of scientific language, but the distinctive nature of scientific language rests in the "wording" as a whole, not just individual vocabulary words (Halliday & Martin, 1993). Technical terms, then, are only part of the whole story of science and the challenges it presents to MLs.

In K-12 science education curricula, textbooks have been shown to be a dominant instructional device (Good, 1993; Weiss et al., 2001). Descriptions of the content-specific language in science textbooks are needed to better understand students' literacy needs in comprehending science textbooks (Saul, 2004; Stevens et al., 2009). Science textbook authors organize and condense science knowledge and information through complex clause structures (Fang, 2006; Fang et al., 2010). Attention to specific language features when reading science textbooks help MLs understand the language of science beyond technical terms.

Writing in Science at the Elementary School Level

U.S. elementary school education is almost entirely a matter of literacy – of learning to read and write (early literacy instruction) and reading and writing to learn the academic content (content area literacy instruction). Students learn and practice beginning reading and writing skills through the elementary grades (grades K–3) (Allington & Johnston, 2002). Starting in the fourth grade, students are expected to have these basic reading and writing skills developed to learn school subjects. However, many upper elementary students in Grades 4 through 5 who can read words accurately and fluently find the literacy task of reading and writing content area texts in school subjects challenging. Most educators would agree that content area writing is associated with the academic content of various subject areas and this kind of writing is essential for students' learning in every subject area, especially for their learning and doing science (Fang et al., 2010). Writing in science is not peripheral but integral to doing and learning science. Science involves the study of natural phenomena, whether observing, recording, experimenting with, describing, or explaining. Scientists engage in writing to record observations, procedures, results, and explanations of experiments so that they can check on the accuracy, completeness, and reliability of their findings – integral aspects of studying natural phenomena.

Writing in science requires the use of unfamiliar technical language and school science-based genres (Christie & Derewianka, 2010; Fang et al., 2010; Haneda, 2000; Haneda & Wells, 2000). These unfamiliar written tasks place new linguistic and cognitive demands on MLs (Bruna & Gomez, 2009; Lee et al., 2008). Content area instruction should provide more instructional support for MLs' scientific literacy development. Writing in science has been emphasized as an essential component of science learning at every stage of the inquiry process (Worth et al., 2009). Because of its centrality to doing and learning science, writing in science is seen as an essential literacy tool for developing students' scientific knowledge and understanding.

To learn to produce effective science written texts expected by school, students need to become familiar with school-based science genres. Among the various genres in science, procedural recounts, procedures, reports, explanations, and expositions are the most recognizable genres in school science textbooks and scientific literacy tasks (Derewianka & Jones, 2016).

Of these five school-based science genres, procedural recount has been identified as a key genre in doing and learning inquiry-based science. Procedural recount is "the prototypical experimental genre, learned in childhood and early adolescence, and remaining important throughout adolescence" (Christie & Derewianka, 2010, p. 181). Procedural recount is the most commonly assigned genre in science classes across the grades and is one of the most recognizable forms used by students in doing and learning science. Therefore, teachers need support in recognizing the organizational structure and language features in this genre so they are better able to familiarize students with this specific genre and construct their procedural recounts

(Fang et al., 2010). Most students do not just pick up the specific genre and language features of school-based science genres, including procedural recounts. Such genre and language features typical of procedure recounts will not be understood or learned unless students are specifically taught. Table 6.1 displays the purpose, stages, and language features of the procedural recount genre, accompanied by a sample text of the features typical of the procedure recount genre.

Table 6.1: Genre, Purpose, Stages, and Language Features

Genre	Purpose	Stages	Language features
Procedural Recount	– To recount in order and with accuracy – To record the aims, steps, results, and conclusion of a scientific activity already conducted	◆ Aim (Materials) ◆ Record of events ◆ Conclusions	◆ Declarative sentences ◆ Use of passive voice to suppress actor ◆ Doing verbs ◆ Past tense ◆ Time connectors

Sample Text	
To demonstrate that plants need air *2 pill bottles (one with a cup)* *50 Beans* *Water*	Aim Materials required
What we did: *First we soaked 50 beans. Then we filled both bottles with the soaked beans and put a little water in the bottom of each. Next we put the cap tight on one of the bottles and left the other open. Finally we shook the water over the beans.* What we observed: *The seeds [in the bottle with the cap off] started to sprout.*	Record (What we did/What we observed)
Plants need air to grow.	Conclusions

(Adapted from Christie & Derewianka, 2010, p. 155).

The above table and sample text both display the features typical of the procedural recount genre. A procedural recount records the aim, steps, results, and conclusions of a specific scientific experiment already conducted. The components include the *Aim*, which is where the writer states what the purpose of the scientific experiment is and includes information about materials or equipment to be used; the *Record of Events*, which is where the writer records what was done in a sequenced way; and the *Conclusion*, which is where the writer constructs the general conclusion based on the experiment results.

LACI in the Classroom: Exploring the Language of Science with MLs

The teacher featured in this chapter, Karla Dixon, worked with me in Indiana for several years implementing LACI and LACI's TLC in her classroom. At the time of the study, Mrs. Dixon had been teaching fourth grade for six years at Campus University School District. Mrs. Dixon taught in a school district with 30% culturally and linguistically diverse (CLD) students and 70% White from non-ELL backgrounds. Many of the CLD students came from families whose parents are associated with the nearby university, including children of international students and immigrants. Over the course of four years, the implementation of LACI in Mrs. Dixon's classroom took several forms that I have called "periods." Period 1 focused on reading science texts and developing lessons to address the challenges of science, then moved on to Period 2, addressing writing instruction about science experiments. Period 3 focused on talking science or the classroom discourse about science that supported and challenged MLs (see Lan & de Oliveira, 2019, and de Oliveira & Lan, 2014, for more details about each period). At the time of the study, Mrs. Dixon had just completed a master's degree in Literacy and Language Education.

Though we have collected multiple lesson plans for activities that she implemented, the examples used in this chapter come from the writing science period. During this period, Mrs. Dixon's class consisted of five Asian-origin MLs classified by the school district as English Language Learners at different English language proficiency levels – one Level 2, two Level 3, and two Level 4 on a 1–5 scale of English language proficiency, three Latino students who were previously designated as ELLs and at the time of writing were at Level 5, and 17 White students. With almost half of her class being

MLs, Mrs. Dixon wanted to improve her teaching of reading and writing in science as she noted that this was particularly challenging discipline for her MLs.

Mrs. Dixon followed the implementation framework for lesson planning and delivery, presented in Chapter 7. Before designing language-based lessons for her classroom, Mrs. Dixon selected key texts to work on with students. I use excerpts from her classroom teaching to exemplify implementation of LACI in the teaching of science. This chapter is guided by the following questions:

1. How does a fourth-grade teacher incorporate LACI's TLC in her teaching of science writing?
2. What is the nature of a fourth-grade teacher's guidance through interaction in the context of shared experience – writing a procedural recount about a science inquiry activity?

A Unit Plan Focused on Mass, Density, and Volume

The unit plan for a series of lessons carried out in Mrs. Dixon's classroom presents specific information about how she used LACI's six Cs of support within the TLC. Mrs. Dixon planned various science activities focused on the concepts of mass, density, and volume. In implementing LACI's TLC, Mrs. Dixon primarily focused on the Deconstruction and Joint Construction phases. Because these two stages are seen as the most critical for writing development (Caplan, 2019; Humphrey & Macnaught, 2011), it is important to show how they work in a general education classroom with MLs in the content area of science.

Mrs. Dixon planned several interactions that drew upon the different six Cs of support to engage students in understanding these science concepts. Table 6.2 shows a unit plan with lessons that took six days in Mrs. Dixon's classroom.

Table 6.2: Mrs. Dixon's Unit Plan

Grade Level: Fourth grade
Subject Area: Science
Lesson Title: *Mass, Density, and Volume*
Duration of the Lesson: 6 days

ELD Standard(s)/WIDA Standards e.g., WIDA or state ELPD standard[s] that are the target of student learning. (Note: Please list the **number and text of** each standard that is being addressed.)	English Language Development Standard 2: English Language Learners communicate information, ideas, and concepts necessary for academic success in the content area of Science
CCSS or State Content Standard What CCSS standard(s) are most relevant to the learning goals?	**Indiana Science Standards – Fourth Grade Process Standards** Students will work on observing the world around them and taking part in scientific investigations. They will develop communication skills that allow them to share their findings. They will work on making predictions, coming up with useful questions, and formulating tests. Class time will be devoted to planning and performing investigations, both as individual students and in groups. Scientific tools will be used, along with measurements. Students will learn how to test their predictions and ensure that they're maintaining accurate records. They will recognize patterns and compare results with initial predictions.

Content Objectives (related to the subject matter central focus)	Students will be able to distinguish between mass, density, and volume.
Language Objectives (related to key language function, task, or skill)	Students will examine the differences in three definitions that are very similar to understand the differences between three scientific concepts. Student will read and write a procedural recount after they conduct a science experiment using the three concepts.
Prior Academic Knowledge and Conceptions What knowledge, skills, and concepts must students already know to be successful with this lesson?	Students need to be familiar with the concept of matter (including the 3 states of matter – liquid, solid, and gas) and space

Instructional Strategies and Learning Tasks

Description of what the teacher (you) will be doing and/or what the students will be doing.

Introduction _____ Minutes How will you start the lesson to engage and motivate students in learning?	**LACI's TLC Phase 1: Building Shared Knowledge of the Topic** Day 1 Mrs. Dixon displayed a chart with the 3 words: Mass, Volume, and Density. She asked the students, "What do you know about these three words?" The students, sitting in groups of 3–4, were given a few minutes to discuss the words with their group members (*Connection and Community and Collaboration*). After the students were given some time, the class discussed the words while the teacher wrote their input under the words on the chart.
Instruction _____ Minutes **Highlighted LACI's TLC Phase:** Sustained Reading **Procedures:** specific details regarding what the students will do during the lesson (practice/application) **LACI 6 Cs of Support:** *Connection:* What will you do to connect the lesson to students' prior academic learning, backgrounds and experiences?	**LACI's TLC Phase 2: Sustained Reading** Day 1 (continued) After writing on the chart, the class began reading together the section on how matter is measured (pp. 322–327). Mrs. Dixon did an interactive reading aloud activity along with a discussion of observations about definitions (*Classroom Interactions*) Day 2 The class finished reading the section together. The teacher asked the students if they learned anything new about mass, volume, and density. She added the students' input in the chart paper in another color (*Connection*) Day 3 The teacher asked the students to look back at the pages that they have read together over the last couple of days, starting with page 322. Under the subject heading "mass" the teacher asked the students to pinpoint the sentence that gives the definition of mass. After students gave their responses, the teacher led a short discussion on how the students were able to choose a sentence. The teacher used sentence strip paper to copy the sentence. Mrs. Dixon then went on to have the students follow the same steps for volume and density. (*Challenge and Code-Breaking*). After the sentence strips were written for each, the teacher displayed them on the board. She asked the students to name each part of these sentences: the participant, process, and scientific description (*Challenge and Code-Breaking*).

Culture: How will you link the new content skills and concepts to students' cultural and linguistic resources to support academic learning? *Challenge*: What aspects of disciplinary literacy will you address? Which higher-order thinking and reasoning skills will you focus on? *Code-Breaking*: What will you do to explicitly teach ways of doing school, academic literacy, and disciplinary, linguistic, and cultural codes of content learning? How will you model the language forms/vocabulary/function/skills?	The teacher had students help her cut the sentence strip paper into the sections (*Community and Collaboration* and *Code-Breaking*). Together, the class analyzed each of the sentences, discussing the similarities and differences between them (*Code-Breaking*). The class looked back at their chart together to determine if anything that they initially thought about, any of the words, should be deleted. The class also discussed what should remain. The sentences should be: 1. **Mass *is* the measure of the amount of matter in an object.** 2. **Volume *is* the amount of space that matter takes up.** 3. **The amount of mass in a certain volume of matter *is* a property called density.** **Added Phase: Inquiry-Science Project with an Experiment** Day 4 Between the sustained reading and the deconstruction of a mentor text, Mrs. Dixon conducted the first part of an experiment to incorporate inquiry-based science into the lesson. The experiment was about layers of liquids to show that different liquids have different densities. Students wrote what they observed as a pretest. Day 5 The next day students read more from the textbook about density and reviewed concepts such as mass, weight, and volume, introduced the day before. **LACI's TLC Phase 3: Deconstruction** ◆ Focus on talking about the language features of the Record stage Before Day 5, Mrs. Dixon met with Dr. de Oliveira to select a mentor text that was more characteristic of the procedural recount genre. We developed this mentor text from one of the texts collected from Mrs. Dixon's students who wrote about Experiment 1. Day 5 For the Deconstruction phase, Mrs. Dixon projected the mentor text on the whiteboard. She talked about the language features of the Record stage. 1. Mrs. Dixon read aloud the mentor text projected on the whiteboard 2. Mrs. Dixon raised questions about which language features make the mentor text good. (*Code-Breaking*)

Community and collaboration: How will you engage students in collaboration and build a community of practice? *Classroom interactions*: How will you use "interactional scaffolding" in the classroom? Plan for the use of oral discourse to prompt elaboration, build academic literacy, and move discourse and learning forward. **Closure**	◆ Students immediately noticed **some words that show Time Relationships (first, then…)** ◆ Students then noticed **the repeated use of action verbs (e.g., pour, settle)** ◆ Mrs. Dixon supported students to develop their sense and responsibilities to audience and **being specific in naming the ingredients** 3. Mrs. Dixon asked students to paste the mentor text on their science journals/notebooks and highlighted together (naming "first, then, finally…" as Time/Sequence/Order/Transition words; having words highlighted in different colors, grouping words together, talking about Materials/Objects, Verbs etc) (*Code-Breaking*) Mrs. Dixon and the class then prepared for the Joint Construction of the Conclusion stage (take the level up to "why" question) **LACI's TLC Phase 4: Joint Construction** ◆ Focus on their joint construction of the Conclusion for Experiment 1, the first part of the experiment, and why students need to write in the Procedural Recount organization (familiarize students with the scientific genre) Day 6 1. Mrs. Dixon and the class reviewed Experiment 1 (a close look at the cups) (*Connection*) 2. They then reviewed the Record stage (students noticed the past tense and tried to explain the reasons why the person used past tense writing up the Record stage) (*Code-Breaking*) 3. Mrs. Dixon led a Joint Construction of the Conclusion stage of experiment 1. (*Code-Breaking*) Mrs. Dixon then did Experiment 2, the 2nd part of the experiment. She placed objects – paper clip, a piece of rubber band, Styrofoam Ball – into the cups.

(Continued)

(Continued)

	LACI's TLC Phase 6: Independent Construction*
	Mrs. Dixon then discussed Procedural Recount genre and what students were expected to write in which stage – Materials, Aim, Record, Conclusion. Students wrote up their Procedural Recount for Experiment 2, the 2nd part of the experiment. (*Phase 5 Collaborative Construction was not included)
Assessment/ Evaluation (Formative and/or Summative)	Writing of procedural recount after Experiment 2, the 2nd part of the experiment
Extension	Extension: Conducting a different experiment focusing on density (the soda test; the soap test, or the gummy bear test)

LACI's TLC Phase 1: Building Shared Knowledge of the Topic

To start building shared knowledge of the topic, Mrs. Dixon displayed a chart with the three words: Mass, Volume, and Density. She asked the students, "What do you know about these three words?" The students, sitting in groups of 3–4, were given a few minutes to discuss the words with their group members. Here we see the Cs of *connection* and *community and collaboration* featured. After the students were given some time, the class discussed the words while the teacher wrote their input under the words on the chart.

LACI's TLC Phase 2: Sustained Reading

After writing on the chart, the class began reading together the section on how matter is measured (Scott Foresman, 2006, pp. 322–327). Mrs. Dixon did an interactive reading aloud activity along with a discussion of observations about definitions. These featured the C of *classroom interactions*.

The class finished reading the section together and Mrs. Dixon asked students to tell her if they learned anything new about mass, volume, and density. She added the students' input in the chart paper in another color, using the C of *connection* to connect to what students learned the previous day. The next day, Mrs. Dixon asked the students to look back at the pages that they read together over the last couple of days, starting with page 322. Mrs. Dixon asked the students to pinpoint the sentence that gives the definition of each concept under each subject heading *mass, volume*, and *density*. After students gave their responses, Mrs. Dixon led a short discussion on how the students were able to choose a sentence. Table 6.3 presents the text selection that the class read. Sentences with definitions that students selected are underlined.

Mrs. Dixon used sentence strip paper to copy each sentence that had a definition. These are examples of the use of the C of *challenge* and the C of *code-breaking*. Mrs. Dixon displayed the sentence strips on the board. She asked the students to name each part of these sentences: the participant, process, and scientific description, using the C of *code-breaking*. Students were already familiar with the functional metalanguage *participant, process*, and *scientific description*, having done multiple code-breaking activities that used this metalanguage prior to this lesson. It is important to note that Mrs. Dixon selected "scientific description" because all of the sentences that she had selected contained relating processes (*is*) that contained a definition which can be seen as a description of the participant introduced as the Subject of each clause. This helped students identify the critical information presented in the full definition and understand the relevant science concepts for this unit.

Table 6.3 Text Selection with Definitions of Mass, Volume, and Density

---

Lesson 2: How is matter measured? (pp. 322, 324, 326)

Mass

Scientists use mass because they want a measurement that will not change if the object is moved to a different location. Mass is the measure of the amount of matter in an object. The mass of an object does not change unless matter is added to or removed from it. (second paragraph Mass on p. 322)

Volume

Take a deep breath. As your lungs fill with air, you can feel your chest expand. This change in your lung size is an increase in volume. Volume is the amount of space that matter takes up. (first paragraph of Volume on p. 324)

Density

Sometimes you need to know how much mass is in a certain volume of matter. Suppose a friend asks you, "Which has more mass, a piece of wood or a piece of steel?" Your first response might be, "How big is each piece?" In order to compare the masses of two objects, you need to use an equal volume of each. The amount of mass in a certain volume of matter is a property called density. For example, if the pieces of wood and steel are the same size, the pieces of steel have more mass and a greater density than the wood.

Finding Density

You find the density of a substance by dividing its mass by its volume. The units often used for the density of solids are grams per cubic centimeter. You write density as a fraction: $\dfrac{\text{mass in grams}}{\text{volume in cubic centimeters}}$. The density of water is 1 because 1 gram of water has a volume of 1 cubic centimeter. (p. 326)

Mrs. Dixon led the class in cutting the sentence strip paper into the sections and together the class analyzed each of the sentences, discussing the similarities and differences between them:

1. Mass is the measure of the amount of matter in an object.
2. Volume is the amount of space that matter takes up.
3. The amount of mass in a certain volume of matter is a property called density.

The class analyzed the sentences as the following:

Participant	Process	Scientific Description
Mass	is	the measure of the amount of matter in an object
Volume	is	the amount of space that matter takes up.
The amount of mass in a certain volume of matter	is	a property called density.

Added Phase: Inquiry-Science Project with an Experiment

Between the sustained reading and the deconstruction of a mentor text, Mrs. Dixon led her students to carry out Experiment 1 in groups to observe layered liquids, incorporating inquiry-based science into the lesson. This experiment was about layers of liquids to show that different liquids have different density. At the beginning of Experiment 1, Mrs. Dixon briefly outlined what the students were expected to do – pour four different liquids into a cup and observe what would happen. She distributed one empty clear plastic cup and four different liquids to each group of students. Then each group was guided to carefully pour corn syrup, dishwasher soap, water with red food coloring, and corn oil – in that order – into the cup. After all four liquids had been poured into the cup, Mrs. Dixon asked students to discuss with their group what had happened in the cup. Then one student from each group was asked to share what they had observed from Experiment 1. Based on their observations and classroom discussions of the results of Experiment 1, students were asked to write down what they had observed and thought about Experiment 1, as their first text. The next day students read more from the textbook about density and reviewed concepts such as mass, weight, and volume, introduced the day before. These examples show Mrs. Dixon's focus on disciplinary literacy. This is part of a collaborative activity in which students were engaged, exemplifying the C of *community and collaboration*.

Sample Text 1 by a Multilingual Learner

I selected writing samples of one ML to identify how our collaboration around LACI impacted this student's writing development. Ji Soo is originally from Korea and was 10 years old at the time of this work. Ji Soo was classified as ELL at a Level 3 on a 1–5 scale of English proficiency and had been just integrated into Mrs. Dixon's classroom when our collaboration began. Mrs. Dixon noted to us that Ji Soo, who seemed to have high oral English proficiency and the ability to write personal stories and narratives in English language arts, struggled to write about science experiments.

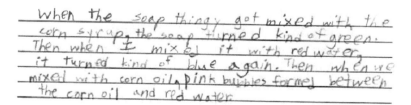

When the soap thingy got mixed with the corn syrup, the soap turned kind of green. Then when I mixed it with red water, it turned kind of blue again. Then when we mixed with corn oil, pink bubbles formed between the corn oil and red water

Figure 6.1 Ji Soo's Text After Experiment 1.

This short analysis of Ji Soo's text showed Mrs. Dixon that he needed specific instruction in writing that would allow him to produce effective procedural recounts, learning to better record the explicit and accurate experiment materials and steps/results of a specific experiment already conducted. Therefore, what came next in terms of activities, drawing her students' attention to key language features and organization of procedural recounts, including how to accurately and explicitly describe experiment materials, steps, and conclusion, was instrumental for Ji Soo and the other students in Mrs. Dixon's classroom (for more information about the analysis and Mrs. Dixon's application of the TLC, see de Oliveira & Lan, 2014).

LACI's TLC Phase 3: Deconstruction

For the Deconstruction phase, Mrs. Dixon projected the mentor text on the whiteboard. She, under the pressure of limited class time, placed more emphasis on one key stage of the Procedural Recount – the Record. Mrs. Dixon wanted to make students more aware of the language features the mentor text used in the Record stage to record events in order and with more precision. She focused, then, on connectors and vocabulary choices and technicality to name specific experiment materials. The full mentor text is presented on Table 6.4.

Figure 6.2 shows the Record stage of the mentor text projected on the board.

Mrs. Dixon, together with her students, highlighted the important language features the mentor text writer used in the Record stage. Two examples of how the teacher and students explicitly talked about these language features as well as their function in procedural recounts are evident in the following classroom interactions. In the first example, accompanying the mentor text projected on the whiteboard, Mrs. Dixon clearly used the C of *code-breaking* when leading the class in a discussion of how the temporal connectors such as *first, then, next,* and *finally* in the mentor text functioned to "make their observations clear" and "give some sort of order." First, Mrs. Dixon had each student get a highlighter and typed copy of the mentor text. The teacher and students, with highlighters in hands, identified the words and organizational structures characteristic of the Record stage. The classroom transcript (Example 1) reveals how the teacher supported all students, including MLs, in analyzing the language choices the writer made to express sequences of the experiment already conducted in the classroom, with a specific focus on temporal connectors.

Table 6.4 Mentor Text Developed from Students' Written Texts about Experiment 1

Procedural Recount Stages	Text
Materials required	Corn syrup Dishwasher soap Water with red food coloring Corn oil Clear plastic cups
Aim	To demonstrate that different liquids have different density
Record (Observations/What we did)	First, we poured corn syrup into the cup. Then, we poured dishwasher soap into the cup. The dishwasher soap just settled on the corn syrup. Next, we poured water with red food coloring. This water settled on the soap. Finally, we poured corn oil. It settled on the water. The liquids layered on top of one another.
Conclusion	Layers of liquids are formed according to their density. The liquids that have lower density settle on top of the liquids that have higher density.

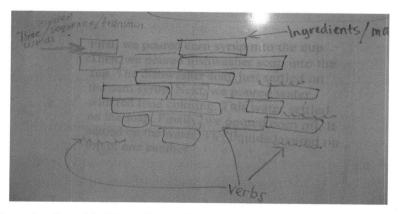

Figure 6.2 Deconstruction of the Mentor Text by Mrs. Dixon.

Example 1   Explicit Talk about Temporal Connectors in the Procedural Recount

1. Mrs. Dixon: Okay, now when you look at this [mentor text projected on the whiteboard]. Are there some words that stick out? That make their observations clear? That give some sort of order? That make it easier to read? Because when you explain what you observe in science experiments, it's important how you lay out, what kind of order you put your words in. What did you notice? Is there something that makes it easier to read? That's my question – is there anything here to make it easier to read? What do you think?
2. Gloria: First, then, next, finally…
3. Mrs. Dixon: Yes! Look at the words she noticed right away. These words – first, then, next, and finally, why did these words stick out to you? Jay?
4. Jay: Because they are like, they just, they are kind of making things kind of flow together.
5. Mrs. Dixon: Okay, they make it flow. Okay, what else they tell us? Ryan? So it gives us a flow. Anything else those words can help you with?
6. Ryder: It shows which they poured first, which they poured next.
7. Mrs. Dixon: Okay, I think you are going to say about something. It shows the time… when each of these occurs, so putting us in the order. Those are really good words. So as soon as I read this explanation, I was really impressed with that.
8. … [Teacher and students continue talking about other kinds of words]
9. Mrs. Dixon: What do we want to call these words in red? [Teacher points to first, then, next, finally]. What do you think? What kind of words are they?
10. Students: Time words, sequence words.
11. Mrs. Dixon: Time or sequence words, maybe even transition word.
12. Felipe: Order.
13. Mrs. Dixon: Order words.

The example shows how Mrs. Dixon focused on the Record stage of the mentor text. This exchange exemplifies several Cs of support. First, Mrs. Dixon is using *classroom interactions* to focus on *code-breaking*. The C of *challenge* can also be seen in this example, as students are discussing challenging concepts. Mrs. Dixon is drawing on students' backgrounds and experiences to discuss language features, an example of the C of *connection*. She starts out by asking students if they recognized any key words in the text which made the Record stage "clear" or "give some sort of order". One student, Gloria, a ML, immediately responded *first, then, next, finally*. Mrs. Dixon uses the interactional scaffolding move *purposeful repetition* when she repeats what Gloria answered accompanied by another move *moving the discourse forward* when she asks students to explain "why did these words stick out to you?", thereby encouraging students to think about the function these words have in the mentor text. Then another student, Jay, specified the function of these words by saying "they are kind of making things kind of flow together." Mrs. Dixon continues using the interactional scaffolding move *moving the discourse forward* when asking "what else they tell us?... Anything else those words can help you with?" Ryder, another ML, then stated these words could function to identify the sequence of the poured liquids in the Experiment 1 conducted earlier. After recognizing these words which function to construct the sequential connectors of the Record stage, Mrs. Dixon and students named these words *time words, transition words, or order words*, thereby drawing their attention to the language features characteristic of procedural recounts in science that typically connect the experiment steps sequentially, namely, time and sequence connectors such as *finally, previously, next, secondly, lastly*, and *as*. Naming the recognized language features of the mentor text is significant because it allowed students and especially MLs to attach deeper meanings to the recognized language features and to expand their awareness of these language patterns and their functions in the procedural recount.

In the second example, accompanied by the mentor text projected on the whiteboard, Mrs. Dixon continued leading the class in a discussion of how the specific names of experiment materials function to help readers figure out exactly what they used for Experiment 1. The classroom transcript (Example 2) reveals how the teacher supported all students in analyzing the writer's language choices in naming the specific experiment materials of a procedural recount.

Example 2   Explicit Talk about Naming Experiment Materials

1. Mrs. Dixon: You know something else I think is important. This person was really specific to say what exactly we used for this experiment. What do I mean by saying that? So when somebody was reading this the first time, and trying to figure out what exactly we did… if somebody was trying to figure out what we did, they would have very good ideas because they also, this person listed what?

2. Students: Names of it.

3. Mrs. Dixon: Put the names of what?
4. Students Liquids.
5. Mrs. Dixon: Yes, they were very specific in naming the ingredients. Okay, some people turned it in and only said "we put liquids together and layers were formed." But this person took the time to say "first, this is the first step we did and we used corn syrup" "we used…" People called it dishwasher soap, some people said dish soap. A couple of different things. But look at this, this person gives me the exact ingredients… I got corn syrup, dishwasher soap, I got my red food coloring here.
6. Students: Water, corn oil.
7. Mrs. Dixon: I got corn oil. It talked about the soap here… the words of materials, the ingredients we used.
8. … [Mrs. Dixon and students continue talking about other kinds of words.]
9. Mrs. Dixon: What about those words in blue that we see that person includes in his explanations? [the words *corn syrup, dishwasher soap, water with red food coloring, corn oil* used by writer]
10. Students: ingredient, objects…
11. Mrs. Dixon: Ingredient, you could say that, there is no only one right answer. Material, objects used, good!

Mrs. Dixon engaged in *code-breaking* with students as she directed their attention to other specific words, the names of experiment materials. These words help readers, who do not share the same context of observing Experiment 1, get a sense of which materials Mrs. Dixon and the students used. This *code-breaking* with students supported them in analyzing the language choices used by the writer in recording the experiment materials. The teacher instructed students to identify and highlight those words. Mrs. Dixon said the students "were very specific in naming the ingredients" and reported these words back to the class: *corn syrup, dishwasher soap, red food coloring, corn oil*. After recognizing these words, which function to construct the specific names of experiment materials in the Record stage, Mrs. Dixon and her students named these words as ingredients, objects, or material. Such a process of recognizing and naming the specific words help students become more aware of the exact functions of these words in the text. Once the students had practiced analyzing and naming the language choices, they turned their attention to analyzing and revising their own texts. The next day, Mrs. Dixon and her students jointly constructed the Conclusion stage based on the results and their discussion about Experiment 1. Ideally, a teacher deconstructs an entire mentor text with students and then jointly constructs an entire new text of the same genre with the class. But Mrs. Dixon considered the conclusion to be a key stage in the procedural recount genre and decided to jointly construct it with her students.

The examples above show how teachers like Mrs. Dixon can develop understanding of the role of language in science learning. Mrs. Dixon was introduced to ways of a talking about language through the implementation of LACI. She used specific metalanguage not only to discuss lesson design and conduct text analysis but also to implement lessons in her classroom.

LACI's TLC Phase 4: Joint Construction

Before jointly constructing the Conclusion stage, Mrs. Dixon and the class reviewed Experiment 1. They then reviewed the Record stage. Students noticed the past tense and tried to explain the reasons why the person use past tense writing up the Record stage. Mrs. Dixon led a Joint Construction of the Conclusion stage of Experiment 1. Figure 6.3 shows the teacher in front of the room writing on the whiteboard as she jointly constructed the conclusion with students.

Figure 6.3 Joint Construction of Conclusion After Experiment 1.

Example 3 shows a classroom example of Mrs. Dixon's Joint Construction with the class:

Example 3   Joint Construction of the Conclusion of Experiment 1

1. Mrs. Dixon: *Now* we talked about this a little bit yesterday… and somebody said that the conclusion has something to do with density. Okay. If we want to say it has something to do with density and liquids, what could we say for the conclusion? Let's just talk about the conclusion for this experiment. This is what happened [pointed to the Record stage]. What we can conclude from this and let's use the word "density." You don't have to be specific but just think about the liquids, why they would form the layers. [T tried to jointly construct the Conclusion part with her students in front] Why would they form those layers?

2. Luis: Because… how much they weigh… and what's their thickness.

3. Mrs. Dixon: Yeah, so if you would like to use that… again. Weight, thickness. Let's fill in the word density somewhere. What could we say as the conclusion? Some liquids

4. Maria: Are more dense, have more density than others.

5. Mrs. Dixon: Okay. We can say something about that. [writing on the board] "*Some liquids are more dense than others.*" Okay! Who can remember what's density? You did your posters! Can we figure which of these liquids is denser? The ones on the top or the ones on the bottom? Which are the ones that are more dense? We can make a conclusion here. Raise your hand if you think the ones on the top are more dense? Raise your hand if you think the ones on the bottom are more dense! [most Ss raised their hands for the 2nd option] You are correct, okay, those liquids that floated to the bottom… so which are the liquids that are more dense? Look at here, we can see which one layered on which one. We had our cup. How did they layer? What was on the very bottom?

6. Students: Corn syrup.

7. Mrs. Dixon: Corn syrup. Can you guys remember the consistence of that? When we poured it, it was super thick. It took a while to pour out of that. Then our next layer was…?

8. Students: Dishwasher soap.
   [Overlapping discussion]

9. Mrs. Dixon: Was it the red water?

10. Students: No, it wasn't.

11. Students: It was soap.

12. Mrs. Dixon: Okay, it was soap. Okay, a little thicker… our next one is…

13. Student: the dishwasher soap was that little purple

14. Mrs. Dixon: It turned the water purplish.

15. Students: Red water.

16. Mrs. Dixon: Is it the red water?
[Overlapped discussion]

17. Mrs. Dixon: And then… what sat on the very top?

18. Students: Corn oil.

19. Mrs. Dixon: *Now*, based on our observations, could we improve that conclusion? Could we add a little bit more detail to it? All we've said was some liquids are more dense than others. If we were to look at our experiment, could we say specifically to this experiment which liquids are more dense? You should be able to… I just wrote a chart up there, too [on whiteboard] some liquids are more dense than others. How could we make that even better? If we look at what happened in our experiment, Brianne is thinking about it. I love it, I can tell who is really thinking about this. Let's make this better. What can we say instead? Sandro is thinking about it!

20. Sandro: Hmmm.

21. Mrs. Dixon: Make it even better. How can we make it better?
[Students suggest ideas]

22. Mrs. Dixon: Okay, keep going with that. Do you need to talk with your neighbors a little bit more… talk to your neighbors for 15 seconds about this topic [Students talked with their group members about the Conclusion] Okay, freeze! I am going to start our conclusion with the word layers! What did we find out about layers? When were layers made here, how did the layers form? What's that to do with density? We are going to make this a little more detailed here! Sandro?

23. Sandro: we could explain which liquid is more dense… like have an introduction to it…

24. Mrs. Dixon: Absolutely, let's have an introduction here. So… *Layers are formed*… [writing on the whiteboard] I like what he said… He was looking back at… exactly how layers were formed. So *layers are formed according to their density* [writing it on the whiteboard]. So we could even say in our experiment… corn syrup is more dense than soap, which is more dense than the red water, which is more dense than the oil, right? We could be specific like that… tell exactly what happened in this. This is what we've learned based on this… experiment… so liquids have formed. So if we know that the ones with the highest density settle on the bottom,

25. Student: The ones with lowest density settle on the top…

26. Mrs. Dixon: To the top. So when you think of the conclusion. You have to come up with what is the experiment? What we are learning from this experiment

Teacher-led, whole-class Joint Construction was an opportunity for Mrs. Dixon to not only co-construct the conclusion with students but also review what happened during Experiment 1. She starts this co-construction using the C of *connection* to link to what they discussed the day before, *"We talked about this a little bit yesterday"* (Turn 1). This also represents the use of the C of classroom interactions, with the interactional scaffolding move *linking to prior experience and pointing to new experiences* because Mrs. Dixon is explicitly connecting students' previous learning to current instruction, preparing students for what follows. Then she proceeds to ask specifically, "What could we say for the conclusion?" This starts the conversation with a lot of prompting by the teacher, also reminding students where they were in the genre and what they were going to do next. When Mrs. Dixon says, *"If we want to say it has something to do with density and liquids, what could we say for the conclusion?"*, she is connecting her expectation to have the concept of *density* and the materials used *liquids* as part of the conclusion. In addition, when she says, *"Let's just talk about the conclusion for this experiment. This is what happened* [pointed to the Record stage]. *What we can conclude from this and let's use the word 'density'"* she is providing the appropriate level of scaffolding to get students to discuss what needs to be included in the conclusion. With the addition of the prompt *"You don't have to be specific but just think about the liquids, why they would form the layers. Why would they form those layers?"* Mrs. Dixon is guiding students to think about both content and language simultaneously, a key aspect of the C of *code-breaking*. She is directing students to use the word density and reminding them of the science content that they learned during the experiment, *"Just think about the liquids. Why would they form those layers?"* With the use of *"Why would they form those layers?"* she is also helping students remember the experiment and what they concluded based on what they observed. This task has the appropriate level of challenge for students, as they engage in classroom interactions with the teacher which incorporates the Cs of *challenge* and *classroom interactions*.

Two students, Luis and Maria, both MLs, suggest ideas and Mrs. Dixon takes this opportunity to write on the board *"'Some liquids are more dense than others'"* (Turns 2–4). She then proceeds with a reminder to students about the word density and which liquids were denser. Mrs. Dixon and the students continue to consider the different liquids and how they layered in the cups. She transitions back to the conclusion by using an emphatic *"now…"*, a common feature of classroom discourse to move from one task to another. She asks students to improve the conclusion by adding more details to it. By stating, *"could we say specifically to this experiment which liquids are more dense?"* she is again connecting the content of the experiment with the language that they should be using in the conclusion.

Mrs. Dixon uses classroom interactions to guide students and their thinking. In Turn 19, the use of *"How could we make that even better… Let's make this better. What can we say instead?"* she is using the interactional scaffolding move *moving the discourse forward* to ask students to continue to improve the conclusion. A few seconds later, she says *"How can we make it better?"* After students have a little time to discuss with partners (*community and collaboration*), Mrs. Dixon gets their attention again and guides them to how she is going to start the "improved conclusion" (as she writes this on the whiteboard):

> *I am going to start our conclusion with the word layers! What did we find out about layers? When were layers made here, how did the layers form? What's that to do with density? We are going to make this a little more detailed here!*

Notice now how Mrs. Dixon went from a general question (e.g. *"How can we make it better?"*) to more specific guidance for the writing, asking students what they found out about the layers, how the layers form and connect these to the concept of density that they learned. This opportunity to connect the science content with the language to express that content is extremely important for students and a critical component of the Joint Construction phase. The talk about language associated with the science content is clear in what Sandro is contributing, *"we could explain which liquid is more dense... like have an introduction to it"* which Mrs. Dixon takes on, reaffirms with *"Absolutely!"* and then writes on the whiteboard: *layers are formed according to their density*, saying this out loud for all to hear. She continues on to explain,

> *So we could even say in our experiment ... corn syrup is more dense than soap, which is more dense than the red water, which is more dense than the oil, right? We could be specific like that...tell exactly what happened in this*

All of these connections to the science content are essential for all students, and especially MLs, so the conversation about the observations and how to write those observations out can be understood in the context of this collaborative activity of jointly constructing this text. She ends the Joint Construction activity by reminding students about what to add in the Procedural Recount genre, what is the experiment and what they are learning from this experiment.

This example is a clear illustration of the principle "guidance through interaction in the context of a shared experience". The guidance provided by Mrs. Dixon through interactions with students was critical in connecting what students learned in the experiment (the 'science') to how the class could express that learning (the 'language'). Three levels of scaffolding were observed in this Joint Construction: *Macro*-level support with the use of LACI's TLC and inclusion of several Cs of support; *Meso*-level support with structured directed assistance focused on content and language simultaneously during the Joint Construction of the conclusion; and *Micro*-level support offered by the teacher through careful solicitation of ideas and use of interactional scaffolding moves to connect to prior learning and move the discourse forward facilitated the process for students' suggestions and teacher negotiation. This was an example of a high-challenge, high-support activity as students were faced with high challenge, bringing together specialized knowledge of science as observed during the science experiment, with a high level of support with significant teacher direction.

After this Joint Construction activity, Mrs. Dixon led her students to do Experiment 2, placing objects, including paper clips, a piece of rubber band, and a Styrofoam ball, into the cups with layered liquids formed in Experiment 1. In order to familiarize her students with the structure of procedural recount, the teacher projected the procedural recount genre stages on the whiteboard and explicitly talked about the four stages with her students: Materials, Aim/Purpose, Record, and Conclusion.

LACI's TLC Phase 6: Independent Construction

Mrs. Dixon then discussed the Procedural Recount genre and what students were expected to write in which stage - Materials, Aim, Record, Conclusion. The last task was for students to construct their individual texts in the procedural recount genre based on what they did and observed in Experiment 2. With their explicit talk about certain language choices made by the mentor text writer and the four stages of procedural recounts, the students were encouraged not only to understand but also to appropriate the language choices in developing their texts. Students wrote up their Procedural Recount the second part of the experiment.

In our work together for several years, over and over again, Mrs. Dixon reminded me of the difficulties with reading and writing the science textbook and write about science and the need for greater explicitness about how to engage students with science texts. Teachers like Mrs. Dixon can benefit from an approach such as LACI if it is introduced in teacher education programs systematically and applied by teachers in their classrooms.

Sample Text 2 by a Multilingual Learner

Let's look at what Ji Soo was able to produce after the implementation of LACI's TLC. Next, we see significant development in this ML's use of language in procedural recounts, including his greater control of naming experiment materials and using temporal connectors.

As Mrs. Dixon deconstructed the mentor text and explicitly talked about the language of the mentor text with highlighters (see Example 1 and Example 2), she brought specific attention to the way the writer of the mentor text recorded events in order (temporal connectors) and with precision (naming experiment materials). The analysis of Ji Soo's text after the implementation of LACI's TLC reflects his increasing ability to record events with precision and in order, especially his greater control of naming experiment materials and using temporal connectors. First, and perhaps most notably, the analysis of Ji Soo's text demonstrates his increasing use of field-specific vocabulary, or technical terms, in naming experiment materials. Figure 6.4 shows that Ji Soo learned to list the experiment materials with more precision; for example, he used *dishwater soap* to name one liquid in the text instead of his previous, more colloquial choice *the soap thingy*. This vocabulary includes not just technical participants in naming the experiment materials *dishwater soap* and *Styrofoam ball* but also more precise processes in recording the events. He expanded his use of processes by using words such as *poured, mixed, put, floated,* and *sank* in Text 2, whereas he primarily relied on the process *poured* in Text 1. Ji Soo's choices of these technical terms in participants and processes also construct an important difference in the topics; Ji Soo's Text 1 primarily focused on the

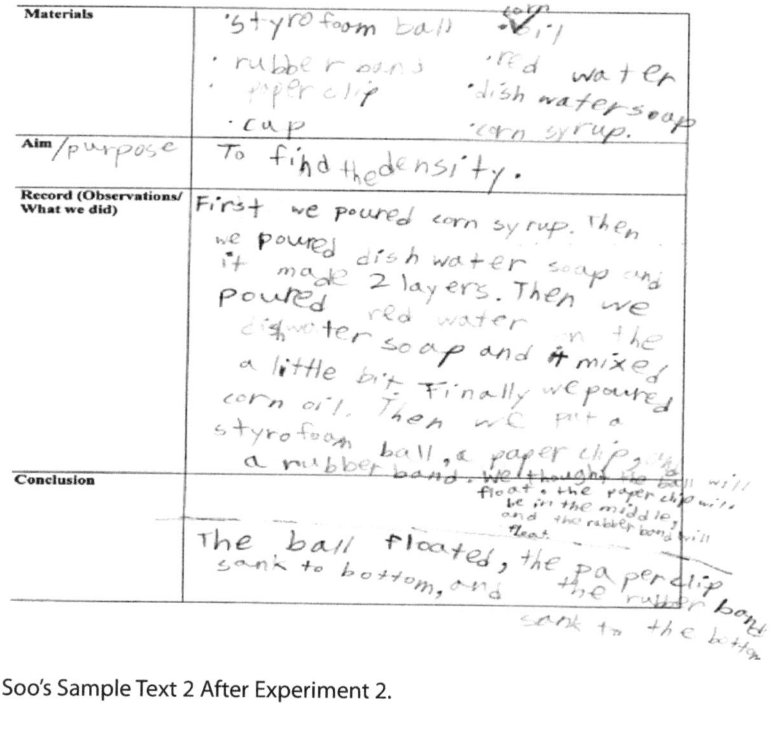

Materials	·styrofoam ball ·rubber band ·paper clip ·cup ·corn oil ·red water ·dish water soap ·corn syrup.
Aim/purpose	To find the density.
Record (Observations/ What we did)	First we poured corn syrup. Then we poured dish water soap and it made 2 layers. Then we poured red water on the dishwater soap and it mixed a little bit. Finally we poured corn oil. Then we put a styrofoam ball, a paper clip, and a rubber band. We thought the ball will float. the paper clip will be in the middle, and the rubber band will float.
Conclusion	The ball floated, the paper clip sank to bottom, and the rubber band sank to the bottom

Figure 6.4 Ji Soo's Sample Text 2 After Experiment 2.

change of liquid color, whereas his Text 2 focused on how the layers of liquids formed from Experiment 1 and how the placed objects floated or sank in the layers of liquids.

Second, it seems that the teacher's deconstruction and explicit talk about the language of the model text strengthened Ji Soo's ability to link his ideas in the texts by using temporal connectors. The analysis of Ji Soo's Text 2 reveals his increasing use of temporal connectors *first*, *then*, and *finally* to link his ideas and especially to record events in order. Compared to his repeated use of *then when* to link his ideas in Text 1, Ji Soo used a variety of temporal connectors to record sequentially the poured liquids of Experiment 1. While the connectors do not appear once in Text 1, after the implementation of LACI's TLC, they appear at the beginning of the record stage of Text 2.

Putting into Practice

Analyzing a Case Study: Second-Grade Science

The following case study depicts a second-grade classroom in a school in California. MLs are divided up at random among the classrooms in this school. As you read, imagine yourself in Luna's place.

> For a science lesson on the states of matter, a second-grade teacher, Mrs. Paul, began with a whole-class discussion where she described the characteristics of solids to the children.
>
> "Solids don't change," she stated.
>
> She then introduced liquids, at which point Luna, classified as a Level 2 EL, linked the two states by offering an acute observation: "Ice cream can be liquid," she pointed out.
>
> The teacher conceded that this was true and then said, "What I meant was that solids don't change shape."
>
> Then Mrs. Paul moved on, asking for other examples.
>
> Luna's ice cream comment actually suggested another science concept: heat affects the rate of melting a solid to a liquid. Luna had combined language and prior experience to offer her observation. When asked about expanding the science unit to include hands-on activities involving the freezing and melting of different substances, Mrs. Paul said, "The standards just say they have to know 'solid, liquid, gas' so that's all I'm doing. Besides, the multilingual learners can't handle any more than that. It will overload them."

Discussion Questions:

1. What kind of learning does the teacher think multilingual learners are capable of?
2. What was this lesson like from Luna's point of view?
3. What science learning was accomplished by the lesson? How could this have been made more productive for Luna?
4. How could the teacher have connected language and science content in this lesson?
5. How could the teacher have used LACI's six Cs of support in this lesson? Give specific examples.
6. How could the teacher have implemented LACI's TLC in this classroom? Give specific examples.

7

Implementing LACI in the Classroom

This book has identified several academic language features of the content areas for MLs at the elementary school level and shows the importance of teachers developing a better understanding of how authors construct disciplinary knowledge. This work recognizes that MLs need opportunities for interaction in meaningful contexts supported by explicit attention to language itself. Several examples throughout the chapters show how a **language-based approach to content instruction (LACI)** implements a *functional approach to language development*, providing a simultaneous focus on the meanings that are made (the "content") and the language through which the meanings are expressed.

A key aspect for all teachers is knowledge about how the language of a specific discipline differs from other disciplines. Every discipline uses academic language in specific ways. These differences have to do with the nature of the discipline itself. Enabling MLs to recognize the different meanings presented through different language choices highlights the importance of focusing on the role of language in developing disciplinary knowledge in different content areas.

Teachers need more than to respond to MLs' needs. They need the knowledge about language necessary to identify potential academic language demands and address them in teaching. To help MLs gain access to and participate in experiences involving the use of academic language, teachers can engage in closer reading of their materials and develop a better understanding of the language through which meanings are expressed.

DOI: 10.4324/9781003264927-7

Academic language is more than vocabulary. Knowledge of an academic vocabulary word is not enough for MLs to fully grasp the range of meanings presented in content area texts. As shown through the examples presented throughout this book, it is important for teachers to understand that the ways in which content area texts are constructed can be made explicit to MLs so they can see how language works in each content area. Teachers can engage all students in discussions about text in meaningful ways. If textbooks are used in the classroom, teachers do not need to engage in language analysis of entire textbooks. This would be impossible. But even deconstructing a short passage can assist MLs in their reading of the content areas. This kind of language-based approach to content instruction supports learning as MLs continue to develop their language skills.

Engaging with the academic language of texts and exploring their language choices contributes to MLs' learning in three ways: they engage more deeply with knowledge about content; they learn about the connections an author makes with readers; and they learn about how language can be organized through cohesive links. These are some of the ways that the areas of meaning that students experience early in schooling are constructed.

One of the main goals of this work is to enable teachers to make grade-level content accessible to MLs so they can be more proactive in helping MLs learn the ways language is used to construct subject-matter knowledge. Efforts to change the academic language of the content areas are counterproductive, as *all* students will need to deal with the specialized knowledge presented in the disciplines to fully participate in school. Learning the language of the academic community allows individuals to have access to this community's meaning-making practices.

This final chapter presents an application framework (based on de Oliveira & Schleppegrell, 2015) that teachers can follow as they plan instruction using LACI. This framework can guide teachers' application of LACI in their classrooms as they plan instruction for their MLs.

A Language-Based Approach to Content Instruction (LACI): An Application Framework for Teachers

LACI emphasizes teaching content through language, which provides MLs with access to grade-level content while simultaneously supporting language development. The following application model can guide teachers' integration of LACI in their classrooms as they set goals based on key concepts, select texts to work with students, analyze these texts, and plan instruction for their MLs.

Steps in Using LACI to Select Texts and Language Features

1. Setting goals, based on key concepts and motivating the learning	2. Selecting a text	3. Analyzing a text	4. Planning instruction with a focus on language and content
Set particular goals based on key concepts and standards that students will need to develop. Specify the content knowledge that students need to develop.	Identify a text. This could be two or three paragraphs that have significant content information related to the key concepts and the main points you want to make. Carefully read the text, keeping in mind the following two questions: ◆ What is most important for students to learn from the selection you have chosen? Write at least one *guiding question* that will guide your teaching of this content. ◆ What language challenges in the text may make it difficult for students to understand the content?	Use Table 7.1 to identify the language focus and features of the text. ◆ What are the most significant language focus and features in this particular text for this particular topic? ◆ Identify 2–3 language features that will help students understand the content, based on the table.	This step is focused on planning how to draw students' attention to language features, as they are encountered in the text. Use these additional steps to guide your planning: ◆ Consider the main points necessary to understand the text with students. ◆ Write some discussion questions or a list of important questions/points that can be used to guide students in examining the language features and main points. Use the **LACI Planning Guide for Incorporating the Six Cs of Support** to guide your planning with the six Cs and/or to scaffold existing lessons. Use the **LACI's Teaching and Learning Cycle Planning Tool** to guide your planning for incorporating LACI's TLC into your units of study. Use the **LACI Unit Plan** to guide your planning of a unit of study or series of lessons using LACI.

Table 7.1: Areas of Meaning, Questions to Guide Language Focus, and Language Focus

Area of Meaning	Questions to Guide Language Focus	Language Focus
Presenting content	1. What is the text/image about? 2. What are the key concepts developed in the text/image?	Sentence constituents: ◆ Participants ◆ Processes ◆ Circumstances
Enacting a relationship with the reader	3. What is the author's perspective? 4. How does the author of this text/image interact with the reader/viewer?	Mood choices: ◆ Declarative ◆ Interrogative ◆ Imperative Modality Evaluative Meanings
Constructing a cohesive message	5. How is the text/image organized? 6. How does the text/image construct a cohesive message?	Given/New Patterns Cohesion

LACI Planning Guide for Incorporating the Six Cs of Support

This guide is based on the 6 Cs of Support, a framework for scaffolding learning for multilingual learners using a Language-based Approach to Content Instruction (LACI). The 6 Cs encompass techniques to scaffold learning. The purpose of this guide is to assist educators in identifying opportunities in curriculum and instruction to better scaffold language development and content-area learning for multilingual learners.

Connection: What activities connect the lesson to students' prior academic learning, backgrounds, and experiences?		
Examples	**Briefly describe existing examples from the lesson**	**Briefly describe possible enhancements**
Connect to previous discussion		
Connect to previous lesson		
Encourage recall of prior learning		
Ask questions to connect experiences to lesson		

Other ways the lesson connects to students' prior academic language, backgrounds and experiences?		

Culture: How does the lesson link the new content skills and concepts to students' cultural and linguistic resources to support academic learning?		
Examples	**Briefly describe existing examples from the lesson**	**Briefly describe possible enhancements**
Home language use		
Connect to students' interests, home lives and experiences, and issues of personal and community importance		
Other ways the lesson links new content skills and concepts to students' cultural and linguistic resources to support academic learning		

Code-Breaking: What will the teacher/students do to explicitly teach/learn ways of doing school, academic literacy, and disciplinary, linguistic, and cultural codes of content learning? How does the teacher model the language functions and associated language features?		
Examples	**Briefly describe existing examples from the lesson**	**Briefly describe possible enhancements**
Use of language objectives		
Vocabulary instruction/word learning strategies		
Modeling reading strategies		
Analyzing and annotating a mentor text (e.g., deconstruction)		
Teacher facilitated joint construction		
Jointly analyzing and editing student writing		

Discussing the purpose and organization of a genre (e.g., argument)		
Making comparisons between English and home languages and/or different linguistic styles for positive transferring		
Other ways the teacher/students explicitly teach/learn ways of doing school, academic literacy, and disciplinary, linguistic, and cultural codes of content learning		

Challenge: What aspects of disciplinary language and literacy does the lesson address? Which higher-order thinking and reasoning skills does the teacher focus on?		
Examples	**Briefly describe existing examples from the lesson**	**Briefly describe possible enhancements**
Maintain high academic standards and expectations while simultaneously providing high levels of support		
Engage students in higher-order questions		
Use grade-level texts while providing supports		
Include activities that require students to analyze and evaluate events or practices and/or create products		
Teach students to think metalinguistically to reflect on how language construes perspectives in texts and how language positions people, etc.		
Other ways the lesson addresses aspects of disciplinary literacy or focuses on higher-order thinking and reasoning skills		

Collaboration and community: How does the teacher engage students in collaboration and build a community of practice where all students are valued and participate?		
Examples	**Briefly describe existing examples from the lesson**	**Briefly describe possible enhancements**
Incorporate routines and interactions that build community and mutual respect (e.g., students are comfortable participating, turn-taking, sharing)		
Use cooperative learning strategies or activities where students can work together		
Implement student-centered activities		
Include varied participant structures		
Other ways the lesson engages the students in collaboration and build a community of practice where all students are valued and participate		

Classroom interactions: How will the teacher use "interactional scaffolding" in the classroom?		
Examples	**Briefly describe existing examples from the lesson**	**Briefly describe possible enhancements**
Link to prior experience and pointing to new experiences		
Recap		
Appropriate		
Recast		
Use cued elicitation		
Move conversation forward		
Probe		
Elaborate		
Clarify		
Repeat purposefully		

LACI's Teaching and Learning Cycle Planning Tool

LACI's Teaching and Learning Cycle Phases	Possible Activities
Building Shared Knowledge of the Topic ◆ engaging students in discussion about the topic that will be the focus of various activities ◆ finding out what they know about the topic ◆ beginning to develop shared understandings.	◆ Identifying current knowledge of the topic ◆ Guided discussions about the unit's topics and themes ◆ Hands-on activities such as science experiments ◆ Teacher-guided activities that involve bridging (e.g. shifting between everyday and more academic language to support students; use of classroom interactions with interactional scaffolding moves; dialogic teaching to move the discourse forward) ◆ Multimodal activities that involve examining images and visuals and image-text relationships ◆ Brainstorming and mind mapping ◆ Think-pair-share ◆ Field trips ◆ Videos ◆ Guest speakers ◆ Research activities, such as jigsaw and notetaking ◆ Skimming/scanning material ◆ Anchor charts

Sustained Reading

◆ reading carefully selected texts which can be two to three paragraphs or longer texts, depending on the purposes for reading.

◆ continuing to build knowledge of the topic, now with an emphasis on further developing MLs' experiences

◆ going through a series of reading practices with students

◆ *Reading Aloud*: Teachers read texts aloud to children

◆ *Interactive Reading Aloud*: Teachers read texts aloud to children and occasionally and selectively pause for conversation and invite students to discuss key ideas, images, illustrations, text features, interesting details, and language.

◆ *Modeled Reading*: Teachers model, verbally, how they would read the text themselves, including reading the text aloud to students while they listen and observe and demonstrating how they would read a text with challenging sentences, thinking aloud about how they might tackle them and allows students to see a purpose in learning to read.

◆ *Shared Reading*: Teachers share a text that is visible to the entire class in an interactive reading experience. Students join in or share the reading while guided and supported by the teacher.

◆ *Guided Reading*: Teachers provide differentiated support for students' developing reading proficiency as they move to new texts at increasingly challenging levels of difficulty in a small-group practice.

◆ *Collaborative Reading*: Pairs or groups of students do structured reading activities while the teacher is working with a particular group.

◆ *Independent Reading*: Students will be doing activities independently (similar to collaborative reading but students are reading independently).

Exploring the language of the text
Possible questions to use:

◆ What is this section of the text about?

◆ How does the author introduce and develop a concept in an informational text? An explanation? An argument?

◆ How does this character change as the story moves along?

◆ How does the author interact with the reader?

◆ How has the author structured this text?

Deconstruction	

◆ introducing mentor texts in a specific genre that students are expected to read and write (e.g., imaginative recount, procedural recount, biographical recount)
 	
◆ guiding students to deconstruct these texts through:
   ❑ demonstration
   ❑ modeling
   ❑ discussions about their purpose, text structures (stages), and language features typical of a specific genre
 	
◆ building up students' knowledge of the content information (i.e., setting context).
 	
◆ developing a shared metalanguage (e.g. purpose and name of the genre, the labeling of stages, and the terminology used for the various language features).
	◆ Exploring the **social purpose** for writing (e.g. narrating, informing, explaining, arguing)
	
	◆ Identifying the **typical key stages** that the text goes through in achieving its purpose
	
	◆ Identifying **optional phases** within stages
	
	◆ Carrying out discussions related to **how the text is organized** and other linguistic styling and organizational choices
	
	◆ Identifying **language features** (only between 2 and 3 depending on length and text complexity)

Joint Construction	
◆ working together as a class (teacher and students) to co-construct a text in the same genre similar to the mentor texts already explored in the deconstruction phase	◆ Developing an overview of the text with students' help
	◆ Focusing on a particular stage of the text
◆ using the language features of the specific genre about which students are learning	◆ Developing a paragraph
	◆ Demonstrating language choices by recasting what students offer in oral language into more written-like language
◆ providing a bridge for students between their everyday language and the academic language of school	◆ Asking questions to request student responses
	◆ Making suggestions
◆ attending to text organizational issues such as purpose, stages, and language features.	◆ Discussing how a specific language choice might be better than another
	◆ Moving the discourse forward by asking students to say more or extend their ideas
◆ scribing by the teacher; writing by everyone	◆ Focusing on choices about the whole text, paragraph or sentence structure
◆ engaging students for MLs' language development at various levels of English language proficiency	◆ Reminding students of the stages of the genre and typical genre features
◆ demonstrating how to construct a good example of the genre they are learning	◆ Referring back to the deconstructed text as the class composes a new text together
◆ preparing for joint construction is critical for MLs so that they have had time to prepare and are ready to contribute	

Collaborative Construction

- bridging between the joint construction and independent construction phases
- conducting pair or group activities for students to work together to develop a new, single text
- focusing on one stage or more for the collaborative construction
- working with other students in pairs or small groups
- brainstorming and negotiating ideas
- co-writing in pairs or small groups
- revising
- further scaffolding as needed by the teacher, drawing on understandings developed in previous lessons.

- Introducing the collaborative construction activity
- Selecting partners/groups for the writing task
- Modeling the collaborative writing phase
- Engaging students in writing conferences
- Encouraging student presentations

Independent Construction	
• working independently to construct own texts in the specific genre.	◆ Students brainstorm ideas for writing own text
• minimizing teacher their support, scaffolding, and guidance	◆ Students use graphic organizers and other classroom resources independently
• conducting additional research if writing a text that is on a different topic from the topics of the other phases but involves the same genre	◆ Students self-monitor time and progress
• referring to the deconstructed mentor text, the jointly constructed text, and the collaboratively constructed text to now write a text by themselves independently. Considering audience, editing the text, and expanding their language choices.	◆ Students write independently
• Consulting with the teacher and conferences with peers about writing	◆ Teacher provides scaffolding as needed
• proofreading texts to attend to spelling, punctuation, and other mechanics.	
• presenting guidelines for students to revise, edit, and proofread their texts.	

LACI Unit Plan

Grade Level:
Subject Area:
Lesson Title:
Duration of the Lesson:

ELD Standard(s)/WIDA Standards e.g., WIDA or state ELPD standard[s] that are the target of student learning. (Note: Please list the **number and text** of each standard that is being addressed.)	
CCSS or State Content Standard What CCSS standard(s) are most relevant to the learning goals?	
Content Objectives (related to the subject matter central focus)	
Language Objectives (related to key language function, task, or skill)	
Prior Academic Knowledge and Conceptions What knowledge, skills, and concepts must students already know to be successful with this lesson?	
Instructional Strategies and Learning Tasks *Description of what the teacher (you) will be doing and/or what the students will be doing.*	
Introduction _____ Minutes How will you start the lesson to engage and motivate students in learning?	**LACI's TLC Phase 1: Building Shared Knowledge of the Topic**

Instruction _____ Minutes **Highlighted LACI's TLC Phase(s)**: **Procedures**: specific details regarding what the students will do during the lesson (practice/application)	**LACI's TLC Phase 2: Sustained Reading**
LACI 6 Cs of Support: *Connection*: What will you do to connect the lesson to students' prior academic learning, backgrounds and experiences? *Culture*: How will you link the new content skills and concepts to students' cultural and linguistic resources to support academic learning? *Challenge*: What aspects of disciplinary literacy will you address? Which higher-order thinking and reasoning skills will you focus on? *Code-Breaking*: What will you do to explicitly teach ways of doing school, academic literacy, and disciplinary, linguistic, and cultural codes of content learning? How will you model the language forms/vocabulary/function/skills? *Community and collaboration*: How will you engage students in collaboration and build a community of practice? *Classroom interactions*: How will you use "interactional scaffolding" in the classroom? Plan for the use of oral discourse to prompt elaboration, build academic literacy, and move discourse and learning forward. **Closure**	**LACI's TLC Phase 3: Deconstruction** **LACI's TLC Phase 4: Joint Construction** **LACI's TLC Phase 5: Collaborative Construction** **LACI's TLC Phase 6: Independent Construction**
Assessment/Evaluation (Formative and/or Summative)	
Extension	

Next, I provide some examples of how teachers can plan instruction using LACI. Though teachers may choose to move through a unit of instruction in multiple ways, this section shows how they might go through steps to plan instruction using LACI. The four steps of the application framework can be taken to promote a central role for language in the content classroom, but how they are realized in lessons will depend on your students, context, content, and goals.

An Application Framework for Teachers

Step 1: Setting goals, based on key concepts, and motivating the learning
The first step in this framework is to set particular goals based on key concepts that students will need to learn. Specify the content knowledge that students need to develop. For instance, a science teacher might select to focus on the process of pollination. Their goals are to set the context for the students to understand this process and how it happens.

Step 2: Selecting a text

The second step is to identify a text – this could be two to four paragraphs that have significant content information related to the key concepts and the main points the teacher wants to make. Carefully read the text, keeping in mind the following two questions.

- ◆ What is most important for students to learn from the selection you have chosen? Write at least one *guiding question* that will guide your teaching of this content.
- ◆ What language challenges in the text may make it difficult for students to understand the content?

Here we might imagine the science teacher introducing the selected text about pollination that the class will work with over the next week or two. The guiding question could be "What is pollination?" For example, a text that she might select may have *definitions*, *descriptions*, and *relating verbs*. She might suggest that in reading, talking, and writing about the text over the next week, they will focus on how the author uses the language of *definitions* and *descriptions* and identify nouns such as *flowers, stamen, pollen, pistil, ovary, seeds*, verbs such as *have, is, form, happens*, and connectors such as *when*. Students can then use these features in their writing. For instance, the teacher might select the following four paragraphs that have significant content information. This text is from *Harcourt Science* (Harcourt, 2005) and is part of the chapter entitled "Plant Growth and Adaptations," and appears as part of lesson 3, "How Do Plants Reproduce?" This section is called "Plant Life Cycles" and describes the ways in which plants reproduce and how seeds are spread.

Plants from Seeds

Have you ever planted seeds in a garden? Seeds form in the cones of conifers. Seeds also form in the flowers of flowering plants. When a flower dries up and falls away, fruit forms around the young seeds. The fruit protects the seeds. Inside each seed is a tiny plant and the food it needs to start growing.

Seeds are the first part in a flowering plant's life cycle. To begin to grow, seeds need warmth, water, and air. Most seeds don't get what they need, so they don't grow. However, when a seed has its needs met, it **germinates**, or sprouts. Seedlings that sprout in soil may keep growing. They grow to become adult, or mature, plants. The mature plants form flowers.

Flower Parts and Seeds

Flowers have parts that work together to make seeds. The **stamen** makes pollen, a kind of powder. The top of the **pistil** collects pollen. The bottom of the pistil is the ovary where seeds form. An apple core is an apple tree ovary.

Seeds form after a flower is pollinated. **Pollination** happens when pollen is carried from a stamen to a pistil by wind or animals. For example, bees, birds, and bats feed on nectar, a sweet liquid in some flowers. Pollen sticks to the animals' bodies. When they leave or visit another flower, the pollen is transferred to the pistil.

Text Excerpt from *Harcourt Science* (Harcourt, 2005, pp. A84–85)

Step 3: Analyzing a text
Use Table 7.2 to identify the language focus and features of the text.

◆ What are the most significant language focus and features in this particular text for this particular topic?
◆ Identify 2–3 language features that will help students understand the content, based on the table.

Table 7.2: Areas of Meaning, Questions to Guide Language Focus, and Language Focus

Area of Meaning	Questions to Guide Language Focus	Language Focus
Presenting content	1. What is the text/image about? 2. What are the key concepts developed in the text/image?	Sentence constituents: ◆ Participants ◆ Processes ◆ Circumstances
Enacting a relationship with the reader	3. What is the author's perspective? 4. How does the author of this text/image interact with the reader/viewer?	Mood choices: ◆ Declarative ◆ Interrogative ◆ Imperative Modality Evaluative Meanings
Constructing a cohesive message	5. How is the text/image organized? 6. How does the text/image construct a cohesive message?	Given/New Patterns Cohesion

This section describes and highlights some language features in the science text, which is from a fourth-grade textbook. I selected more than 2–3 language features to highlight here to show all of the potential of this text and provide several examples of what teachers can focus on with students.

Presenting Content
From Words to Sentences: Technical Terms and Definitions
Key concepts in this text are used as participants. These participants are technical terms, a common feature of the language of science. Technical terms are essential for constructing the distinctive nature of scientific language. This analysis revealed that these terms often are defined, explained, or paraphrased and appear typically in bold, as in the sample passages. In science textbooks, definitions are used often when technical terms need to be introduced and described.

In the selected text, the technical terms *germinates* and *pollination* are both defined and appear in bold. Some other terms that students must be familiar with and understand in this excerpt are *seeds, cones, conifers, flowers, stamen, pollen, pistil, ovary*, and *nectar*, but not all of these terms are in bold face.

The technical term *pollen* is defined as *a kind of powder*. But this explanation occurs right after the technical term and is set out by only a comma. Identifying *a kind of powder* as a definition could be an excellent point for discussion with students. Because this word is not in bold face, it may not be easily recognized as an important term. But *pollen* is a very relevant term for MLs if they are to understand the process of pollination. Another key technical term in this passage is *seedlings*. This technical term is never defined or explained, although it is also important for understanding *adult plants*, which appears in the next sentence.

Enacting a Relationship with the Reader
From Everyday to Academic: Everyday Meanings and Words with Specialized Meanings

The text starts out with a question, "Have you ever planted seeds in a garden?" This is a choice the author made to interact directly with the reader by using the interrogative mood. Questions like this are a common feature of textbooks, especially in the lower elementary grades. They become less common in the upper elementary and secondary grades. This feature can be seen as an attempt to make the content more accessible to students, to connect to students' everyday language, and to spark students' interest in the topic. The use of the pronoun *you* also exemplifies this attempt to connect to students. Right after this introductory question, however, a sentence with several technical terms is already introduced and, from then on, the language of science is dense and packed, as will be described.

Constructing a Cohesive Message
From Common Usage to Science Usage: Connectors with Specific Roles

The connector *or* in science has two very specific and distinct roles. The first role is introducing explanations or paraphrases, rather than indicating alternatives – more commonly used in everyday language (Fang, 2006) – as is the case in the clause *When they leave or visit another flower* in the selected text. The technical term *germinates*, for instance, is followed by a connector, *or*, and a paraphrase, *sprouts*, in an attempt to paraphrase the more technical term. In this case, however, the word used as a paraphrase is itself a technical term and may still be difficult for students to understand. The second role for the connector *or* is the introduction of more abstract or technical terms. One example found in the text appears in the sentence *They grow to become adult, or mature, plants*. Here *or* is used to introduce the more technical term *mature*. This dual role of the connector *or* in science constitutes another important point to discuss with students who may understand the connector as indicating alternatives or choices, which is common in more everyday language.

From Simple to Complex: Noun Groups and Zig-Zag Structuring

Both simple and complex noun groups appear in science writing. Expanded and complex nominal groups – those that have pre-modifiers and post-modifiers – are typically present in science texts. Expanded nominal groups function to pack a lot of information in a single lexical item. In the sentence *Temperature is a measure of the average energy of motion of the particles in matter* (Harcourt, 2005, p. E43), an expanded and complex nominal group is given as the definition for temperature: *a measure of the average energy of motion of the particles in matter*. This nominal group has as its head the noun, *measure*; *a* is a pre-modifier and *of the average energy of motion of the particles in matter* are post-modifiers. Such meaning accumulation allows science texts to pack more lexical content per sentence. This high lexical density of science texts presents challenges for MLs.

The selected text contains many nouns, most of which are the technical terms referred to earlier. These nouns have different structures which are shown in Table 7.3. These nouns have specific roles in text structuring and must be understood in the context of the entire passage, not as isolated terms.

Table 7.3 Noun Group Structure

Type of Noun Group	Sample Text Examples
Noun (with head only)	*seeds* *fruit* *pollination*
Pronoun	*you* *they* *it* *this* *these*
Noun with pre-modifiers	***a** garden* **the young** *seeds* **this pollen** *tube*
Noun with post-modifiers	*seedlings* **that sprout in the soil** (*that sprout in the soil* is a relative clause that adds information about the head *seedlings*) *parts* **that work together to make seeds** (*that work together to make seeds* is a relative clause that adds information about the head *parts*)
Noun with pre- and post-modifiers	***the thick bottom** part **of the pistil called the ovary***

Table 7.4 shows the zig-zag movement found from one sentence to the next in the text. The noun groups are underlined and include simple nouns (noun with head only), pronouns, nouns with pre-modifiers, and nouns with post-modifiers.

All of these noun groups are important for the understanding of this science topic and must be understood in the context of this passage. The majority of nouns are introduced and referenced back within the text itself, with the exception of the pronoun *you*, which is a reference outside of the text. These referential relations need to be understood by MLs who must be able to track and connect these referrers so they can fully comprehend this text. For instance, in the sentence *Inside each seed is a tiny plant and the food it needs to start growing*, the referent for the pronoun *it* may be difficult for MLs to understand. In this case, *it* refers back to *a tiny plant*. This sentence also has an unusual pattern since it starts with a circumstance indicating place, *inside each plant*. Teachers would need to deconstruct a sentence like this with MLs to help them understand the important information presented.

Table 7.4 Nouns, Noun Groups, and Zig-Zag Structuring in Text

Have you ever planted seeds in a garden? Seeds form in the cones of conifers. Seeds also form in the flowers of flowering plants. When a flower dries up and falls away, fruit forms around the young seeds. The fruit protects the seeds. Inside each seed is a tiny plant and the food it needs to start growing.

Seeds are the first part in a flowering plant's life cycle. To begin to grow, seeds need warmth, water, and air. Most seeds don't get what they need, so they don't grow. However, when a seed has its needs met, it germinates, or sprouts. Seedlings that sprout in soil may keep growing. They grow to become adult, or mature, plants. The mature plants form flowers.

Flower Parts and Seeds

Flowers have parts that work together to make seeds. The stamen makes pollen, a kind of powder. The top of the pistil collects pollen. The bottom of the pistil is the ovary where seeds form. An apple core is an apple tree ovary.

Seeds form after a flower is pollinated. Pollination happens when pollen is carried from a stamen to a pistil by wind or animals. For example, bees, birds, and bats feed on nectar, a sweet liquid in some flowers. Pollen sticks to the animals' bodies. When they leave or visit another flower, the pollen is transferred to the pistil.

The noun *pollination* is an example of a nominalization, introduced in Chapter 2 as a resource for the construction of nouns. The noun *pollen* is introduced in the first paragraph of the section. Then *pollinated* is used as a verb in the passive voice construction *is pollinated* in the second paragraph. *Pollination* is used as a nominalization to refer to the process being described in the two paragraphs. Nominalization allows writers to package information into a single unit and then use this in subsequent paragraphs to expand the explanation. Understanding what nominalizations mean is challenging for all students, but may be particularly challenging for MLs.

The zig-zag patterning appears as words are first introduced and then either repeated or referred to within the passage. For instance, *seeds* is first introduced in the question that appears at the beginning of the paragraph. This word is repeated again in the second sentence and throughout the passage. Pronouns are used as referrers, so linking pronouns to their specific referents can be a reading strategy to work on with MLs. These internal references are important for the information flow of the paragraph and the text as a whole, and is an important feature to highlight with students.

Step 4: Planning instruction with a focus on language and content
This step is focused on planning how to draw students' attention to language features, as they are encountered in the text. Use these additional steps to guide your planning:

- ◆ Consider the main points necessary to understand the text with students.
- ◆ Write some discussion questions or a list of important questions/ points that can be used to guide students in examining the language features and main points.
  - Use the **LACI Planning Guide for Incorporating the Six Cs of Support** to guide your planning with the six Cs and/or to scaffold existing lessons.
  - Use the **LACI's Teaching and Learning Cycle Planning Tool** to guide your planning for incorporating LACI's TLC into your units of study.
  - Use the **LACI Unit Plan** to guide your planning of a unit of study or series of lessons using LACI.

After building background knowledge so students remember what important science concepts they discussed before reading the text (***Connection***), the teacher leads them in activities where they focus in on the ways the author has presented technical terms and their definitions as well as the noun groups (some of which are technical terms!) and how they are used to structure the text. They unpack the written language, using the metalanguage of *technical terms, definitions, participants*, and *zig-zag structuring*. The teacher introduces the text along with the metalanguage for discussing the text in meaningful ways, drawing on students' cultural and linguistic resources (**Culture**). The class can identify some technical terms and associated definitions and talk about why identifying these is important in science. The focus at this point, though, is engaging students in talking about the text, drawing on their background knowledge and motivating their interest (**Culture, Classroom Interactions, Challenge**). The class engages in a read-aloud activity that introduces them to the text.

After the students have read the text for understanding, the teacher leads them in activities where they focus on the ways the author has presented *participants* in the text, as these are central to understanding how pollination occurs and all of the different parts of a plant that are involved in it (**Codebreaking**). They unpack the written language, looking at how participants are presented as technical terms and other noun groups and how the author creates zig-zag structuring in the science text. Now that the students have had an opportunity to focus on the forms, use, and meanings, the teacher keeps a focus on participants throughout the remainder of the unit of instruction. She will be alert to identify when students use various technical terms and other noun groups as participants and will draw attention to them, restating what the students say and highlighting the use of language relevant to understanding and using participants. Students will be given opportunities to work together using other kinds of relevant texts and will help each other remember how participants are introduced and developed in different ways (**Community and Collaboration**). When the teacher sees that the students now are using participants and the language they have learned for talking about these, she gives them written assignments that call for them to this language feature.

A Unit Plan with *I Hate English!*

Table 7.5 presents a unit plan for the picture book *I Hate English!*, introduced in Chapter 2.

The focus of this unit is on identifying processes (*doing, thinking,* and *feeling*) to explain how Mei Mei feels, and how her feelings change as the story progresses. By identifying thinking and feeling processes that explain how Mei Mei feels and by focusing on doing processes that

Table 7.5 A Unit Plan with *I Hate English!*

Grade Level: Third grade
Subject Area: English Language Arts
Lesson Title: Exploring Feelings in *I Hate English!*
Duration of the Lesson: 2 days

ELD Standard(s)/WIDA Standards e.g., WIDA or state ELPD standard[s] that are the target of student learning. (Note: Please list the **number and text** of each standard that is being addressed.)	English Language Development Standard 2: English Language Learners communicate information, ideas, and concepts necessary for academic success in the content area of Language Arts
CCSS or State Content Standard What CCSS standard(s) are most relevant to the learning goals?	CCSS.ELA-Literacy.RL.1.1 Ask and answer questions about key details in a text. CCSS.ELA-Literacy.RL.1.2 Retell stories, including key details, and demonstrate understanding of their central message or lesson. CCSS.ELA-Literacy.W.1.3 Write narratives in which they recount two or more appropriately sequenced events, include some details regarding what happened, use temporal words to signal event order, and provide some sense of closure.
Content Objectives (related to the subject matter central focus)	Students will be able to identify processes (*doing, thinking, and feeling*) to explain how Mei Mei feels, and how her feelings change as the story progresses.
Language Objectives (relate d to key language function, task, or skill)	Students will be able to write a narrative recount using the language of doing/relating/thinking/feeling/saying processes and relate them to circumstances (prepositional phrases) to explore how Mei Mei's feelings change throughout the story.
Prior Academic Knowledge and Conceptions What knowledge, skills, and concepts must students already know to be successful with this lesson?	Feeling words, language, culture, family, immigrants
Instructional Strategies and Learning Tasks *Description of what the teacher (you) will be doing and/or what the students will be doing.*	
Introduction 30 Minutes How will you start the lesson to engage and motivate students in learning?	**LACI's TLC Phase 1: Building Shared Knowledge of the Topic** The teacher began the lesson by connecting to students' backgrounds and experiences which later connected to Mei Mei and the *I Hate English!* story. The teacher posed several questions including; Does anyone speak a language besides English? How did you learn English? When you were still learning English, how did you feel when you were at ___ and everyone around you was speaking English? (*Connection and Culture*)

(Continued)

Table 7.5 (Continued)

Instruction	LACI's TLC Phase 2: Sustained Reading, *I Hate English!*
60 + 60 Minutes (2 periods of 60 min each) **Highlighted LACI's TLC Phase:** Sustained Reading **Procedures:** specific details regarding what the students will do during the lesson (practice/application) **LACI 6 Cs of Support:** *Connection:* What will you do to connect the lesson to students' prior academic learning, backgrounds and experiences? *Culture:* How will you link the new content skills and concepts to students' cultural and linguistic resources to support academic learning? *Challenge:* What aspects of disciplinary literacy will you address? Which higher-order thinking and reasoning skills will you focus on? *Code-Breaking:* What will you do to explicitly teach ways of doing school, academic literacy, and disciplinary, linguistic, and cultural codes of content learning? How will you model the language forms/vocabulary/function/skills? *Community and collaboration:* How will you engage students in collaboration and build a community of practice?	The teacher and students will read through the text together without stopping. After reading, the teacher will direct students on a picture walk of the text. During the picture walk, the students will look at the illustrations and identify the feelings expressed by the main character's (Mei Mei) face and gestures and make connections between the text and the images (*Challenge*). The teacher will emphasize the way the illustrations show how Mei Mei feels. The teacher might say, for example, "Let's look at page 4 together where Mei Mei is at school in New York. Look at her face. Tell me what you think she is feeling? Why?" (*Code-breaking*) After the picture walk, students will work in small groups to identify the places where Mei Mei used Chinese/English and the processes. They also discuss how Mei Mei felt and why she felt this way (*Community and Collaboration*). a) Students identify the places where the processes took place. The teacher writes different locations on the blackboard and assigns the location to each group. **First location: In the Library (used as a model)** **Group 1: Hong Kong (pp. 2, 10)** **Group 2: Chinatown in New York (pp. 2–3);** **Group3: School in New York (pp. 4–6)** **Group 4: Chinatown Learning Center (pp. 7–9; 14–17)** **Group 6: Jones Beach (pp. 11–12)** **Group 5: At Home (pp. 18–19)** **Group 6: Classroom in New York (pp. 20–23)** **Group 7: In the street (pp. 24–27; 30)** b) The teacher gives each group a handout. The purpose of the handout is to develop the language to name Mei Mei's feelings in different locations (e.g., anxiety, apprehension, shock, tension, surprise, excitement, pride; Students' Talk: Mei Mei is sad/upset/shocked/happy/excited/proud). **Where did it take place?** **What was happening?**

Classroom interactions: How will you use "interactional scaffolding" in the classroom? Plan for the use of oral discourse to prompt elaboration, build academic literacy, and move discourse and learning forward.

Closure

In what language? Circle one.	
in Chinese	in English
How did Mei Mei feel?	
Draw Mei Mei's face	**Use words to describe Mei Mei's feelings.**
What words in the book tell you how Mei feels?	
Why did Mei Mei feel this way?	

c) Prior to starting the handout, the teacher draws a similar chart on the blackboard and models for the students how to fill it out using "The First Location: In the Library." The teacher emphasizes that some emotions can be expressed through description of body language or actions, or by what Mei Mei says or thinks. (*Code-breaking*)

d) The teacher elicits answers and develops a chart on the board with the whole class. (*Community and Collaboration*)

e) The students copy the chart (pre-writing).

Examples of:

- *doing processes:* moved, looked, talked, happened, makes, fight, will go, bang, keeps, took, wouldn't work, helped
- *relating processes:* was, is, stands, is not like
- *thinking processes:* didn't know, thought, understood, forgot, knew about, thought about, didn't know, knew, don't think, couldn't think about
- *feeling processes:* hate, didn't want to move, loved, seemed to fly, didn't want to listen, wanted to move, didn't want to hear, felt, dreamt about, woke up shouting, don't care!, don't want to go/ask/have/read/talk, wanted to tell, liked, couldn't stand [it], want to talk, didn't care
- *saying processes:* said, wouldn't speak, could say, didn't ask

f) Using the chart off the board, the teacher leads the whole-class discussion asking *why* and other questions (*Challenge*). The students copy information in the *why* column of their handouts.

Examples of Teacher-Leader Questions:

- Why did Mei Mei hate English?
- How did she learn to speak English?
- How did she learn to read and write in English?
- Why did her feelings begin to change?
- What can help Mei Mei to begin to love English?

Table 7.5 (Continued)

Other Questions (relating to students' experiences) (*Culture and Connection*):

◆ Can you speak other languages besides English? (Ask students to speak in another language and/or teach each other in a different language.)

◆ Have you ever been in a situation when everybody spoke another language? How did you feel? What help did you need?

◆ Is it good to know one or two languages, and why?

LACI's TLC Phase 3: Deconstruction

The teacher displays the mentor text on the smartboard for everyone to see. The mentor text is below.

When Mary was a little girl, her family moved to Paris, the capital of France. Mary did not know why. She liked Paris and people but everything was in French. French was a strange language, not like English. Mary loved English, and thought that she wouldn't speak French in school. But everything in school was in French. She did not understand what the teacher said in French, and she could not find friends because her classmates did not understand what she said. Once she heard a song in French, and she liked the music. Her teacher said, "Do you want to sing the song?" Mary loved music, she loved singing. She said, "Yes." But she had to learn how to sing in French. French seemed lonely, she thought in English. But Mary decided to try…

The teacher asks: What is the purpose of the text? (To tell what happened.) Who is involved? When did it happen? Where did it happen? What was going on? How did Mary feel? Why do you think so? Have you been to Paris? (The teacher shows Paris on the map.) What country/ies have you been to? (Show it/them on the map.) Who knows French? Would you like to know French, and why? Why is it good to know English and French? (*Challenge, Code-breaking*)

a) The teacher pays attention to the following language features:

◆ Places and characters (nouns; pronouns: e.g. *she* instead of *Mary*);

◆ Processes: (doing/relating/thinking/feeling/saying) in the simple past tense;

◆ Use of linking words to identify the time (When Mary was a little girl; once);

◆ Circumstances (prepositional phrases) (e.g. in English, in French);

◆ Some descriptive features or words (e.g. a lonely language)

◆ Words that have cultural meanings (not in this text)

LACI's TLC Phase 4: Joint Construction

The teacher decides with the students on the topic they will write about (it has to be a recount).

a) The teacher asks: Look at the chart that we discussed yesterday. What is the story (personal recount) like? What do you think we should talk about next?

b) Constructing the text together with students and writing it on the blackboard, the teacher engages the class, asks for students' contributions, writes on the board, suggests new words, and negotiates the language of the text. The teacher discusses the language of the story and its functions (e.g. nouns/pronouns, processes in the simple past tense, prepositional phrases, the feelings and how they changed, and why) (*Code-breaking*)

The topic selected by the teacher and students was What Happened When I Visited The Museum. Because this was a shared experience for this group of students (they had just gone to a museum the week before), this was a good topic for them to write about.

Possible other topics for personal recount genre:

◆ My First Day in a New Country
◆ How Joaquin Became a Writer
◆ How Elizabeth Found a New Friend

LACI's TLC Phase 5: Collaborative Construction

Students write together in pairs on one of the topics above to practice writing a personal recount. They brainstorm a list of events that happened before they start writing.

LACI's TLC Phase 6: Independent Construction

Students will now have the opportunity to apply what they have learned by writing their own text independently. The teacher will select one of the topics above that was not previously selected for joint construction.

Assessment/Evaluation (Formative and/or Summative)	Formative evaluation is embedded in the lesson as students work on reading and writing tasks, both individually and collaboratively with peers and the teacher. The summative assessment is the individual writing assignment.

explain the actions that occur in different cultural and linguistic settings, students can better understand how Mei Mei's emotions developed and changed. For example, Mei Mei felt she was smart "in *her* school in Hong Kong. In Chinese"; she began to hate English when her family moved to New York. As a result, "she wouldn't speak in school," "everything was in English, and she would not speak English." By identifying circumstances that are prepositional phrases with an emphasis on languages, students can better understand how Mei Mei's feelings develop from her resistance to speak English to the use of the English language. For example, in the beginning, Mei Mei hated English, as she "said in her head *in Chinese.*" Later, English began to seem "interesting even it [the story] was *in English*"; eventually, Mei Mei "talked for twenty-two minutes without stopping. *In English.*" While the language focus for a specific unit will highly depend on the selected text, here we can see the importance of character development in picture books which can be a powerful focus in English language arts. A chart like the one in Table 7.6 can help teachers identify feelings and consider questions to promote discussion for inclusion in the unit plan.

Table 7.6: Activity for Teachers Based on the Book *I Hate English!*

Please fill out the chart and think of questions that can promote discussion.				
Participants	**Processes (doing, relating, thinking, feeling, and saying)**	**Circumstances (prepositional phrases)**	**Feelings**	**Questions to promote discussion**

This unit plan features all six Cs of support. The C of code-breaking is emphasized, with a focus on doing, thinking, and feeling processes as well as circumstances associated with those processes. The teacher carefully planned the implementation of LACI's TLC incorporating all phases. The Sustained Reading phase helped students understand the various places where Mei Mei was and the feelings associated with those places, and identify how Mei Mei's feelings changed as her experiences changed throughout the book.

Conclusion

This book presented a **language-based approach to content instruction (LACI)**, a teacher preparation model developed over the past 20 years through research in content area classrooms with MLs. LACI implements a *functional approach to language development*, providing a simultaneous focus on language and meaning. Because language is a meaning-making system used to achieve social goals (de Oliveira & Schleppegrell, 2015; Halliday & Matthiessen, 2014), a focus on language in content classrooms helps teachers understand how knowledge is created across content areas. LACI places emphasis on language learning in the content classroom. With a focus on content *through* language, instruction for MLs is accomplished in meaningful ways in a general education classroom with the use of LACI. Raising teachers' awareness about the academic language demands of learning content can help them more effectively contribute to the language development of MLs in their general education classes.

LACI's Teaching and Learning Cycle (TLC), drawing on all Cs of support for scaffolding to design instruction for MLs, applies genre-based pedagogy based on SFL in high-challenge, high-support classrooms with high expectations and purposeful scaffolding for the explicit teaching necessary for MLs' language and content development. As a pedagogical framework, it provides learners with explicit knowledge about language to break down academic language and build up MLs' knowledge, skills, and abilities for continued access and success.

LACI's TLC enables teachers to identify the language demands of the texts and tasks assigned, explicitly teach MLs the genres of schooling, focus simultaneously on language and content learning, and utilize classroom interactions to build scaffolding throughout the cycle.

LACI focuses on disciplinary learning as teachers and students explore the language of the content areas – as they are written – without simplification. As MLs explore and "unpack" – or **break down** – academic language in texts, they discover both the language and content they are using and developing. This language exploration develops their awareness of how language works as teachers support MLs to notice, analyze, and practice discipline-specific reading and writing.

One of the major points presented in this book is the idea of *accessibility*. This book uses the notion of making content *accessible* to mean **providing access to the academic language that constructs disciplinary knowledge in the content areas**. MLs need access to the dense and abstract language of the content areas. This is a matter of social justice; if MLs are not given opportunities to engage and participate in experiences involving the use of academic language, they will continue to be at a disadvantage. LACI enables MLs to manipulate language as it is written, without simplification, and develops teachers' understanding about how disciplinary discourse is constructed. Using language analysis to focus on content, and working with teachers who are knowledgeable about content, LACI promotes a focus on language in ways that reveal and uncover the many and varied meanings that texts present.

Appendix

CCSS Text Type, WIDA Key Language Uses, Genre Families, Genres, Purposes, Stages, and Language Features

CCSS Text Type	WIDA Key Language Uses	Genre Family	Genre	Purpose	Stages	Language Features
Narrative	Narrate	Stories	Personal Recount	to share sequence of events	Orientation Record of Events	Sequenced in time Individual nouns are common
			Imaginative Recount	to engage readers in a problem/complication and resolving it	Orientation Complication Resolution	Sequenced in time Individual nouns are common
		Histories	Autobiographical Recount	to chronicle own significant life events	Orientation Record of stages	Sequenced in episodes Individual nouns are common
			Biographical Recount	to chronicle others' significant life events	Orientation Record of stages	Sequenced in episodes Individual nouns are common
			Historical Recount	to chronicle stages in history	Background Record	Sequenced in episodes Group nouns are common
Informational/Explanatory	Inform	Procedures	Simple Procedure	to instruct someone how to do experiments, observations, and other tasks	Materials Instructions	Imperative mood Individual nouns
			Procedural Recount	to record steps taken to carry out experiments, tasks, and observations	Aim Materials Record of events Conclusions	Sequenced by task General and abstract nouns
		Reports	Descriptive Report	to classify and describing a phenomenon or place	Classification (phenomenon) OR Positioning (place) Description	General and Abstract nouns Doing and Relating verbs
			Classifying Report	to classifying and describe types of phenomena	Classification Types	General and Abstract nouns Doing and Relating verbs
			Compositional Report	to describe parts and wholes	Classification Components	General and Abstract nouns Doing and Relating verbs

			Genre	Purpose	Stages	Language features
Argumentative	Explain	Explanations	Historical Account	to explain historical events	Background / Account of events	Sequenced in episodes / Group nouns are common / Evaluative language
			Sequential Explanation	to explain a sequence (generalized phenomena)	Phenomenon / Explanation	Present tense / Time expressions to sequence events
			Conditional Explanation	to explain alternative causes and effects	Phenomenon / Explanation	General and abstract nouns / Verbs show cause and effect / Topic-appropriate organization
			Factorial Explanation	to explain factors (multiple causes) that contribute to a particular outcome	Outcome / Factors	General and abstract nouns / Verbs show cause / Topic-appropriate organization
			Consequential Explanation	to explain multiple effects	Phenomenon: cause / Explanation: conseq.	General and abstract nouns / Verbs show effects / Topic-appropriate organization
	Argue	Arguments	Exposition	to persuade audience to agree with a position on an issue	(Background) / Thesis / Arguments / Reinforcement of Thesis	Abstract and generalized nouns / Beginning of paragraphs refer to thesis through shared vocabulary
			Discussion	to inform audience of different perspectives and persuade them to agree with position on an issue	Background / Issues / Perspectives / Position	Abstract and generalized nouns / Beginning of paragraphs refer to thesis through shared vocabulary
		Text Responses	Review	to evaluate a literary, visual or musical text	Context / Description of text / Judgement	Thinking, Feeling, Doing, and Relating verbs / Individual nouns / Evaluative language
			Interpretation	to interpret the message of a text	Evaluation / Synopsis of text / Reaffirmation	"Showing" verbs / Evaluative language
			Critical Response	to challenge the message of a text	Evaluation / Deconstruction / Challenge	Simple evaluative adjectives / Reasons described in dependent clauses

References

Abedi, J., & Lord, C. (2001). The language factor in mathematics tests. *Applied Measurement in Education*, 14(3), 219–234.

Achinstein, B., Athanases, S., Curry, M., Ogawa, R., & de Oliveira, L. C. (2013). These doors are open: Community wealth and health as resources in strengthening education for lower-income Latina/o youth. *Leadership*, 42(5), 30–34.

Achugar, M., Schleppegrell, M. J., & Oteiza, T. (2007). Engaging teachers in language analysis: A functional linguistics approach to reflective literacy. *English Teaching: Practice and Critique*, 6(2), 8–24.

Alexander, R. (2008). *Essays on pedagogy*. Routledge.

Allington, R. L., & Johnston, P. H. (2002). *Reading to learn: Lessons from exemplary fourth-grade classrooms*. Guilford Press.

Arizpe, E., & Styles, M. (2015). *Children reading picturebooks: Interpreting visual texts*. Routledge.

Athanases, S. (2012). Maintaining high challenge and high support for diverse learners. *Leadership*, 42(1), 18.

Athanases, S. Z., & de Oliveira, L. C. (2011). Toward program-wide coherence in preparing teachers to teach and advocate for English language learners. In T. Lucas (Ed.), *Teacher preparation for linguistically diverse classrooms: A resource for teacher educators* (pp. 195–215). Routledge.

Bank et al. (2013). *The United States: Its regions and neighbors* (student edition). McGraw-Hill.

Beck, I. L., & McKeown, M. G. (1994). Outcomes of history instruction: Paste-up accounts. In M. Carretero & J. F. Voss (Eds.), *Cognitive and instructional processes in history and the social sciences* (pp. 237–256). Lawrence Erlbaum Associates.

Bland, J. (2013). *Children's literature and learner empowerment: Children and teenagers in English language education*. Bloomsbury.

Boaler, J. (2006). How a detracked mathematics approach promoted respect, responsibility, and high achievement. *Theory Into Practice*, 45(1), 40–46. doi:10.1207/s15430421tip4501_6

Boehm, R., Hoone, C., McGowan, T., McKinney-Browning, M., Miramontes, O., & Porter, P. (2000). *Harcourt Brace social studies*. Harcourt School Publishers.

Brisk, M. E. (2015). *Engaging students in academic literacies: Genre-based pedagogy for K-5 classrooms*. Routledge.

Brisk, M. E., & Tian, Z. (2019). A developmental and contextual perspective on academic language. In L. C. de Oliveira (Ed.), *The handbook of TESOL in K-12* (pp. 41–54). Wiley.

Brock, C. H. (2007). Exploring an English language learner's literacy learning opportunities: A collaborative case study analysis. *Urban Education, 42*(5), 470–501.

Brooks, K., & Thurston, L. P. (2010). English language learner academic engagement and instructional grouping configurations. *American Secondary Education, 39*(1), 45–60.

Brown, A. L., & Campione, J. C. (1994). Guided discovery in a community of learners. In K. McGilly (Ed.), *Classroom lessons: Integrating cognitive theory and classroom practice* (pp. 229–270). MIT Press.

Bruna, K. R., & Gomez, K. (Eds.). (2009). *The work of language in multicultural classrooms: Talking science, writing science*. Routledge.

Bruner, J. (1983). The acquisition of pragmatic commitments. In R. Golinkoff (Ed.), *The transition from prelinguistic to linguistic communication* (pp. 27–42). Lawrence Erlbaum Associates.

Bunch, G. (2006). "Academic English" in the 7th grade: Broadening the lens, expanding access. *Journal of English for Academic Purposes, 5*(4), 284–301. doi:10.1016/j.jeap.2006.08.007

Caplan, N. A. (2019). Learning through language: A response to Polio, "Keeping the language in second language classes". *Journal of Second Language Writing, 46*, 100677. doi:10.1016/j.jslw.2019.100677

Caplan, N. A., & Farling, M. (2017). A dozen heads are better than one: Collaborative writing in genre-based pedagogy. *TESOL Journal, 8*(3), 564–581.

Carrasquillo, A., Kucer, S. B., & Abrams, R. (2004). *Beyond the beginnings: Literacy interventions for upper elementary English language learners*. Multilingual Matters.

Celedon-Pattichis, S., & Ramirez, N. G. (Eds.). (2012). *Beyond good teaching: Advancing mathematics education for ELLs*. National Council of Teachers of Mathematics.

Cenoz, J., & Gorter, D. (2021). *Pedagogical translanguaging*. Cambridge University Press.

Christie, F., & Derewianka, B. (2010). *School discourse: Learning to write across the years of schooling*. Continuum.

Clark, D. (2022). *Percentage of pupils whose first language is not English in England 2015 2021*. Retrieved from https://www.statista.com/statistics/330782/england-english-additional-language-primary-pupils/

Charles, R. I., Crown, W., & Fennel, F. S. et al. (2005). *Indiana mathematics Scott Foresman Addison Wesley*. Pearson Education.

Cochran-Smith, M. (2004). *Walking the road: Race, diversity, and social justice in teacher education*. Teachers College Press.

Coffin, C. (2006). *Historical discourse: The language of time, cause, and evaluation*. Continuum.

Cohen, E., Lotan, R., & Holthuis, N. (1997). Organizing the classroom for learning. In *Working for equity in heterogeneous classrooms: Sociological theory in practice* (pp. 31–43). Teachers College Press.

Cooper, R., & Slavin, R. (2001). *Cooperative learning programs and multicultural education: Improving intergroup relations*. Information Age Publishing.

Daniel, S., Martin-Beltrán, M., Peercy, M. M., & Silverman, R. (2016). Moving beyond yes or no: Shifting from over-scaffolding to contingent scaffolding in literacy instruction with emergent bilingual students. *TESOL Journal*, 7(2), 393–420. doi: 10.1002/tesj.213

Davison, C., & Williams, A. (2001). Integrating language and content: Unresolved issues. In B. Mohan, C. Leung, & C. Davison (Eds.), *English as a second language in the mainstream* (pp. 51–70). Pearson Education.

de la Pena, M. (2015). *Last stop on market street*. G.P. Putnam's Sons.

de Jong, E. J., & Harper, C. A. (2005). Preparing mainstream teachers for English-language learners: Is being a good teacher good enough? *Teacher Education Quarterly*, 32(2), 101–124.

de Jong, E. J., Harper, C. A., & Coady, M. R. (2013). Enhanced knowledge and skills for elementary mainstream teachers of English language learners. *Theory into Practice*, 52(2), 89–97.

de Oliveira, L. C. (2007). Academic language development in the content areas: Challenges for English language learners. *INTESOL Journal*, 4 (1), 22–33.

de Oliveira, L. C. (2010). Nouns in history: Packaging information, expanding explanations, and structuring reasoning. *The History Teacher*, 43(2), 191–203.

de Oliveira, L. C. (2011). *Knowing and writing school history: The language of students' expository writing and teachers' expectations*. Information Age Publishing.

de Oliveira, L. C. (2012). The language demands of word problems for English language learners. In S. Celedón-Pattichis & N. Ramirez (Eds.), *Beyond good teaching: Advancing mathematics education for ELLs* (pp. 195–205). National Council of Teachers of Mathematics.

de Oliveira, L. C. (2016). A language-based approach to content instruction (LACI) for English language learners: Examples from two elementary teachers. *International Multilingual Research Journal*, 10(3), 217–231.

de Oliveira, L. C. (2017). A genre-based approach to L2 writing instruction in K-12. *TESOL Connections*. Retrieved from http://newsmanager.commpartners.com/tesolc/downloads/features/2017/2017-07-TLC.pdf

de Oliveira, L. C. (2020). Planning and application using a language-based approach to content instruction (LACI) in multilingual classrooms. *MinneTESOL Journal*, *36*(2). Retrieved from https://minnetesoljournal.org/journal-archive/mtj-2020-2/planning-and-application-using-a-language-based-approach-to-content-instruction-laci-in-multilingual-classrooms/

de Oliveira, L. C., & Athanases, S. Z. (2017). A framework to reenvision instructional scaffolding for linguistically diverse learners. *Journal of Adolescent & Adult Literacy*, *61*(2), 123–129.

de Oliveira, L. C., & Beatty, J. (2023). Antiracist linguistic practices in history curriculum. In P. Friedrich (Ed.), *The anti-racism linguist: A book of readings*. (pp. 135–145). Multilingual Matters.

de Oliveira, L. C., Braxton, D., & Gui, J. (2021). Planning for instruction using a language-based approach to content instruction for multilingual learners. *Journal of English Learner Education*, *13*(1), 2.

de Oliveira, L. C., & Dodds, K. N. (2010). Beyond general strategies for English language learners: Language dissection in science. *The Electronic Journal of Literacy through Science*, *9*(1), 1–14. Retrieved from http://ejlts.ucdavis.edu/article/2010/9/1/beyond-general-strategies-english-language-learners-language-dissection-science

de Oliveira, L. C., Gilmetdinova, A., & Pelaez-Morales, C. (2015). The use of Spanish by a monolingual kindergarten teacher to support English language learners. *Language and Education*, *29*(6), 1–21.

de Oliveira, L. C., & Iddings, J. (Eds.). (2014). *Genre pedagogy across the curriculum: Theory and application in U.S. classrooms and contexts*. Equinox Publishing.

de Oliveira, L. C., Jones, L., & Smith, S. L. (2020). Interactional scaffolding in a first-grade classroom through the teaching–learning cycle. *International Journal of Bilingual Education and Bilingualism*, 1–19. DOI: 10.1080/13670050.2020.1798867

de Oliveira, L. C., Jones, L., & Smith, S. L. (2021). A language-based approach to content instruction (LACI) for multilingual learners: Six cs of scaffolding in first grade. *Journal of Language, Identity & Education*, 1–16.

de Oliveira, L. C., & Lan, S.-W. (2014). Writing science in an upper elementary classroom: A genre-based approach to teaching English language learners. *Journal of Second Language Writing*, *25*(1), 23–39.

de Oliveira, L. C., & Schleppegrell, M. J. (2015). *Focus on grammar and meaning*. Oxford University Press.

de Oliveira, L. C., Smith, S. L., Jones, L., & Rossato de Almeida, C. (2018). Strategies for working with image–text relations in picture books. In N. Guler (Ed.), *Optimizing elementary education for English language learners* (pp. 177–195). IGI Global.

de Oliveira, L. C., & Westerlund, R. (2021). A functional approach to language development for dual language learners. *Journal of English Learner Education, 12*(1), 1–23.

de Oliveira, L. C., & Westerlund, R. (Eds.). (2023). *Scaffolding for multilingual learners in elementary and secondary schools.* Routledge.

de Oliveira, L. C., & Yough, M. (Eds.). (2015). *Preparing teachers to work with English language learners in mainstream classrooms.* Information Age Publishing and TESOL Press.

Derewianka, B., & Jones, P. (2016). *Teaching language in context* (2nd ed). Oxford University Press.

Ebe, A. (2011). Culturally relevant books: Bridges to reading engagement for English language learners. *Insights on Learning Disabilities, 8*(2), 31–45.

Eggins, S. (2004). *Introduction to systemic functional linguistics.* A&C Black.

Egi, T. (2010). Uptake, modified output, and learner perceptions of recasts: Learner responses as language awareness. *Modern Language Journal, 94*(1), 1–21.

Fang, Z. (2006). The language demands of science reading in middle school. *International Journal of Science Education, 28*(5), 491–520.

Fang, Z. (2017). Academic language and subject area learning. In K. Hinchman & D. Appleman (Eds.), *Adolescent literacy handbook of practice-based research* (pp. 323–340). Guilford Press.

Fang, Z., Cao, P., & Murray, N. (2020). Language and meaning making: Register choices in seventh- and ninth-grade students' factual writing. *Linguistics and Education, 56.* doi:10.1016/j.linged.2020.100798

Fang, Z., Lamme, L. L., & Pringle, R. M. (2010). *Language and literacy in inquiry-based science classrooms grades 3–8.* Corwin Press.

Fang, Z., & Schleppegrell, M. J. (2008). *Reading in secondary content areas: A language-based pedagogy.* University of Michigan Press.

Fang, Z., & Schleppegrell, M. J. (2010). Disciplinary literacies across content areas: Supporting secondary reading through functional language analysis. *Journal of Adolescent & Adult Literacy, 53*(7), 587–597.

Fine, C. G. M. (2022). Translanguaging interpretive power in formative assessment co-design: A catalyst for science teacher agentive shifts. *Journal of Language, Identity & Education, 21*(3), 191–211.

Fuson, K. C. (2009). *Math expressions.* (Grade 4) (Vol. 1). Houghton Mifflin Harcourt School Publishers.

García, O. (2015). Translanguaging and abecedarios ilegales. In T. M. Kalmar (Ed.), *Illegal alphabets and adult biliteracy: Latino migrants crossing the linguistic border, expanded edition* (pp. 131–136). Routledge.

García, O., & Kleyn, T. (2016). Translanguaging theory in education. In *Translanguaging with multilingual students* (pp. 9–33). Routledge.

Gebhard, M. (2019). *Teaching and researching ELLs' disciplinary literacies: Systemic functional linguistics in action in the context of U.S. school reform.* Routledge.

Gee, J. (1996). *Social linguistics and literacies: Ideology in discourses.* Routledge.

Gerofsky, S. (2004). *A man left Albuquerque heading east: Word problems as genre in mathematics education* (Vol. 5). Peter Lang.

Gibbons, P. (2006). *Bridging discourses in the ESL classroom: Students, teachers and researchers.* A&C Black.

Gibbons, P. (2009). *English learners, academic literacy, and thinking: Learning in the challenge zone.* Heinemann.

Gonzalez, N., Moll, L. C., & Amanti, C. (2005). *Funds of knowledge: Theorizing practices in households, communities, and classrooms.* Routledge.

Good, R. (1993). Science textbook analysis. *Journal of Research in Science Teaching, 30*(7), 619.

Gort, M., & Sembiante, S. (2015). Navigating hybridized language learning spaces through translanguaging pedagogy: Dual language preschool teachers' languaging practices in support of emergent bilingual children's performance of academic discourse. *International Multilingual Research Journal, 9*(1), 7–25.

Gunderson, L. (2007). *English-only instruction and immigrant students in secondary schools: A critical examination.* Lawrence Erlbaum Associates.

Gunderson, L. (2009). *ESL(ELL) literacy instruction: A guidebook to theory and practice* (2nd ed.). Routledge.

Halliday, M. A. K. (1978). *Language as social semiotic.* Edward Arnold Publishers, Ltd.

Halliday, M. A. K., & Martin, J. R. (1993). *Writing science: Literacy and discursive power.* Falmer.

Halliday, M. A. K., & Matthiessen, C. M. I. M. (2014). *An introduction to functional grammar* (4th ed.). Routledge.

Hamman-Ortiz, L., Santiago Schwarz, V., Hamm-Rodríguez, M., & Gort, M. (2022). Engaging teachers in genre-based pedagogy for writing arguments: A case study of shifts in practice and understanding. *TESOL Quarterly.* Retrieved from https://onlinelibrary.wiley.com/doi/epdf/10.1002/tesq.3156

Hammond, J. (2006). High challenge, high support: Integrating language and content instruction for diverse learners in an English literature classroom. *Journal of English for Academic Purposes, 5*, 269–283.

Hammond, J. (2009). High challenge, high support programmes with English as a second language learners: A teacher–researcher collaboration. In J. Miller, A. Kostogriz, & M. Gearon (Eds.), *Culturally and linguistically diverse classrooms: New dilemmas for teachers* (pp. 56–76). Multilingual Matters.

Hammond, J. (2023). Scaffolding: Implications and equity for diverse learners in mainstream classes. In L. C. de Oliveira & R. Westerlund (Eds.), *Scaffolding for multilingual learners in elementary and secondary schools* (pp. 9–28). Routledge.

Hammond, J., & Gibbons, P. (2005). Putting scaffolding to work: The contribution of scaffolding in articulating ESL education. *Prospect, 20*(1), 6–30.

Haneda, M. (2000). Modes of student participation in an elementary school science classroom: From talking to writing. *Linguistics and Education, 10*(4), 1–27.

Haneda, M., & Wells, G. (2000). Writing in knowledge-building communities. *Research in the Teaching of English, 34*, 430–453.

Hansen, L. (2006). Strategies for ELL success. *Science and Children, 43*(4), 22–25.

Harcourt (2004). *Harcourt math. Indiana edition*. Harcourt.

Harcourt. (2005). *Harcourt science. Indiana edition*. Harcourt.

Harniss, M. K., Dickson, S. V., Kinder, D., & Hollenbeck, K. L. (2001). Textual problems and instructional solutions: Strategies for enhancing learning from published history textbooks. *Reading & Writing Quarterly, 17*(2), 127–150.

Hedges, H., Cullen, J., & Jordan, B. (2011). Early years curriculum: Funds of knowledge as a conceptual framework for children's interests. *Journal of Curriculum Studies, 43*(2), 185–205.

Hernández, A. C., Montelongo, J. A., & Herter, R. J. (2016). Using Spanish–English cognates in children's choices picture books to develop Latino English learners' linguistic knowledge. *The Reading Teacher, 70*(2), 233–239.

Herrera, S. (2015). *Biography-driven culturally responsive teaching*. Teachers College Press.

Herrera, S. G., Perez, D. R., & Escamilla, K. (2015). *Teaching reading to English language learners: Differentiated literacies* (2nd ed.). Allyn & Bacon/Pearson.

Hogg, L. (2011). Funds of knowledge: An investigation of coherence within the literature. *Teaching and teacher education, 27*(3), 666–677.

Honigsfeld, A., McDermott, C., & Cordeiro, K. (2018). Preparing social studies and ESOL teachers for integrated language and content instruction in support of ELLs. In L. C. de Oliveira & K. Obenchain (Eds.), *Teaching history and social studies to English language learners: Preparing pre-service and in-service teachers* (pp. 127–158). Palgrave Macmillan.

Humphrey, S. (2021). The role of teachers' disciplinary semiotic knowledge in supporting young bi/multilingual learners' academic and reflexive multiliteracies. *Language and Education, 35*(2), 140–159, DOI: 10.1080/09500782.2020.1772282

Humphrey, S., Droga, L., & Feez, S. (2015). *Grammar and meaning: New edition*. Primary English Teaching Association Australia.

Humphrey, S., & Macnaught, L. (2011). Revisiting joint construction in the tertiary context. *Australian Journal of Language and Literacy, 34*(1), 98–115.

Indiana State Department of Education. (2015). *Non-English speaking program*. Indiana Department of Education. Retrieved from http://www.doe.in.gov/lmmp/pdf/non-english-speaking/allocation_history.pdf

Johnson, E. M. (2019). Choosing and using interactional scaffolds: How teachers' moment-to moment supports can generate and sustain emergent bilinguals' engagement with challenging English texts. *Research in the Teaching of English, 53*(3), 245–269. Retrieved from https://library.ncte.org/journals/rte/issues/v53-3/30036

Jones, L., & de Oliveira, L. C. (2022). Collaborative writing with young multilingual learners. *Journal of English Learner Education, 14*(1). Retrieved from https://stars.library.ucf.edu/jele/vol14/iss1/2

Kanno, Y., & Applebaum, S. D. (1995). ESL students speak up: Their stories of how we are doing. *TESL Canada Journal, 12*(2), 32–49.

Karim, A., & Rahman, M. M. (2016). Revisiting the content-based instruction in language teaching in relation with CLIL: Implementation and outcome. *International Journal of Applied Linguistics and English Literature, 5*(7), 254–264.

Keefer, N., Lopez, J., Young, J., & Haj-Broussard, M. (2020). Gathering funds of knowledge: An elementary social studies unit plan for bilingual settings. *Social Studies and the Young Learner, 33*(2), 14–19.

Keenan, S. (2004). Reaching English language learners: Strategies for teaching science in diverse classrooms. *Science and Children, 42*(2), 49–51.

Khote, N. (2018). Translanguaging in systemic functional linguistics: A culturally sustaining pedagogy for writing in secondary schools. In R. Harman (Ed.), *Bilingual learners and social equity* (pp. 153–178). Springer.

Lado, A. (2012). *Teaching beginner ELLs with picture books: Tellability*. Sage.

Lado, A., & Hauth, C. (2022). Selecting picture books for EL beginners in Panama: Tellability. *The Reading Teacher, 75*(6), 767–775.

Lan, S. W., & de Oliveira, L. C. (2019). English language learners' participation in the discourse of a multilingual science classroom. *International Journal of Science Education, 41*(9), 1246–1270.

Lave, J. & Wenger, E. (1991). *Situated learning: Legitimate peripheral participation*. Cambridge University Press.

Lee, E. (2020). Translingualism in the teaching of English: Theoretical considerations and pedagogical implications. In P. Vinogradova, & J. K. Shin

(Eds.), *Contemporary foundations for teaching English as an additional language* (pp. 121–147). Routledge.

Lee, O., Maerten-Rivera, J., Penfield, R. D., LeRoy, K., & Secada, W. G. (2008). Science achievement of English language learners in urban elementary schools: Results of a first-year professional development intervention. *Journal of Research in Science Teaching, 45,* 31–52.

Levine, E. (1989). *I Hate English!* Scholastic.

Li, N., & Peters, A. W. (2020). Preparing K-12 teachers for ELLs: Improving teachers' L2 knowledge and strategies through innovative professional development. *Urban Education, 55*(10), 1489–1506.

Liang, X., Mohan, B. A., & Early, M. (1997). Issues of cooperative learning in ESL classes: A literature review. *TESL Canada Journal, 15*(2), 13–23.

López, F., & Santibañez, L. (2018). Teacher preparation for emergent bilingual students: Implications of evidence for policy. *Education Policy Analysis Archives, 26*(36).

Lotan, R. (2007). Developing language and mastering content in heterogeneous classrooms. In R. M. Gillies, A. F. Ashman, & J. Terwel (Eds.), *The teacher's role in implementing cooperative learning in the classroom* (pp. 184–199). Springer.

Lucas, T., & Grinberg, J. (2008). Responding to the linguistic reality of mainstream classrooms: Preparing all teachers to teach English language learners. In M. Cochran-Smith, S. Feiman-Nemser, & J. McIntyre (Eds.), *Handbook of research on teacher education: Enduring issues in changing contexts* (3rd ed., pp. 606–636). Lawrence Erlbaum Associates.

Lyster, R., & Izquierdo, J. (2009). Prompts versus recasts in dyadic interaction. *Language Learning, 59*(2), 453–498.

Malik, S. A. (2017). Revisiting and re-representing scaffolding: The two gradient model. *Cogent Education, 4*(1), 1–13, DOI: 10.1080/2331186X.2017. 1331533

Mariani, L. (1997). Teacher support and teacher challenge in promoting learner autonomy. *Perspectives, 23*(2). Retrieved from http://www. learningpaths.org/papers/papersupport.htm

Martin, J. R. (2002). Writing history: Construing time and value in discourses of the past. In M. J. Schleppegrell & M. C. Colombi (Eds.), *Developing advanced literacy in first and second languages: Meaning with power* (pp. 87–118). Lawrence Erlbaum Associates.

Martin, J. R. (2003). Making history: Grammar for interpretation. In J. R. Martin & R. Wodak (Eds.), *Re/reading the past: Critical and functional perspectives on time and value* (pp. 19–57). John Benjamins.

Martin, J. R. (2009). Genre and language learning: A social semiotic perspective. *Linguistics and Education, 20*(1), 10–21.

Martin, J. R., & Rose, D. (2005). Designing literacy pedagogy: Scaffolding democracy in the classroom. *Continuing Discourse on Language: A Functional Perspective, 1,* 251–280.

Martin, J. R. & Rose, D. (2008). *Genre relations: Mapping culture.* Equinox.

Martin, J. R., & Wodak, R. (2003). Introduction. In J. R. Martin & R. Wodak (Eds.), *Re/reading the past: Critical and functional perspectives on time and value* (pp. 1–16). John Benjamins.

Martinez, R., Hikida, M., & Durán, L. (2015). Unpacking ideologies of linguistic purism: How dual language teachers make sense of everyday translanguaging. *International Multilingual Research Journal, 9,* 26–42.

Martiniello, M. (2008). Language and the performance of English-language learners in math word problems. *Harvard Educational Review, 78*(2), 333–368.

McNeil, L. (2012). Using talk to scaffold referential questions for English language learners. *Teaching and Teacher Education, 28*(3), 396–404.

Mead, J. (2021). *Teachers' experiences incorporating English language learners' funds of knowledge into scripted curricula.* Unpublished Dissertation, Georgia State University. Retrieved from https://scholarworks.gsu.edu/mse_diss/104

Mercer, N. (2000). *Words and minds: How we use language to think together.* Routledge.

Michell, M. (2021). *How many English as an additional language or dialect (EAL/D) learners are there in Australian schools?* Retrieved from https://tesol.org.au/how-many-english-as-an-additional-language-or-dialect-eal-d-learners-are-there-in-australian-schools/

Moje, E. B., Ciechanowski, K. M., Kramer, K., Ellis, L., Carrillo, R., & Collazo, T. (2004). Working toward third space in content area literacy: An examination of everyday funds of knowledge and discourse. *Reading Research Quarterly, 39*(1), 38–70.

Moll, L. C., Amanti, C., Neff, D., & Gonzalez, N. (1992). Funds of knowledge for teaching: Using a qualitative approach to connect homes and classrooms. *Theory into Practice, 31*(2), 132–141.

Molle, D., de Oliveira, L. C., MacDonald, R., & Bhasin, A. (2021). Leveraging incidental and intentional vocabulary learning to support multilingual students' participation in disciplinary practices and discourses. *TESOL Journal, 12*(4), 1–13. DOI: 10.1002/tesj.616

Moore, J., & Schleppegrell, M. (2014). Using a functional linguistics metalanguage to support academic language development in the English Language Arts. *Linguistics and Education, 26,* 92–105.

Morrison, V., & Wlodarczyk, L. (2009). Revisiting read-aloud: Instructional strategies that encourage students' engagement with texts. *The Reading Teacher, 63*(2), 110–118.

National Center for Education Statistics. (2020). *English language learners in public schools*. Retrieved from https://nces.ed.gov/programs/coe/indicator_cgf.asp

National Council of Teachers of English. (2020). *NCTE position paper on the role of English teachers in educating English Language Learners (ELLs)*. NCTE. Retrieved from https://ncte.org/statement/teaching-english-ells/

National Governors Association Center for Best Practices & Council of Chief State School Officers. (2010). *Common core state standards*. Authors.

Nieto, S. (2000). *Affirming diversity: The sociopolitical context of multicultural education* (3rd ed.). Longman.

O'Halloran, K. (2005). *Mathematical discourse: Language, symbolism and visual images*. Continuum.

O'Halloran, K. L. (2015). The language of learning mathematics: A multimodal perspective. *The Journal of Mathematical Behavior, 40*, 63–74.

Ortega, L. (2013). Ways forward for a bi/multilingual turn in SLA. In S. May (Ed.), *The multilingual turn: Implications for SLA, TESOL, and bilingual education* (pp. 32–52). Routledge.

Osborn, T. A. (Ed.). (2007). *Language and cultural diversity in U.S. schools: Democratic principles in action*. Rowman & Littlefield Education.

Osborne, M. P. (2002). *Magic tree house collection: #4*. Listening Library.

Otheguy, R., García, O., & Reid, W. (2015). Clarifying translanguaging and deconstructing named languages: A perspective from linguistics. *Applied Linguistics Review, 6*(3), 281–307. doi:10.1515/applirev-2015-0014

Paris, D., & Alim, H. S. (Eds.). (2017). *Culturally sustaining pedagogies: Teaching and learning for justice in a changing world*. Teachers College Press.

Paxton, R. J. (1999). A deafening silence: History textbooks and the students who read them. *Review of Educational Research, 69*(3), 315–339.

Peercy, M. M., Martin-Beltrán, M., Silverman, R. D., & Nunn, S. J. (2015). "Can I ask a question?" ESOL and mainstream teachers engaging in distributed and distributive learning to support English language learners' text comprehension. *Teacher Education Quarterly, 42*(4), 33–58.

Pimm, D. (1987). *Speaking mathematically: Communication in mathematics classrooms*. Routledge.

Ravitch, D. R., & Finn, C. E. (1987). *What do our 17-year-olds know? A report on the first national assessment of history and literature*. Harper & Row.

Roberts, J., & Eady, S. (2012). Enhancing the quality of learning: What are the benefits of a mixed age, collaborative approach to creative narrative writing? *Education 3–13, 40*(2), 205–216.

Rose, D., & Martin, J. R. (2012). *Learning to write, reading to learn: Genre, knowledge and pedagogy in the Sydney School*. Equinox.

Saul, E. W. (2004). *Crossing borders in literacy and science instruction: Perspectives on theory and practice*. International Reading Association.

Scarcella, R. (2002). Some key factors affecting English learners' development of advanced literacy. In M. J. Schleppegrell & M. C. Colombi (Eds.), *Developing advanced literacy in first and second languages: Meaning with power* (pp. 209–226). Lawrence Erlbaum Associates.

Schleppegrell, M. J. (2001). Linguistic features of the language of schooling. *Linguistics and Education, 12*(4), 431–459.

Schleppegrell, M. J. (2004). *The language of schooling: A functional linguistics perspective.* Lawrence Erlbaum Associates.

Schleppegrell, M. J. (2013). Systemic functional linguistics. In J. P. Gee & M. Handford (Eds.), *The Routledge handbook of discourse analysis* (pp. 47–60). Routledge.

Schleppegrell, M. J., Achugar, M., & Oteíza, T. (2004). The grammar of history: Enhancing content-based instruction through a functional focus on language. *TESOL Quarterly, 38*(1), 67–93.

Schleppegrell, M. J., & Colombi, M. C. (Eds.). (2002). *Developing advanced literacy in first and second languages: Meaning with power.* Lawrence Erlbaum Associates.

Schleppegrell, M., & de Oliveira, L. C. (2006). An integrated language and content approach for history teachers. *Journal of English for Academic Purposes, 5*(4), 254–268.

Scott Foresman. (2006). *Scott Foresman Science (Indiana).* Pearson Education.

Seltzer, K. (2019). Reconceptualizing "home" and "school" language: Taking a critical translingual approach in the English classroom. *TESOL Quarterly, 53*(4), 986–1007.

Shafer Willner, L., Gottlieb, M., Kray, F. M., Westerlund, R., Lundgren, C., Besser, S., Warren, E., Cammilleri, A., & Cranley, M. E. (2020). Appendix F: Theoretical foundations of the WIDA English language development standards framework, 2020 edition. *In WIDA English Language Development Standards Framework, 2020 Edition.* Wisconsin Center for Education Research at the University of Wisconsin–Madison.

Steele, C. M., & Aronson, J. (1995). Attitudes and social cognition. *Journal of Personality and Social Psychology, 69*(5), 797–811.

Stevens, L. P., Jefferies, J., Brisk, M. E., & Kaczmarek, A. S. (2009). Linguistics and science learning for diverse populations: An agenda for teacher education. In K. Richardson Bruna & K. Gomez (Eds.), *The work of language in multicultural classrooms: Talking science, writing science.* (pp. 291–315). Routledge.

Swain, M. (2001). Integrating language and content teaching through collaborative tasks. *Canadian Modern Language Review/La Revue Canadienne Des Langues Vivantes, 58*(1), 44–63. doi:10.3138/cmlr.58.1.44

Thornton, S. J. (1991). Teacher as curriculum-instructional gatekeeper in social studies. In J. P. Shaver (Ed.), *Handbook of research on social studies teaching and learning* (pp. 237–248). Macmillan.

Tian, Z., & Shepard-Carey, L. (2020). (Re) imagining the future of translanguaging pedagogies in TESOL through teacher–researcher collaboration. *TESOL Quarterly, 54*(4), 1131–1143.

Toohey, K., & Day, E. (1999). Language-learning: The importance of access to community. *TESL Canada Journal, 17*(1), 40–53.

Turner, E. E., Aguirre, J., McDuffie, A. R., & Foote, M. Q. (2019). Jumping into modeling: Elementary mathematical modeling with school and community contexts. *North American Chapter of the International Group for the Psychology of Mathematics Education.*

Valenzuela, A. (1999). *Subtractive schooling: U.S.-Mexican youth and the politics of caring.* State University of New York Press.

van Lier, L. (2004). *The ecology and semiotics of language learning: A sociocultural perspective.* Kluwer Academic Publishers.

Viesca, K. M., Strom, K., Hammer, S., Masterson, J., Linzell, C. H., Mitchell-McCollough, J., & Flynn, N. (2019). Developing a complex portrait of content teaching for multilingual learners via nonlinear theoretical understandings. *Review of Research In Education, 43*(1), 304–335.

Villegas, A. M. & Lucas, T. (2002). *Educating culturally responsive teachers: A coherent approach.* State University of New York Press.

Vygotsky, L. S. (1978). *Mind in society.* Harvard University Press.

Walqui, A. (2006). Scaffolding instruction for English language learners: A conceptual framework. *International Journal of Bilingual Education and Bilingualism, 9*(2), 159–180.

Walqui, A. (2019). Shifting from the teaching of oral skills to the development of oracy. In L. C. de Oliveira (Ed.), *The handbook of TESOL in K-12* (pp. 181–198). Wiley.

Walqui, A., & Schmida, M. (2023). Reconceptualizing scaffolding for English learners: An ecological/sociocultural perspective. In L. C. de Oliveira & R. Westerlund (Eds.), *Scaffolding for multilingual learners in elementary and secondary schools* (pp. 29–47). Routledge.

Weiss, L., Banilower, E., McMahon, K., & Smith, P. (2001). *Report of the 2000 national survey of science and mathematics education.* Horizon Research.

WIDA. (2020). *WIDA English language development standards framework,* 2020 edition: Kindergarten–grade 12. Board of Regents of the University of Wisconsin System.

Wilson, K., & Devereux, L. (2014). Scaffolding theory: High challenge, high support in academic language and learning (ALL) contexts. *Journal of Academic Language and Learning, 8*(3), A91–A100.

Wong Fillmore, L. (1991). When learning a second language means losing the first. *Early Childhood Research Quarterly, 6,* 323–346. doi:10.1016/S0885-2006(05)80059-6

Wood, D., Bruner, J. S., & Ross, G. (1976). The role of tutoring in problem solving. *Child Psychology & Psychiatry & Allied Disciplines.*

Worth, K., Winokur, J., Crissman, S., Heller-Winokur, M., & Davis, M. (2009). *Science and literacy: A natural fit: A guide for professional development leaders.* Heinemann.

Yarrow, F., & Topping, K. J. (2001). Collaborative writing: The effects of metacognitive prompting and structured peer interaction. *British Journal of Educational Psychology, 71*(2), 261–282.